WITHDRAWN

THE STRUGGLE FOR SURVIVAL

VOLUME 53

THE CHRONICLES
OF AMERICA SERIES
ALLAN NEVINS
EDITOR

WILLIAM J. NIVEN, JR.
ASSISTANT EDITOR

THE RIGHT NUMBERS . . . IN THE RIGHT PLACES

From the painting by Elizabeth Olds. Reproduced from *Fortune*, January, 1943, by special permission of the Editors.

THE STRUGGLE
FOR SURVIVAL

A CHRONICLE OF ECONOMIC
MOBILIZATION IN WORLD WAR II
BY ELIOT JANEWAY

NEW HAVEN: YALE UNIVERSITY PRESS
TORONTO: GLASGOW, BROOK & CO.
LONDON: GEOFFREY CUMBERLEGE
OXFORD UNIVERSITY PRESS

1951

CONTENTS

CONTENTS

ILLUSTRATION

THE STRUGGLE FOR SURVIVAL

. .

CHAPTER I

ROOSEVELT'S GAMBLE

One morning in 1939, Montague Norman, the fabulous governor of the Bank of England, dropped by the American Embassy in London for an informal chat with Ambassador Joseph P. Kennedy.

"I see that you folks in the United States are contemplating industrial mobilization," he snorted. "Who's going to run it? God Almighty?"

Who *was* going to run it? The American people—Lincoln's people—were imperfect, impressionable, undisciplined, unpredictable. From Lincoln's time and before, instinct and experience had taught them characteristic and sometimes contradictory habits of playing politics, doing business, dealing with the world overseas and fighting wars. Now totalitarianism was challenging them to mobilize politics, business, diplomacy and war into a coordinated and interrelated war economy. Overnight, these four distinct forms of activity which had always operated separately had to be combined and unified into a new and overriding Governmental operation, which had no familiar name but whose impact was to be felt in every aspect of living and, as Montague Norman's question suggested, was to strain every quality of leadership. Mobilization, clearly, had to be run by experts; and, just as clearly, foremost among the problems awaiting expert analysis was that of reckoning with the attitudes—with the incentives and inhibitions—of the people.

In America, reckoning with the people is called politics, and is at once suspect and sacrosanct. Suspect because the essence of politics is compromise: sacrosanct because compromise is the essence of life. Many books have been written about the principles of politics, but none about the politics of principle. Yet principles no less than people live by compromise. Witness the sturdy integrity of the anti-slavery principle during the era of Clay and Lincoln. It submitted to compromise and it survived the compromisers.

Politics is the art of improvising third alternatives to dilemmas. And idealism embodies a dilemma, for by pointing men toward the unattainable, it destines them to frustration and threatens constantly to disintegrate into schizophrenia. Idealists, therefore, live under greater pressure to reckon with politics than politicians do to compromise with ideals. Hence the pressure upon idealism to conjure up a politics of its own: hence the politics of principle, personified by Franklin D. Roosevelt, which mere politicians and, indeed, mere idealists cannot understand.

The politics of principle stabilizes idealism and mobilizes it to stabilize society. Only idealism can— that is, only idealism disciplined and matured by the politics of principle. For to the people any new idealism is suspect, and with good reason. On the one hand, idealists are notoriously susceptible to corruption by contact with power. And, on the other, idealists innocent of the realities of power are all too often irresponsible and self-defeating provocateurs of reaction. Therefore, crusaders need any credentials they can get from politicians. The American political system enables the people to use idealism without being used by the idealists. For it puts the people in position to bargain constantly for a *quid pro quo* between ideals and expedients, and for the politics of principle as opposed to mere politics on the one hand and mere principle on the other.

Thus, the democratic process compromises idealism. But it also commits society to meet idealism half way. Every society teaches people to live by principles. What gives American politics its characteristic cultural form is its way of forcing principles to live with people. Again and again, it forces the purest of principles to take on the impure characteristics of life; and, again and again, this very process of alloying principle with living imperfection purifies the purposes of society. Like a reciprocating engine driving its pistons back and forth, the democratic process hammers principles against pressures and pressures against principles until at last the people find themselves deriving moral guidance from principles which in turn derive their moral authority from the people.

The Founding Fathers were concerned to erect safeguards for the people. But they felt as deeply the need to erect safeguards against the people. And all the historic rules of thumb describe our ingenious arrange-

ment of constitutional checks and balances as a carefully designed model of representative government, as
a republic and not a democracy, as a delegation of
power from the people and not a sharing of power
with them. Nevertheless, to such a mercurial but
prophetic figure as Roosevelt, who at the slightest
provocation was ready and able to rise above both
politics and principle, the American political system
offers a standing invitation to operate a crisis presidency by the technique of pure democracy—by provoking participation from the people instead of by
imposing discipline upon them, by manipulating the
complications of the American political system and
the American war economy to free instead of to frustrate the energies and the passions of the masses.

PITTED against Roosevelt in Europe and Japan was a
stupendous essay in the dramatics of authority. Roosevelt's answer was to invoke the authority of dramatics.
In fact, the most eloquent measure of his political
genius is to be found in the impresario's instinct which
prompted him, even in wartime, to handle the intricate
controls and the cruel pressures of modern mass society as casually as if he were operating within the
intimate confines of a Greek city state.

The era of big government, of what may be called
total politics, began with Roosevelt's first Administration. And big government—subject as it is to the unpredictable and uncontrollable sanctions of public
opinion—complicates and intensifies the traditional
problem of the American politician: to apply ideals
to politics and politics to ideals. American democracy

judges politicians by their ability to symbolize the moral aspirations of society while manipulating its political pressures. It rewards politicians who pass the test of idealism and it heeds idealists who pass the political test. It measures statesmen as if they were aldermen and aldermen as if they were statesmen.

Franklin Roosevelt was not the first American President who earned his freedom to be a statesman with his political winnings. Nor did he plan America's transformation into a welfare state. On the contrary, he and the transformation happened to America at the same time. Cicero says that one of the distinctive qualities of great generals is luck; and Roosevelt's luck in being thrust into the Presidency at the very climax of the crisis of "Normalcy" struck the authentic note of a commanding and new greatness. His emotional affinity for the unfamiliar agencies of total politics not only explains Roosevelt's success: it explains why his success always seemed so natural.

The truth is that democracy offers a more flexible and durable vehicle for inspired leaders than dictatorship. Inspired leaders—whether vicious or noble—are, by definition, unpredictable. Dictatorships, depending as they do on literal obedience to minutely subdivided and standardized directives, harden into a state of brittleness and in time of crisis tend to break apart under the impact of the turbulent personalities to whom they are dedicated. But democracies, although they average great men down to average size, hunger for leadership and rise spontaneously to its challenge. If inspiration demoralizes dictatorships, it literally organizes—it galvanizes—democracies.

By the same token, dependence upon organization disorganizes democracies. The dramatics of pure democracy can be evoked, but never systematized. In normal times democracy needs no substitute for inspiration, and in emergencies there is no substitute for inspiration. Politicians who are primarily men of mind and not of heart—Charles Evans Hughes was a prime example—are not in demand during quiet years and are suspect at moments of tension. The people simply do not trust men of the calculating type, not even those who happen to mean well. Only leaders who work by instinct and not by blueprint manage to generate dramatic passions among the masses. And, no matter what the system of government, the attachments which bind the people to these men of glands and heart are equally instinctive. In a democracy, the power of these dominant figures—of the dashing ones as well as the tragic ones—rests on this intangible, almost mystical force and on it alone.

The dramatics of democracy called for the devices of democracy, and Roosevelt applied them. Every cross-current and conflict in the country was bound to express itself in the home front. It was Roosevelt's responsibility to appoint men representative of every competing interest. If he had relied on conventional methods of launching a mobilization program, he would have appointed a staff of emergency administrators and dealt with the people through them. But he realized that he would have to appoint many men whom he did not know, and, in self-protection, he wanted to deal with them through the people. The conventional approach would have invited the people to judge him by the performance of his appointees: it would have made him the prisoner of his appointees. But Roosevelt wanted his employees to be his prisoners. And in fact, his hold on the popular imagination allowed him to claim credit for the successes of the mobilization effort and to blame the leaders he appointed for its failures. From the White House, the problem of mobilization could never seem as simple as Roosevelt's appointees invariably regarded it, and it could never be solved by the simple expedient of his delegating his powers to them. What Roosevelt delegated, accordingly, was always responsibility and never authority.

To say that the President imprisoned his own appointees, gave them public responsibility without corresponding authority to act, and made them scapegoats in order to preserve the people's confidence in his own leadership may make him seem a most unscrupulous manipulator; indeed, on the personal level, he did love to manipulate. But back of his tortuous manipulations there was a straightforward and essentially democratic premise. Running through each of his experiments and surviving them all was a simple and abiding faith that the country could be trusted to lead its leaders toward mobilization.

Roosevelt discovered as early as anyone that Germany's secret weapon was scientific mobilization, so-called. But he was as clearly aware of its limitations as of its strength—it counted people as so many units of national energy without ever reckoning with them as human beings. Now Roosevelt had a genius for dealing with masses of people in the aggregate as if

they were so many individuals sitting across a table
from him. If he had a secret weapon, it was his flair
for reckoning with human beings. Fortunately, the
war was won by human beings and not by units of
national energy manipulated on calculating machines.
Roosevelt was incapable of mobilizing the home front
by following any scientific blueprint filed, German-
fashion, in minutely divided pigeonholes and guaranteed by the experts to substitute for inspiration, luck,
judgment, stamina, individual genius and whatever
else it is that drives a people on to make history. And
the American people are incapable of making history
by following a blueprint. By the same token, they are
realistic enough to trust measures of emergency which
allow for the pressures and the accidents of politics.
What Roosevelt stirred up by the adroit mingling of
politics with principles and principles with politics
was nothing less than the dormant energies and incentives of democracy. Even before Pearl Harbor these
energies had begun to provide the affirmation of faith
by works which generated the momentum of mobilization.

Mobilization needed all the momentum that could
be generated. Fascism had a tremendous head-start,
and more than Roosevelt's dramatics had to be produced to overcome it. To be sure, fear and anxiety
were mounting, but not fast enough. Too many Americans had not yet taken alarm, and, of those who had,
too many did not know what to fear—surrender to
the spirit of totalitarianism or to a totalitarian enemy.
Public opinion was tending to swing over to Montague
Norman's view that for Fascism mobilization was

vitalizing while for democracy it was impossible. Roosevelt set out to convince the country that democracy could mobilize and still remain democracy. But to do so, he knew, America needed time.

ANY judgment upon Roosevelt's leadership of the home front must allow for the double standard by which he worked. Politically, Roosevelt's performance was professional; technically, it was amateurish. Again and again, his administrators disorganized the home front. But this neither alarmed Roosevelt nor upset him. Instinctively he avoided the political traps his administrative failures were constantly springing upon him. At diverting the political storms agitated by the failures of his appointees, Roosevelt had no equal. In fact, he found it easier work and better politics to cope with each political crisis in turn than to face technical problems before they festered into political crises. The more clumsily the men to whom he entrusted responsibility for the home front mismanaged it and the more perversely he himself manipulated the technical problem away from a workable solution, the more dexterously he balanced himself on his pedestal and the more dynamically he led the home front forward.

The performance exasperated his critics, who mistakenly denounced him as a radical confused by theories. But in fact Roosevelt was no more a radical than was Queen Elizabeth. Never was a political freebooter more cynical about all theories. That Roosevelt was not an orderly administrator is an unarguable fact; and no fact could be more misleading. The trouble was not that Roosevelt tried to master the administrator's trade and failed. Nor, on the other hand, was it that, as Chief Executive, he scorned good housekeeping as such. The explanation goes deeper. Temperamentally, the man could not bring himself to believe that good administration ever accomplished or prevented anything. He simply did not believe in Planning—with a capital P—as the answer to the problems of society. And he certainly did not believe in the Planners who looked down their noses at people for being people and at politicians like himself for catering to them.

No doubt, legend will confuse coincidence with cause, and Roosevelt will be credited with having established Government as the dominant entity in American life. What he actually did was to keep pace with a revolution that no man was big enough to have started or stopped. He was able to control the new controls of big government, not because he adhered to a theory about power but because he was an artist and power was his métier. His critics were convinced that he wanted to strait-jacket what is called the enterprise system into a planned society—they saw him as a simple Trilby in the hands of such a masterful Svengali as Henry Wallace, and to the end they persisted in distorting the role of Harry Hopkins into that of a zealous doctrinaire, although the fact is that Hopkins was able to grow into such an effective Presidential shadow because his bent was political and not theoretical.

Even before mobilization installed Government at the economic controls, Roosevelt's critics, observing the impact of big government upon the changing but durable American system, had mistaken it for socialism, just as an earlier generation had mistaken the income tax for socialism. During the great debate of 1939–40, he was widely accused of whipping up a war emergency in order to take over as dictator. And always his critics, agreeing if they but knew it with his most fanatical supporters, believed that Roosevelt was working from an elaborate master-plan. Instead, what inspired this supreme artist of power, what guided him to the mastery of his material, was merely a common-sense assumption about problems: they reduce themselves to people. The philosopher must see problems in the perspective of their past and their future— they are complicated by the past, and they complicate the future. But for the politician only the present exists; and, no matter what may have been done to solve problems in the past, no matter what may be promised to solve them in the future, people must be dealt with in the present. Roosevelt believed in his ability to handle people and he believed in the ability of the people to rise to the crises their leaders fear.

Roosevelt's critics have said—and say—that he mobilized the Washington echelon of the home front on a basis that he better than any knew would not work; that he appointed men to the high command of the home front whom he knew to be incompetent; that he promoted them after they had proven their incompetence to the entire world; that he reorganized and reorganized wartime Washington into a comptroller's hell, into a jungle of confusion and duplication and self-contradiction in which even he ended by feeling lost.

They are right. He did. And yet this irresponsibility —so disastrous on the face of it—did not culminate in disaster. To Roosevelt, as the crisis deepened, as our involvement in it came to seem inescapable, as the battle over isolationism grew more embittered, the important question was the participation of the nation as a whole in its own defense, not the administrative planning for this participation. He dealt, therefore, with the personalities involved in such planning in terms of political pressures, on a minute-to-minute basis. His administrative performance was indeed amateurish. But the message he meant to make clear got through to the people in the end and in time: industrial mobilization for defense was necessary, and if war came only America's industrial mobilization could win it. As long as the country knew this, as long as it was awake to the need for nationwide participation, Roosevelt was willing to let the actual administration of the home front be made into a political side show.

Here is paradox, but it is paradox deeply typical of Roosevelt. He expected to win the war on the home front, but he expected to win it at the cost of the Battle of Washington, which he was perfectly prepared to see lost by the expendables he appointed to its high command. He counted on the home front to win the war and he put it at the bottom of his priorities list. He was sure that America's decisive contribution would have to be made on the home front and he shuffled through its high command men whom he regarded as less formidable and, in at least two cases— Henry Wallace and Donald Nelson—certainly less

reliable than run-of-the-mill political time-serv-
ers.

For Roosevelt was gambling that the home front
would win the war as fast as the war could set it in
motion; and this is exactly what happened. All that
Roosevelt thought important about the home front
was its size. So long as it reached out to include everyone and everything not under direct military authority
on a fighting front, he did not believe that his appointees had to organize it particularly well—the participation of the people would push it forward faster
than any leaders could lead it, and the spontaneous
dramatics of democracy would organize it. So long as
the home front was big at the base, Roosevelt was
willing to bet that he could afford to let it be confused
at the top—and he and he alone had the power, the
genius, the dramatic instinct and, above all, the daring
to make it as big outside Washington and as amor-
phous inside Washington as he pleased.

More than two years before the beginnings of
mobilization, in January, 1937, Roosevelt had asked
Congress: "Will it be said, 'Democracy was a great
dream but it could not do the job?' Or shall we here
and now, without further delay, make it our business
to see that our American democracy is made efficient
so that it will do the job that is required of it by the
events of our time?" But to the end he believed democracy more efficient than efficiency. And to the end
he looked to democracy and not to leaders, to democracy's reservoir of mass energy and faith and not to
the custodians of specialized wisdom, for the answer.

It was his judgment that, given only time, America's

home front would win the war. It was his judgment that the home front—that is, the country—would win through its production and in spite of any high command which pressure or expedience might prompt him to put in charge in Washington. Only on the highest policy-making level—far above that of the home front, far above the diplomatic front and far above even the fighting fronts—did he believe that the country (like the world) was wholly dependent upon Washington for leadership. But there he knew it was safe, for it had him. On the administrative level, however, his realism assumed that, if the country had to depend on Government for leadership, it would lose the war. What justified this gamble—what made it seem safe to the realist—was the time factor which our Allies, armed by the products of American democracy, accounted for. They bought the country the time it needed. It survived, and with it will survive the memory of Roosevelt's dynamic evocation of the dramatics of democracy.

THE first general to whom Lincoln entrusted the responsibility of command was a man named McDowell. Bull Run quickly finished him off. Stettinius, as head of the War Resources Board, was Roosevelt's first director of the home front. He finished himself off—in this capacity at any rate—in less than two months. After McDowell, Lincoln tried McClellan, whose military effort, as distinguished from the political career to which it led, lasted roughly a year, from July, 1861, to August, 1862. Roosevelt's second experiment was called the National Defense Advisory

Commission. Some seven months later, he acknowledged its failure. He began his third term—his first of the war Presidency—by shelving the Commission in much the same way that Lincoln shelved McClellan after the crisis of indecision at Harrison's Landing.

McClellan was followed by Pope, and disaster. The National Defense Advisory Commission was followed by the Office of Production Management, and disaster. Pope was routed in one month, OPM in eight. The elimination of Pope gave McClellan another chance; Roosevelt's action in absorbing OPM into the Supply Priorities and Allocation Board—SPAB—gave the leaders who were failing individually a chance to fail together. McClellan's second chance lasted until the day after the 1862 election, and SPAB lingered on until Pearl Harbor.

Lincoln tried Burnside next. The appointment was made in the full realization that Burnside was unfit and knew it himself. Just so, OPM and SPAB were followed by Donald M. Nelson and the War Production Board. Burnside's lack of competence was demonstrated on the battlefield and he was removed. But the War Production Board was screened for over a year by its remoteness from the fighting fronts overseas. Not until the time approached for America's home front to become the decisive factor along the fighting fronts did WPB fall apart.

By then, Roosevelt had long since stopped worrying about how to organize the home front. It had grown too big and too unruly for this to be possible, or indeed, necessary. The problem of administration in Washington reduced itself to one of keeping peace among the administrators. To keep their quarrels out of the White House and out of the newspapers, Roosevelt appointed Supreme Court Justice James F. Byrnes to head the new Office of War Mobilization and Reconversion—Byrnes was the Assistant President, and he functioned as the Vice President in charge of not rocking the boat. Byrnes immediately loomed up as a leading candidate for the Presidential succession, although Nelson was able to survive for some months as a plausible political aspirant.

Lincoln replaced Burnside with Hooker. This appointment was as transparently political and as admittedly bad as that of Burnside, and its consequences at Chancellorsville were as disastrous. Altogether, Lincoln's maneuvering between Burnside, a Democrat, and Hooker, a radical Republican, wasted nearly eight months of his war Presidency and, of course, many lives. But was it all waste, or did it yield an offsetting balance of faith and power? The people, exasperated and saddened, gradually awakened to a realization that it did. Every pressure group rained abuse on Lincoln from every side, yet his personality towered over all of them. After two years of precarious and defensive war, the politician had begun to exercise moral leadership over the Union. As Sandburg says, the man had become the issue. He never organized the Union for victory—he was too practical to try. Instead, he inspired and provoked it to mobilize the momentum of victory.

The result was inefficient but irresistible. A victory small enough to be organized is too small to be decisive. After one more experiment, this time with Meade,

Lincoln found in Grant a man who personified the brute force that rides momentum through chaos to victory. Grant emerged as the hero of victory and the villain of peace. The chain reaction was inexorable. During the war people looked at the politician in the White House and they saw a person. They lived with the person and created an epic. The Lincoln epic produced a mystic force which disciplined democracy and generated the momentum of victory. Momentum substituted for leadership and in Grant found its characteristic symbol of power. All this took time to happen, and time has not yet been able to undo the damage. Nor will time—or wisdom—quickly undo the damage done by the necessary momentum of our effort to save Russia, which succeeded, and doomed our dream of peace to fail. Thus the epic cycle ran its course. Moral Idealism justified itself in the end as efficiency, and efficiency justified itself as devastation.

The Lincoln-Roosevelt analogy applies equally to the performance of the politician, to the epic of the war President, and to the mystic spell of the martyr in his grave. It applies as well to the winning of each war, and to the loss of each peace. It breaks down under the impact of the politics of the aftermath. Lincoln, plagued by the Senate Committee on the Conduct of the War, picked Senator Andrew Johnson, a member of the Committee, as his running mate in 1864. Johnson served nearly all of Lincoln's second term, at the end of which his former colleagues in the Senate made his renominataion unthinkable: a General took over in his place.

When Roosevelt began to operate the home front,

he assumed that the man credited with managing it would earn the first claim on the succession. But when the time came for the succession to be claimed, it went, not to one of Roosevelt's deputies, but to the Senator credited with having investigated them all. He served all but a few months of Roosevelt's fourth term, at the end of which his former colleagues in the Senate declared his renomination unthinkable and acclaimed a General as his successor. But there the analogy ends. And, in any case, by that time Roosevelt had long since won his bet that the momentum of production outside of Washington would win the war in spite of any and all administrative failure inside Washington.

CHAPTER II

PREPARING FOR PREPAREDNESS

By 1939 the issue of isolationism had begun to divide the country. The great debate has come down to us through the headlines as a contest between internationalism in the Administration and isolationism in Congress. This distortion is a fine example of what Al Smith used to call politics. It is a classic example of Rooseveltian politics. The fact was that Congress had its internationalists and the Administration had its isolationists. The split inside the Administration was at least as representative and as formidable as the split in Congress.

This was understandable. To administrators the foreign policy issue was bound to crystallize as a problem of domestic policy. For six years the crucial question of domestic policy had been to spend or not to spend. The last year before war began in Europe had to all intents and purposes decided the argument against the advocates of spending. This decision the emergency now threatened to reverse. Understandably, therefore, Roosevelt's conservative appointees—and during his most radical phases he always managed to have a number of influential conservatives on tap —sniffed resentfully at internationalism as just another of Roosevelt's spending schemes. They looked at the world of 1939 and saw only the budget that would be needed to pacify it.

The vision of many of Roosevelt's liberal administrators was just as narrow. As a group they too tended to see the world conflict as part of the Battle of the Budget. But instead of welcoming internationalism for the irresistible pressure it would put upon Government to spend, they joined Roosevelt's conservatives in counting its cost—not to the taxpayers, but to their favorite domestic budgets. The New Dealers at this point had won an important and imaginative Wall Street ally in the unusually complicated and unusually able person of James V. Forrestal, then still in private business. He disagreed with their reservations against committing the Government to combat the world crisis, and told them that the practical way to put the New Deal program across was to sell it as Preparedness, not as Reform—indeed, TVA had its beginning under the Defense Act of 1916. In two years Forrestal's judgment was to be vindicated by shortages of all the facilities from dams to dentistry for which the New Dealers had been fighting. But the liberal mind shrank from the temptation to gain the substance by denying the doctrine.

The main convert Forrestal made among the New Dealers was Harry Hopkins and he, with characteristic zealousness, jumped from the WPA point of view to the opposite extreme. Robert Sherwood's book, *Roosevelt and Hopkins,* is a tribute to the force of will which converted Hopkins overnight from a ruthless reformer into a ruthless realist. Now Hopkins was smart, incisive and, like so many politicians, prone to make black-and-white judgments. When he dropped the New Deal, he really dropped it. The men and measures involved in the reform movement of 1933–39 were shoved into a pigeonhole marked "Nuisance."

Although internationalism was not necessarily irreconcilable with liberalism, many die-hard New Dealers felt at the time that it was, and their animosity toward Hopkins, as reported by Sherwood, prompted many of them to join with the conservatives around Roosevelt in resisting the drive to convert the Government to an emergency footing. The die-hard conservatives foresaw the liquidation of property values, and the die-hard liberals foresaw the abandonment of human values. Inevitably, the split in the Administration began to create a new political situation. It was the crisis which sharpened the split, and it was the crisis and only the crisis which could blast open a new mission for Roosevelt. The question was whether it would explode upon the country in time to force the future his devotees demanded. But right down to the eve of the 1940 Democratic Convention, Roosevelt himself persisted in acting as if he only half-believed he would have to run for a third term. More demoralizing than his indecision were his moments of firm resolution not to run again. In July, 1939, as Jim Farley set off for Europe, Roosevelt gave him a promise not to run for a third term in 1940.

This political commitment was as unnecessary as it was to prove mischievous. Whether a third term campaign would be imprudent, or whether it would be inescapable, not Roosevelt but only the logic of the situation would determine; this would not be manifest until spring opened the 1940 political season in America and the fighting season in Europe. Meanwhile, it seemed easier for Roosevelt to invite independent and even hostile action by ambitious Democrats than to force them to support him as an avowed candidate. If he had merely let it be known that only the crisis could draft him—and that the crisis might!—he would have been able to face the public with his Administration united behind him. Instead, he confused the public and invited an anti-Roosevelt conspiracy within the Administration.

The anti-Roosevelt conspiracy and the political stratagems by which Roosevelt defeated it cost America a precious year of preparedness. In the President's mind, the question of running and the question of coping with the crisis were not two questions but one. Because he was unwilling to recognize frankly that the crisis was making him a candidate, he was unable to meet the crisis as it was demanding to be met. If only, to use one of his favorite expressions, he had taken an "Iffy" line, if only he had left the door open to his candidacy in an emergency, he would have obligated himself to prepare the economy for the emergency in the making. He could then have made the progress of preparedness the issue of 1940. Instead, he allowed his opponents to make the scandal of unpreparedness the issue. Yet, if Roosevelt's reluctance to agitate preparedness as a major issue cost him this immediate advantage, it proved shrewd in the end. He knew, in 1939, that the New Deal was still winning politics while war was not. By 1942, he managed to declare a moratorium on the New Deal, but in 1939

his one chance of organizing preparedness was to continue to function as the leader of the New Deal. By
one of the most far-reaching and meaningful paradoxes in history, he survived the New Deal by continuing to symbolize it during the war years; and,
because he symbolized the New Deal when there
could be none, the New Deal in turn survived him.

By 1939, however, the New Deal had been thrown
upon the defensive. The main reason for its loss of
momentum was the calendar: until Roosevelt won his
third term, the American political system knew no
sadder plight than that of a second-term President
finishing out his last two years. Congress invariably
refuses to vote appropriations for "dead ducks." And
legislation and the agencies of Government are utterly
dependent upon appropriations. In 1937, Roosevelt,
fresh from his triumph at the polls, had carried his
fight to Congress. In 1938, infuriated by its resistance
to his reforms, he had tried to purge its leadership.
But now in the spring of 1939, as the administrators
of the New Deal spent the limited funds voted to
them, Congress was carrying the offensive back to the
other end of Pennsylvania Avenue. Strong members of
the Democratic majority, playing double machine
politics with their Republican opposite numbers, had
found a workable, between-election technique for
frustrating Roosevelt's policies without stirring up the
voters. On the assumption that the program of the
New Deal would die a natural political death in 1940,
Congress, unrepentant and unreconstructed, was slashing the departmental and agency budgets submitted

to carry the New Deal from July 1, 1939, to June 30, 1940.

Now the New Deal was never an ideology, as its opponents charged. It was a dollars-and-cents proposition. Any President's power with the people rests on their appreciation of how his Administration has profited them: witness the return of the people to Truman during the boom election of 1948. By early 1939, when domestic reform was still the legislative issue, the conservatives in Congress were preventing Roosevelt from distributing new dividends among the stockholders in the New Deal. He was rediscovering the old rule that the people are mindful of favors yet to come. His popularity fell as his appropriations diminished. "Normalcy" was on the march.

But so was emergency. Soon after his failure to purge the conservative Democrats in the 1938 primaries, Roosevelt had sent their friend—Bernard M. Baruch—on a mission to Europe. On the assumption that secrecy makes for the most publicity, both the White House and Baruch refused to comment on his trip until October. Then, after Munich, the public learned that the President had asked him to verify the intelligence received from Army sources and from Ambassador Joseph P. Kennedy, whom the Senators also respected, that German production of synthetic rubber and oil had made her blockade-proof, and that Britain's arms production was lagging further and further behind Germany's. Both assertions Baruch found to be all too true.

Baruch also verified the extent of the head-start Germany had won in the race for control of the air. A few months later, the Military Intelligence Division of the General Staff revealed how close Germany was to winning by default. For the Luftwaffe commanded five bombers to Britain's one, and eleven to our one. The General Staff Report credited Germany with having 3,353 medium and heavy bombers. In the year of Munich, this was enough. The second power in the air was Russia, whose bomber fleet was estimated at 1,300 to 1,900 planes, which should have taught American Military Intelligence not to be contemptuous of Russia as a military factor. France stood third, with 956 bombers; and Germany's ally, Italy, was right behind with 916. Britain had only 715 bombers, but Japan had 660. And America, with less than half of Japan's strength, was the weakest of all the air powers. Roosevelt was being attacked as a warmonger, and the United States owned 301 bombers! Germany's fighter plane superiority was just as decisive.

Still more ominous, Germany's momentum was enabling her to expand production on a scale greater than that of all the other powers put together. And, although Germany was the one power then in least need of anti-aircraft defense, hers was the one system which had created ground force fire power at home against bombing. These facts and figures apologized for Munich and forecast the Blitz.

Baruch's report was all that Roosevelt needed to justify his differences with the isolationists in his Administration, the most conspicuous of whom was Secretary of War Harry Woodring. By this time Roosevelt was openly feuding with Woodring. Indeed, he had adopted the procedure, unusual even for him, of clear-

ing his growing volume of business with the War
Department through other of its officers than the
Secretary. The office through which he chiefly by-
passed Woodring was that of the Assistant Secretary,
Louis Johnson. A past Commander of the American
Legion and a Roosevelt man, a corporation lawyer and
the West Virginia associate of New Deal Senator
Harley Kilgore, Johnson was exactly the prime mover
Roosevelt needed in 1938 and 1939 to set the War De-
partment in motion and, incidentally, to advertise its
activity to the business and political groups about to
be jolted by its impact.

Admittedly, Johnson was a controversial figure. But
the controversy he then stirred up was good for the
country. Admittedly, he was an inveterate feudist.
But in his dramatic feud with the Secretary of War,
he was as right as he seemed insubordinate. Whatever
may have been the merits of the later charge that
Johnson held back on necessary defense spending in
the crisis of 1949–50, in the crisis of 1939–40 he pressed
vigorously for enough and in time. Whatever may have
been the merits of the charge that he was unfit to be
Secretary of Defense in 1950, in 1939, as Assistant
Secretary of War, Johnson earned a secure place in
history. Where Secretary Woodring was worried by
the growing pressure to spend millions on preparedness, Johnson did not hesitate to agitate for a new
arms program to run into billions. Thanks in good part
to the Baruch Mission, the President was now in position to justify this agitation of Johnson's. He made a
point of asking Baruch if Johnson was an alarmist,
and was assured on the record—and, even more im-

portant, off the record as well—that, however high
Johnson's estimates might seem in Washington, every
realist in Europe knew they were low. Soon Baruch's
spirited support of the Johnson program was the talk
of Washington. The Nazi press attacked him as a warmonger. The American press began to speculate upon
the likelihood that Roosevelt would ask Baruch to return to Washington as civilian coordinator of a national preparedness drive. Roosevelt, delighted that
conservatives in the Senate were pleased with the elder
statesman's new advisory role, was feeling his way
towards the strategic counteroffensive against the
economy bloc on Capitol Hill.

Cautiously, Roosevelt indicated his support for two
elementary measures which Assistant Secretary Johnson was advocating to bring the War Department into
contact with the economy. The first was the so-called
"Educational Orders" Act. Since 1927, the Army had
been lobbying for an appropriation to familiarize key
plants with the munitions it expected to put into mass
production on M-Day. But in spite of the unsatisfactory experience of World War I, in spite of the revela-
tions of its own postwar investigating committees, in
spite of preparedness-minded members of both Parties,
Congress had voted the proposal down in session after
session. Johnson set out to prove that this was "must"
legislation. With Roosevelt's help, he wheedled out of
Congress the Educational Orders Act of 1939, which
authorized expenditures of $2,000,000 a year for five
years. To supplement this, the President felt em-
boldened in January, 1939, to recommend an emergency appropriation of $32,000,000. The program was

hopelessly small and it started hopelessly late, but it stirred up an ominous undercurrent of protest against "militarism." Meanwhile any contribution it made toward familiarizing manufacturers and technicians with the problems of industrial mobilization was over-shadowed by Johnson's whirlwind publicity campaign to awaken the business community as a whole to the reality confronting it.

The second bill for which Johnson was fighting would have authorized an appropriation for the stock-piling of strategic materials. Now the isolationists were ac-cusing Roosevelt of scheming to involve America in another European war. They were working on the generation-old theory that America could remain neu-tral by denying her resources to Germany's enemies; and they were making Roosevelt the target for every grievance accumulated for twenty years against Wood-row Wilson. But the world of 1939 was not the world of 1917. The isolationists of 1939 wanted to keep American industrial products off the Atlantic. Mean-while, the Japanese were by way of keeping off the Pacific the raw materials needed to run America's industrial plant. Nevertheless, the President hardly dared move to secure America's self-sufficiency. On the one hand, the isolationists were counting on this same fancied self-sufficiency to support a policy of neutrality toward Germany in the Atlantic. On the other hand, the President had been afraid to ask the isolationists for permission to make America really self-sufficient against Japan in the Pacific.

In 1938 the Senate Military Affairs Committee had reported a bill to finance a modest four-year program for stock-piling rubber and other strategic imports. The appropriation, to be spread over the entire period, was for only $102,000,000, much less than was needed. But the White House felt obliged to appease so many pressures that it could not even see this bill through. At the insistence of the Bureau of the Budget, the bill was pigeonholed, although at 1938's depressed prices the nominal appropriations involved would have bought considerably more rubber, tin, quinine, and the rest than was possible later on.

In February, 1939, the Senate Military Affairs Committee again voted the stock-pile bill. By March, the bill had reached the House Military Affairs Committee. Here was the historic crisis; here was Roosevelt advancing to meet it; and here, in the corrupt chairman of the House Military Affairs Committee, was Andrew Jackson May, the very personification of the political resistance which the statesman had to pierce. Chairman May was not convinced that Roosevelt was making him a sound business proposition—and business propositions were May's specialty (the stock-piling program, as a matter of fact, competed with one of his own business promotions, a very dubious manganese mining deposit in West Virginia). To placate him, Roosevelt telephoned May to say that he would be willing to cut the amount to be spent the first year from $25,000,000 to $10,000,000. Finally, on June 8, the stock-pile bill became law. A week later, the Administration went back to Congress for permission to spend the full $25,000,000 in the year beginning July 1, 1939.

But in 1939 stock-piling was less urgent than easing

the pressure of farm surpluses. In August, Secretary of Agriculture Henry A. Wallace earmarked well over half a million bales of cotton held over from 1934, which he arranged to barter for British rubber. The deal was imaginative and sound in principle, even though it was inadequate in practice. It corrected neither the cotton surplus nor the rubber shortage. Within a month Hitler was to invade Poland. But not even Henry Wallace was willing to use figures big enough to dispose of the accumulated problems of "Normalcy."

Under cover of Louis Johnson's agitation for Educational Orders and stock-piling, Roosevelt had meanwhile formulated a more general defense program. The Congress which met in January, 1939, expected to starve the New Deal to death. But with the world moving toward war, Roosevelt's problem was ceasing to be how to buy more domestic reform. The spending bills that Congress was resolved to deny him were shrinking into insignificance alongside the sums that anyone could see would be needed to meet the crisis ahead. Accordingly, Roosevelt greeted the Seventieth Congress with a request for a new preparedness budget. "It would be unwise for us to yield to any form of hysteria," he said. "It is equally sensational and untrue to take the position that we must at once spend billions of additional money for building up our land, sea and air forces on the one hand, or to insist that no further additions are necessary on the other." "No responsible officer," the message added, "advocates building up our air forces to the total either of planes on hand or of productive capacity equal to the forces of certain other nations." In January, 1939, majority opinion, far from being alarmed by this statement of policy, accepted it as a guarantee of national security. The New Dealers, instead of jumping aboard this new band wagon as their friend Forrestal had advised them to do, were relieved to find Roosevelt experimenting with his latest project on so moderate a scale.

Thus, having sent Assistant Secretary Johnson far out in front as the advocate of billions for immediate defense and having invoked the prestige of Bernard Baruch in support of Johnson's warnings, Roosevelt in Washington was steering a middle course between his adherents in the War Department and the stand-patters; in the country at large, he was steering the same course between the alarmist minority and the isolationist, pacifist, and liberal majority. For six years he had exploited this technique. Time and again he had used his lieutenants to reach for startling goals; the New Deal programs publicized by them never failed to inspire enthusiasm among his supporters or the wildest fears among his opponents. The enthusiasm strengthened him; the attacks made expendables of his New Deal aides. Then, at the strategic time, after the exchanges between the Roosevelt men and the Roosevelt haters had dramatized the conflict to the general public, Roosevelt invariably compromised for something more than half the gains at issue. Thus, at one and the same time, he contrived to show the mass of voters how much he was winning for them, while convincing opposition opinion that the attacks on him were exaggerated and unfair. The mass of normally Democratic voters believed him to be a passionate partisan of their interests. But to the independent element he was able to protest that he stood only "somewhat to the left of center."

Now, too, he was steering a middle course between his opponents and his mouthpieces, tacking somewhat to the side of the "Roosevelt men." His men were calling for billions. Roosevelt asked Congress for $525,000,000. "Bluff and jitterism," cried Senator Borah—but Congress signed the check in no time at all.

This was the frontal attack. Sensational headlines soon revealed why Roosevelt had been content to mount the attack on such a limited scale. He had another offensive—a flanking movement, already under way. This other offensive exposed the cleavage within the War Department and set off a major explosion in American politics and in world diplomacy. The repercussions early in 1939 set the pattern for the organization of the home front.

On January 23, 1939, the most modern light bomber built in America crashed in flames over the Los Angeles Municipal Airport. One of those injured was Paul Chemidlin of the French Air Ministry. The Douglas Aircraft Company, so reported the Associated Press, "released his [Chemidlin's] name as Smith—a mechanic. "Chemidlin's purpose on the flight was particularly puzzling," the dispatch continued, "because of Federal regulations forbidding the export of any military-type plane until it has been in service in this country for a year, or rejected for national defense use."

On the day the accident was reported, General H. H. Arnold, Chief of the Army Air Corps, was appearing before the Senate Military Affairs Committee on behalf of Roosevelt's requested appropriation. Senator Bennett Clark, of Missouri, a leading isolationist, pounced on the incident. Although Clark was later to be repudiated for his isolationism by the Democratic voters of Missouri in the 1944 primary, he was still, in 1939, a commanding figure under whose fire the most flamboyant generals quailed. "Do you know what this Frenchman was doing in that plane?" he asked General Arnold, in the tone of a housewife finding a mouse in the pantry. "He was out there," the General replied nervously, "under the direction of the Treasury Department, with a view of looking into possible purchase of planes by the French mission." In effect, Senator Clark demanded, "When had the Treasury Department taken over the Army?" General Arnold stammered, "I would suggest that that be gotten from somebody else."

By this time, the Senate Military Affairs Committee and Congress as a whole were aroused. How could a ranking Senatorial committee supervise the operations of its corresponding Department in the Executive if the latter was working under secret orders from another Executive Department? Secretary of the Treasury Morgenthau was called upon for the answer.

One of the Treasury's duties, the Secretary explained, is to act as purchasing agent for the Government. Nothing seemed more logical, he argued, than for its Procurement Division to put its experience in dealing with American manufacturers at the disposal of a friendly Government anxious to place orders here on a large scale. Cross-examination wrung from Secretaries Morgenthau and Woodring the admission that functions ordinarily divided between the Departments of State, War, Navy, and Commerce had come to be centralized in the Treasury, despite the fact that no bona fide Treasury functions (such as the spending or lending of Government money) were involved. From Secretary Morgenthau's elaborate explanation that this was a perfectly conventional Treasury function, his real role in this Rooseveltian maneuver gradually emerged. He was being used to take this function not out of the War Department (where, at this stage of the defense program, it belonged), but out of the Office of the Secretary of War, and thence back into the office of the Assistant Secretary of War (who enjoyed some degree of statutory independence of the Secretary). From the Assistant Secretary of War the new circuit of communication could detour around the Secretary of War and run directly into the busy, growing apparatus of the war Presidency.

The President had asked the Secretaries of War and of the Treasury and the Under-Secretary of State to stay after Cabinet meeting one day and instructed them to clear the projected deal under Morgenthau's direction. The State Department was not asked to name a liaison to work with the Treasury. The Secretary of the Navy named a junior officer. The Secretary of War named Assistant Secretary of War Johnson, who, in the presence of General Arnold, told the Treasury representative that all matters pertaining to contracts for Army-type planes would have to be cleared through his office—not that of Woodring. Thus, the Secretary of State was by-passed; the Secretary of War was clearing through the Secretary of the Treasury; and the Secretary of the Treasury was clearing through the Assistant Secretary of War. Given the strategy Roosevelt was using to regain the initiative in the battle of Washington, this was logical. It split the War Department wide open and established the Commander-in-Chief as the arbitrator of its disputes and, therefore, the effective director of its operations.

BUT meanwhile, all that the average newspaper reader was able to see in this latest Congressional storm was vivid evidence of bickering in Washington and, behind the bickering, of the danger of war. Further cross-examination revealed that the French had $65,000,000 to spend for 1,000 planes on condition of delivery by July 1, 1939. To the Army at that point $65,000,000 and 1,000 planes represented astronomic values. The Treasury, on the other hand, regarded spending on this scale—actually, France had enough dollars to finance the deal—as no more than a beginning. As Morgenthau said in his Diaries, Roosevelt and he regarded the initial Anglo-French orders as so much training for the mass-production effort ahead. But the Army reacted against the proposal that we build 1,000 planes for the French. Despite the fact that six of our then largest plane plants were virtually shut down for lack of orders, the Secretary of War, the Army Chief of Staff, and the Commanding General of the Air Corps feared that we could not meet the

French deadline without delaying work on our 1939 air program.

In December, 1938, the Treasury had prepared a memorandum for the War Department which argued that to take on the French project would gear the aviation industry to produce faster for the Air Corps later in 1939. Assistant Secretary of War Johnson sided with the Treasury (and the White House). His technicians and Secretary Woodring's technicians argued over the Treasury's analysis for a week. Woodring then advised Morgenthau of his objections. Morgenthau replied that the Army attitude was blocking the French deal and appealed to the President.

Mr. President [he records himself as having argued, with characteristic literal-mindedness], if it's your theory that England and France are our first line of defense . . . let's either give them good stuff or tell them to go home, but don't give them stuff which the minute it goes up in the air will be shot down. No sense in selling them that which we know is out of date.

By "good stuff" he was referring specifically to the latest Douglas bomber. When, finally, on January 16, 1939, the President had called a showdown conference at the White House, Woodring defended his position by warning that release of this model to France would embarrass Roosevelt—and the 1939 defense budget. But Johnson, hoping to discredit Woodring and intent on succeeding him as Secretary of War, brought the issue to a head. Roosevelt ordered the administrative log jam broken in favor of Johnson and Morgenthau.

In his Diaries, Morgenthau dismisses the Congressional storm stirred up by the Chemidlin affair as a sensation soon forgotten. But it was more than that. Neither Congress nor the Army forgot the episode. For years it rankled and served as evidence of White House intrigue against the established institutions of national defense. And, more important, it served to crystallize the fundamental division between what might be called the national defense point of view and the global warfare point of view. Suspicion and hostility might have been averted by a more open approach to Congress, but the division could not have been concealed or the viewpoints reconciled.

Certainly, Morgenthau's running debate with Senator Clark clarified the strategy of the flanking movement the White House had designed to supplement direct appropriation for defense. Export orders were to prime the pump for aircraft production. The French, argued Morgenthau, "would pay for the development cost and their orders would be out of the way and delivered before Congress voted the money [for the new Air Corps Program]. . . . All of the development costs would be paid for by the French, and we would get plants into production that are idle now." To the delight of Senator Clark and his isolationist colleagues, no less a personage than the Army Chief of Staff, General Malin Craig, now came forward as the star witness against the White House program.

What right has the Treasury Department . . . to issue orders to the Army?" Senator Robert Reynolds, of North Carolina, asked General Craig.

"None, ordinarily," General Craig replied.

"Do you know of any case where that has ever been done before?" Senator Reynolds persisted.

"No, sir, I do not," the General said.

At this point, Senator Clark took over again.

"Was the memorandum of the Secretary of War in the nature of an objection to this transfer of these latest planes to the French?" he asked.

"The memorandum," explained the Army Chief of Staff, "was in the nature of a protection of the War Department's interest; that is, carrying out the War Department's program."

Secretary Woodring and General Craig charged that the President really had two arms programs, only one of which he had made public. This was the official War Department program (which was a compromise between the conflicting estimates of the alarmists and the stand-patters inside the Department). His secret program—as his Secretary of War and his Army Chief of Staff were informing the Military Affairs Committee—was being withheld from supervision by the responsible heads of the War Department. More sinister still, he was keeping it from Congress too. Presumably he and his bright young men had devised a scheme to finance this program without the formality of an appropriation. How else to diagnose the elaborate subterfuge of using the Treasury to administer a program calling for no Government funds? The White House strategy, Congressional opinion was inclined to agree, was to elude scrutiny by the Congressional Committees empowered to review policy on military affairs, on foreign relations, and on the public finances.

Senator Clark and his fellow isolationists were accusing Roosevelt of conspiring in secret with foreign powers against the national interest, which was to maintain peace. What more deadly confirmation could they have hoped for than that supplied on the record by Roosevelt's ranking military associates? Here were his own Secretary of War and his own Army Chief of Staff warning the Senate that Roosevelt's secret program—his international program—was in the sharpest possible conflict with the official War Department program which Congress was being asked to finance for defense and nothing but defense.

Whatever Roosevelt's failings may have been, he was *not* a dictator. The spectacle of General Craig "protecting" the national security by attacking the Commander-in-Chief spurred Roosevelt to form a clear mental picture of the man to take over as Army Chief of Staff when General Craig reached the retirement age. No matter what other qualities he might value in his next Chief of Staff, no matter what other contributions the next Chief might make, the role for which Roosevelt had to cast him was that of star witness for the Commander-in-Chief at Congressional investigations. And for General Craig he reserved the Chairmanship of the board receiving the applications of gentlemen for commissions. It was a post at which he was happy to allow General Craig to serve for the duration of World War II. Whatever Roosevelt's virtues may have been, he *was* vindictive.

The issue of War Department organization has a long and stormy history. Between World Wars I and II, it crystallized into a conflict between the Assistant Secretary and the General Staff for control of industrial mobilization. As President, Roosevelt had always sided with the Assistant Secretary against the Generals—to paraphrase a famous speech he once made to farmers, he was an Assistant Secretary himself. But now, in the person of General Douglas MacArthur, Roosevelt saw a new and urgent reason for strengthening civilian control of the structure of military command. MacArthur had retired as Chief of Staff when Roosevelt came to Washington. In 1935 he had been made director of national defense for the Philippines Commonwealth, and 1939 found him poised for action in the Philippines, in position to emerge as the symbol of the United States in a war against Japan. While in one way MacArthur's presence on this potential battlefield reassured Roosevelt, in another it irritated him. MacArthur was much more than a mere military genius: he belonged to that select and controversial company of military geniuses whose members through the ages have been possessed of an urge to merge personal destiny with world history.

Cast in any role, MacArthur was an enigmatic figure—and Roosevelt resented other enigmatic men, especially the forceful and self-centered ones who walked in a mystic aura. But in the year of Munich, playing the imperial pro-consul in Manila, MacArthur was beginning to treat Roosevelt as a mere politician, the source of patronage and supply. And, astonishingly enough, Roosevelt responded to this unfamiliar experience by indicating to his War Department advisors that he planned to make MacArthur the Pershing of the coming war. This idea inevitably had the effect of adding to Roosevelt's irritation with MacArthur. While playing with various schemes for diluting this commitment, Roosevelt spent the first part of 1939 quarreling with MacArthur by cable.

This left no doubt that the key to the President's mobilization strategy would be his choice of a successor to General Malin Craig as Chief of Staff on July 1, 1939. MacArthur could be trusted to make Washington a stormier battlefront for the next Chief than ever Pershing had made it for Peyton March in World War I. But Roosevelt did not want a mere counterpoise to MacArthur. On the one hand, he would have to rely on his Chief of Staff for advice more heavily than Wilson had relied on March; on the other hand, the prospective Chief of Staff was not going to be charged with the responsibility of running the coming war, leaving to the President only the fields of moral idealism and international system-building. Roosevelt required his Chief of Staff to be as tough as March was in fighting the White House's battles, but as flexible as March was not in compromising differences between the President and the Congressional chiefs.

The man he picked was George C. Marshall. Just as important, the man he asked to pick Marshall from the eligible upper group of officers was the Assistant Secretary of War. Johnson handled the assignment perfectly. He was able to present Marshall as a professional soldier whom the West Pointers accepted as a member of their club, and yet who was not himself a West Pointer. Marshall was not a political officer, but he had the air of a man whom the members of Congress would believe and accept (and in fact he was to prove the most impressive witness of the

emergency years). His command was Vancouver Bar-
racks, as far from Washington, D.C., as it is possible
to be in the continental United States. The idea of a
Chief of Staff who knew the West Coast appealed to
Roosevelt as an extra qualification for a man who
would have to cope with MacArthur. For, if the Middle Western States were isolationist, the Western Bloc
was intensely anti-Japanese, but remote from Europe.
And a leading Republican publisher of internationalist
convictions, E. Palmer Hoyt, and a Democratic Mayor,
Joseph K. Carson (then both of Portland), joined to
support Louis Johnson's recommendation of Marshall.
This kind of bipartisan endorsement always impressed
Roosevelt.

Convinced that he could use Marshall as a combined deputy and broker, hatchet man and scout,
and that both the soldiers and the politicians would
accept Marshall in this role and still respect him in his
own right, Roosevelt appointed him Acting Chief of
Staff. Woodring had been supporting the candidacy
of General Hugh Drum (for whom Roosevelt never
did find a place in the war).

As the report spread that Roosevelt had snapped, "I'm
tired of hearing Drum beat the drum for Drum,"
Washington gossip buzzed with the word that Woodring was out and Johnson was in as Secretary of War.
As usual, Washington gossip was half-right and, therefore, entirely misleading. Woodring was out at the
White House and, therefore, in as Secretary of War
for another year. Johnson was in at the White House
and, therefore, was a marked man. Roosevelt had

given him real powers—control of the appointment of the wartime Chief of Staff—and thereby disqualified him from enjoying the prestige of the Secretaryship of War. As Jim Farley should have realized, Roosevelt invited men out on his yacht instead of giving them power: he never gave prestige to those who already had power.

Prestige was exactly what the wartime Secretary of War was going to enjoy. If, in addition, he were given a chance to run the Departmental apparatus independently of the White House, he would accumulate enough power to rank as a kind of co-president. But if he were appointed to a conspicuous and dignified office around which the lines of command detoured from the Army into the Office of the President, he would be an exalted public symbol rather than a Presidential rival.

Such a symbol the public was bound to trust at the head of the wartime War Department. It was about to be converted into a kind of gigantic Bourse where all political and business interests would meet a hundred times a day; sometimes to clash, sometimes to combine, but always to make a market for the billions to be given and the sacrifices to be demanded. A year before this happened, while Congress, the pressure groups, and the five percenters licked their chops in anticipation of the day when the War Department would begin to do business as the national pork exchange, Roosevelt reached for the controls behind the trading posts.

He knew exactly where they were. Within a month after he settled on Marshall as his new Chief of Staff,

Roosevelt issued a Military Order—a presidential power very rarely invoked—transferring the Army and Navy Chiefs of Staff, the Aeronautical Board, the Joint Economy Board, and the Army-Navy Munitions Board from the authority of the War and Navy Departments to the direct supervision of the President as Commander-in-Chief. Just as the Joint Board was the instrument of the Chiefs of Staff, so the Army-Navy Munitions Board was operated by the Assistant Secretary of War. And it was through the Assistant Secretary—a civilian, a direct administrative agent of the White House, and the War Department official responsible for the Army-Navy Munitions Board—that Roosevelt proposed to route the lines of command radiating from the White House to the civilian-agencies-to-be. How effectively Roosevelt engineered this organization of direct White House control over the military is documented in Ferdinand Eberstadt's Report to the Secretary of the Navy on the Unification of the Armed Forces.

President Roosevelt had perhaps a greater interest in the detailed handling of our military forces than has been the rule among our Presidents. He appears to have regarded the Joint Chiefs of Staff primarily as advisors to himself on the military conduct of the war. The Joint Chiefs considered that as a body they were responsible only to the President in that field, and there appears to have been no consultation with the Secretaries of War and the Navy regarding the purely military advice they were giving the President.

The Secretaries of War and the Navy were not included on the regular distribution list of Joint Chiefs of Staff papers . . . although the Joint Chiefs of Staff continually dealt with matters for which the Secretaries of War and the Navy were legally responsible.

The situation was accentuated by the desire and need of other departments of the Government to obtain joint military opinion and advice on numerous matters. The State Department desired information on strategic considerations that might affect their policies. The War Production Board desired the same type of information for its purposes in guiding production. The Office of War Mobilization found itself in a similar position.

These agencies adopted the procedure of writing directly to the Joint Chiefs of Staff for their information. The Joint Chiefs responded to these letters frequently without reference to the Secretaries of War and the Navy. The result was a situation where civilian agencies of our Government were conducting major business involving policy with our military service without participation of the Secretaries of War or Navy.

ROOSEVELT had built up a valid administrative reason for wanting both the Chief of Staff and the Assistant Secretary of War to report directly to the White House independently of one another and of the Secretary of War. He had been pressing Congress since 1937 for a Reorganization Act empowering him to coordinate military and civilian functions in the White House. In 1939 he got it. The Reorganization Act of 1939 gave him the essential power he wanted. For it set up the Executive Office of the President, which it authorized him to run by Executive Order. On September 8, 1939, at the end of the first week of war in Europe, Roosevelt issued the historic Executive Order establishing a Presidential apparatus designed to serve as "such office for emergency management as the President shall determine." Although this apparatus

was not given its definitive, official name—Office of
Emergency Management—until May 25, 1940, it became the foundation of the war Presidency, and it
equipped the White House to operate the Joint Chiefs
of Staff and the Army-Navy Munitions Board.

No orthodox recommendations would have enabled
any war President to manage the administrative set-
up, let alone the political problems, accumulated
during the twenty years of drift since Wilson. Roosevelt's orthodox critics never did get clear as to the
administrative responsibility of the war Presidency.
They seemed to be laboring under the impression that
all the Commander-in-Chief had to do was delegate
his powers to a "Czar." But the essential problem of
the war Presidency transcended the power of any
single czar. For it was inescapably dual: how to equate
military and civilian functions and powers. Roosevelt
saw before 1937, as his critics did not even after 1940,
that it was the President's responsibility to operate
above the level of both the military and the civilian
agencies, balancing the powers of each. His responsibility, in short, was less to administer than to manipulate.

It was in August, 1939, that he launched the War Resources Board. It was an essay in manipulation.

test against the Military Order transferring the Joint
Board and Army-Navy Munitions Board into the
Executive Office of the President. This was a measure
of officiency; it intensified the apparatus of the Commander-in-Chief, and that of the Army Chief of Staff
and the strategic defense of navy. This double control Office of the President also grouped together the

CHAPTER III

THE POLITICS OF PREPAREDNESS

HISTORY, with which Franklin Roosevelt maintained
such an intimate alliance, has aided students of his
Presidency by permitting a neat division of his years
in office. The first six years are the time of the New
Deal. The ominous summer of 1939 is the crucial
transition to the war years. As summer ends, Hitler's
invasion of Poland begins preparedness in America,
thus opening a new six-year phase of wartime leadership.

July 1, 1939, brought Roosevelt his first significant
preparedness budget. But immeasurably more significant than the mere size of this first budget was the
use Roosevelt made of it to open a channel for the
tens of billions soon to flow into the war economy. A
sullen and suspicious Congress had granted Roosevelt
a Reorganization Bill and a $525,000,000 defense
budget as two unrelated acts. Roosevelt immediately
combined them. Congress had stormed against the
scheme Roosevelt had devised for organizing aid to
the French. Roosevelt hushed the watchdogs of Capitol Hill by switching the familiar administrative routes
without, however, disturbing their War Department
signposts. The Senate Military Affairs Committee had
been enraged to discover Roosevelt using the Treasury
as his principal defense agency. But no one could pro-

test against the Military Order transferring the Joint Board and Army-Navy Munitions Board into the Executive Office of the President. This was a measure of efficiency: it integrated the apparatus of the Commander-in-Chief with that of the Army Chief of Staff and the Assistant Secretary of War. This new Executive Office of the President also grouped together the Budget Bureau, the National Resources Planning Board, the Office of Government Reports, and the Liaison Office for Personnel Management.

To advocates of business methods in Government, this measure of efficiency seemed as plausible as anything Herbert Hoover might have done. Actually, it was as deceptive as anything Franklin Roosevelt ever did. For it was his simple Military Order which set the pattern of systematic inefficiency in the administration of the home front. Specifically, it enabled the President to create, by Executive Order, emergency agencies—later known as war agencies—which he could control and which the Assistant Secretary of War would operate. The root of the complications to come lay in the new position this Military Order created for the Assistant Secretary. To be sure, a new position was needed for the Assistant Secretary, but it was needed inside the War Department, not inside the White House. Roosevelt's action used a perennial War Department problem to anticipate a new White House problem.

Now the President, in his capacity as President, settles jurisdictional disputes inside Executive Departments as a matter of administrative and political routine. And this particular intra-Departmental squabble had certainly come to be accepted as routine. Like the proverbial crisis of the Hapsburg regime, it was considered "alarming but not serious." Suddenly, however, Roosevelt was making a startling point of intervening in the War Department—not merely as President, but as Commander-in-Chief. And with good reason, though with poor results. For his entire Administration was about to become involved in this intra-Departmental squabble—the civilian amateurs were about to go to war with the military professionals. Both factions were of course indispensable, and Roosevelt was groping for an instrument he could use to mobilize both. How could he provoke each faction to stimulate and at the same time to check the other? Clearly, by manipulating the balance of power between them. Hence his Military Order.

By promoting his second civilian aide in the War Department to the *de facto* position of Presidential chief of staff for the home front, Roosevelt seemed to have given the civilians the advantage over the military. In the past, the demand for a strong General Staff had provoked charges of militarism from Congress. But now Roosevelt had lodged an agency as powerful as the General Staff—the Army-Navy Munitions Board—in the White House under the civilian control of the Assistant Secretary of War. And the Assistant Secretary had exchanged his traditionally junior and insecure place on the periphery of the military hierarchy for that of deputy to the Commander-in-Chief. Just as Roosevelt made the joint chiefs of staff the instrument of direct Presidential control over military matters, so he made the Army-Navy Munitions

Board the corresponding instrument of Presidental control over industrial mobilization matters. The historic Defense Act of 1916 had given the Assistant Secretary control over industrial mobilization and, though subsequent legislation had clouded his title, Roosevelt now reaffirmed it.

Unfortunately, however, in clarifying the position of the Assistant Secretary of War, Roosevelt had complicated the organization of the War Department. Henceforth the Assistant Secretary was to serve in a dual capacity—not only inside the War Department but inside the White House as well. As the second civilian in the War Department, the Assistant Secretary was subordinate to the Secretary. But as the second civilian on the home front, the Assistant Secretary was subordinate only—and directly—to the President. As deputy for the Secretary inside the War Department, the Assistant Secretary's jurisdiction was, by statute, limited to procurement. But as deputy for the President with the war agencies, the Assistant Secretary was empowered to share and even to challenge the authority of the Secretary. At the White House as contrasted with the Departmental level, moreover, control of the home front carried the implicit power to influence military operations.

On the surface, the Military Order transferring the Joint Board and the Army-Navy Munitions Board to the Executive Office of the President may have seemed to be a measure of simple efficiency. But, in reality, it was a model of bad administration, complicated and complicating. At the time, the meaning of the move was obscured by the flash and clash of personality—Roosevelt was streamlining the powers of the Presidency, and Woodring and Johnson were quarreling about how he was to use them. But it was the move, and not the men whom Roosevelt happened to be moving at the moment, that mattered in the end. For by the time its disorganizing impact was felt, both Woodring and Johnson had been replaced by a Secretary and, at that point, an Under-Secretary who, far from being at odds, were intimates—intimates, however, collaborating under a plan of organization which assumed that they would be rivals.

Ordinarily, Roosevelt's ranking appointees in any administrative area were rivals—witness Woodring and Johnson, Hull and Welles in the State Department, Hopkins and Ickes in the public works field, and others too numerous to mention. Roosevelt's normal way of organizing a Department was to split it right down the middle. To this rule the Stimson-Patterson team he put into the War Department in 1940 was the great exception. But Roosevelt worked best when he observed his own highly unorthodox rules. In this case, at any rate, he outsmarted himself. For his 1939 reorganization equipped the apparatus of military command to function in the normal factional way; while his 1940 reshuffle manned it with members of only one faction. Woodring and Johnson balanced the apparatus by working against one another; Stimson and Patterson upset it by working together. The civilian agencies were entrusted to the Assistant Secretary because he was counted upon to fight for his—and their—independence of the Secretary. But what started out as a scheme for balancing civilian against military power ended by producing a concentration of military power. Confronted by the combination of the Secretary and the Assistant Secretary of War, the civilian agencies lost control of the home front to the military; and Roosevelt himself, in spite of all his manipulations, ended by losing the balance of power between the two forces.

From the beginning of the emergency until after Pearl Harbor, the concentration of power in the Office of the Assistant Secretary of War worked as Roosevelt wanted it to: it protected the President against any attempt at usurpation or, indeed, at autonomy by his subordinates, military or civilian. Not until 1942 did it develop into a Frankenstein monster. But then, when the President wanted to centralize control of the home front in an autonomous civilian agency, he found himself a prisoner of the pattern he had set in 1939. For this concentration of power in the Office of the Assistant Secretary of War came to provide the War Department exactly the same protection against the challenge of the civilian agencies that it had originally afforded Roosevelt against the resistance of the military. It was this sharing of power between the White House and the War Department which prevented the War Production Board from exercising its title to control of the home front. In England, the home front was operated by a civilian command enjoying Cabinet rank. But in America the civilian agencies were conceived and controlled as an appendage of the Office of the Assistant Secretary of War and his Army-Navy Munitions Board, and, accordingly, they were forced to fight for control of the functions explicitly assigned to their jurisdiction. Worse still, they were foredoomed to lose the fight.

IN August, 1939, a War Resources Board was appointed to advise the Assistant Secretary of War on how to revise the Industrial Mobilization Plan, and to deal with mobilization problems in general. "Any members appointed to this War Resources Board," warned the staff memorandum prepared in the summer of 1939 for the Assistant Secretary of War,

will be difficult to get rid of for many years if not the right type, hence should be carefully chosen. . . . Since, in the interest of prompt action in an emergency, the final decision on all matters will rest with the Chairman of the Board, he especially should be carefully chosen.

He was, but not to serve the purpose the sober experts of the General Staff had in mind. Their prudent advice assumed that the War Resources Board was going to be run by the man named to head it. Actually, no one but Roosevelt himself was going to run it—that is, if he decided it was going to be worth running. His way of finding out was, characteristically, to follow a pair of premises all his own wherever events, atmospheric conditions, and his flair for manipulation might lead.

The premises were as contradictory as the man, and as pragmatic. Thus—here was the first premise—in launching the War Resources Board, he was assuming the responsibility of leadership. But—and here was the other premise, which in a Rooseveltian equation might be called the paradox factor—this venture in leadership was to be little more than an experiment in predicting public opinion.

The paradox made practical sense, for the moment. After all, Roosevelt designed his first War Board to test public opinion, and not to mobilize the economy. And, certainly, public opinion needed testing. Who could say, in the summer of 1939, how quickly the country was likely to agree with Roosevelt that war was probable? Atmospherically, what was significant about the War Resources Board was its existence. The mere fact of its creation promised sooner or later to put isolationism on trial; and, meanwhile, it put the New Deal on immediate notice of suspension. To serve this grim notice Roosevelt chose not the most reactionary but, on the contrary, the most plausibly progressive of business leaders—Edward R. Stettinius, Jr., of the United States Steel Corporation. Efficiency was now to be expected of the President and, accordingly, efficiency neatly packaged in the person of Stettinius was what he now put on display at the head of his first emergency agency.

The Boards that begin wars rarely finish them. Ventures like the War Resources Board are, of necessity, trial balloons, and the men drafted to fly them in the headlines gamble their reputations against the heaviest of odds. In this particular case, Roosevelt was gambling too; he was staking his future position as a war leader on this first experiment. But his immediate position as a political leader he was not risking at all. For the very fact that the War Resources Board was an administrative speculation, and an audacious one at that, made it a sure-fire political bet for Roosevelt. Its assets were bound to be his, and its liabilities were bound to be charged up to Stettinius and his fellow members. For the Board's achievements the President, and only the President, would get the credit, and only the President would say when. And he would be as free to capitalize the Board's failures. When his famous sense of timing gave the signal, he could write the Board off altogether with thank-you notes to its members.

Stettinius chose as associates three other symbols of business leadership: Walter Gifford, of the American Telephone and Telegraph Company; John Lee Pratt, of General Motors; and General Robert Wood, of Sears, Roebuck, a leader of liberal business opinion in domestic matters and of the America First movement in foreign policy. To round out the public character of the Board, two conservatives not in corporate life were chosen. President Harold G. Moulton, of the Brookings Institution, an effective critic of New Deal economic policies and theories, was expected to deal with the staggering economic problem at hand. President Karl T. Compton, of the Massachusetts Institute of Technology, was to have the nation's scientific and technological resources as his province.

ROOSEVELT had many reasons for choosing Stettinius to head the War Resources Board. To begin with, Stettinius, along with Myron Taylor, had emerged as one of the heroes of the most sensational drama produced by the New Deal—Big Steel's new deal with labor, which had ended the open-shop era in America and split the united front which big business was try-

ing to form against Roosevelt. To Roosevelt, moreover, emotionally involved as he was in the memories
left behind by World War I, young Stettinius was
doubly attractive as the son of his father. Stettinius
Senior was a really able man. He had been J. P. Morgan's expert industrial organizer in the days of the
Morgan firm's empire building. Before emerging as
the key member of the Inter-Allied Munitions Council, the elder Stettinius had served as Assistant Secretary of War. Roosevelt had respected his opposite
number in the War Department and resented its
Chief. For Newton Baker was everything Roosevelt
was not—a leader of the bar, the personification of
all the respectable, conventional virtues, predictable,
sound, and, still more galling to Roosevelt, Wilson's
heir apparent.

These memories of the first World War were understandably vivid to Roosevelt in the summer of 1939.
He recalled scoffing at Secretary Baker and the do-
gooders around him as stuffy and naive, and he recalled
agreeing with J. P. Morgan's clients—the British and
French Governments—that Assistant Secretary Stettinius was the most competent business technician a
politician could wish. But before Roosevelt could
mobilize technicians for his war, he needed a symbol;
and, in the younger Stettinius, he had a symbol at
once promising to repeat the accomplishment of the
elder Stettinius and serving to recall the ordeal of
Woodrow Wilson.

This eager young man was tailor-made for Roosevelt's present purpose. In the first place, at a time
when it was necessary for Roosevelt to make peace

with Wall Street in order to turn a more united
strength against Hitler, he could not have made an
appointment more deferential, at least in outward
appearance, to the House of Morgan, than his choice
of the son of Stettinius. Further, no one could doubt
Stettinius's earnestness. No one would stop to judge
him as an administrator so long as he was on display
as a figure. Everyone was certain to identify him with
the package of respectable efficiency he advertised.
The public could be counted upon to find him as attractive or as repulsive as it found the first War Board
necessary or unnecessary. The White House could
and did use him interchangeably as a mouthpiece and
a scapegoat. The Assistant Secretary of War, accordingly, was given his orders. Casually, almost as an
afterthought to a conference (somehow the important
business of the Roosevelt Administration always managed to be transacted before, between, and after
meetings), the President said one day: "In thinking
about men for this job, don't overlook Ed Stettinius."

Stettinius made an obvious target. But a withering
cross-fire would have opened against anyone appointed to explore the mobilization program. From
one side, any defense effort was bound to be criticized
as bad in itself, and from the other as badly administered. This was bad for Roosevelt's appointees, but
good for him. For it caught the political opposition on
the horns of the dilemma which decided the elections
of 1940, 1944, and 1948: were his critics to oppose the
inevitable or merely to claim they could deal with it
more efficiently? Stettinius personified efficiency. His
appointment was a promise to conservative opinion

that, for the time being at least, the defense program would be organized by the recognized leaders of the business community. The pundits accepted this at face value: they agreed that the crisis was forcing Roosevelt to become practical.

At this stage of developments, the power of the Morgan empire appeared to be strongly resurgent. On the Democratic side, one of its bright young men, Stettinius, was by way of grasping the home front controls. On the Republican side, another was developing into a Presidential candidate: this was the dynamic Indiana farmer and Ohio lawyer, Wendell Willkie. After an early career as a Democratic lieutenant of Newton D. Baker in Ohio, Willkie had become a Republican and a protégé of the Morgans when the New Deal's public utility issue forced Wall Street to fight back in defense of the holding companies, and especially of Commonwealth and Southern. As a Presidential candidate, Willkie aspired to avenge Roosevelt's defeat of Baker in the 1932 Democratic Convention by making Roosevelt's business-baiting the issue of 1940. Willkie, it may be added, perceived that the appointment of Stettinius was a trap for business, but he also saw the necessity for business to rush into it on pain of being caught in the other trap—the trap of isolation.

For a time, Willkie had forced Roosevelt onto the defensive by the vigor with which he stumped the country, hoarsely and relentlessly proclaiming the genius of American business and charging that Roosevelt could not work with businessmen. Now, by a quirk of fate, Roosevelt found a refutation in Stettinius. Even Roosevelt's diabolical imagination could not have conjured up such irony as the House of Morgan grooming this second favorite son to serve him as the answer to the first.

Thus, the pressures of politics and the issues, normally in conflict, merged. Reality supplanted pantomime. Not only did Roosevelt have to show the public at large that he could work with business; just as urgent, he had to show the blocs comprising the New Deal that he was serving them by working with business. The time for the first step forward was at hand. On August 9, 1939, Assistant Secretary of War Johnson and Assistant Secretary of the Navy Edison announced jointly "that the President had approved the formation of a civilian advisory committee to the Army and Navy Munitions Board, to be known as the War Resources Board."

"In an emergency," the Johnson-Edison announcement added, "the War Resources Board would become an executive agency of the Government with broad powers similar to those of the old War Industries Board." But one of the essential qualifications of the old War Industries Board was that it, unlike the War Resources Board, included a ranking representative of labor—Hugh Frayne, general organizer for the American Federation of Labor (Samuel Gompers himself had been one of the seven members of the Advisory Commission of the Council of National Defense, which created the War Industries Board). Thus, the key war agency of the Wilson period had given a place to labor, although organized labor was not then a major political power, and though Wilson himself was a de-

tached, critical, and somewhat condescending patron
of labor. Under the New Deal, by contrast, Roosevelt
had, in a new sense, made himself a leader of labor
and had mobilized it into a huge political army. Yet
now, for some unfathomable reason, when World
War II was threatening to destroy labor as a free and
independent force, the Stettinius Board was being
organized by the War and Navy Departments—not
by the White House!—on a basis which repudiated
the simple, solid precedent Roosevelt himself had
helped the Wilson Administration to set.

Labor's reaction was much less complicated than
Roosevelt's maneuver. The American Federation of
Labor prepared to denounce the new Board. The
attitude of the CIO was expressed by Joseph Curran,
President of the National Maritime Union, who called
on Roosevelt to neutralize his new agency by appointing to it six labor representatives. What Curran did
not realize was that Roosevelt's way of neutralizing
the Board was to restrict its membership to Stettinius
and his five friends. And what Stettinius and his set
did not realize was that they had committed an even
more fatal, if less obviously provocative, blunder. For
not only had they excluded labor from the council of
the nation, they had excluded agriculture as well. If
labor belonged to Roosevelt, agriculture did not; and
if labor was not a first-class power in Congress, agriculture was. Once the economy began to consume the
people's money at a wartime rate, the farm bloc in
Congress was bound to seize the power to purge the
home front agencies. No group of men, accordingly,
who aspired to direct the home front could survive

without the approval of the men the farmers sent to Washington. These farm members could now be counted on to scrutinize the "Morgan Crowd" with more than their normal suspicion and resentment.

Stettinius saw the situation as a honeymoon. But Roosevelt—and Baruch—saw it as an unusually delicate triangle complicated by years of intrigue. Roosevelt and Baruch were not strangers. Nor were they intimates. Wilson's wisest advisor in practical as well as in ideological matters had been Mr. Justice Brandeis, toward whom Roosevelt himself later developed a conspicuously filial relationship. Brandeis had warned Wilson of the danger that too much of the nation's war business might fall into the hands of the Morgan group or some other clique. Yet no one knew better than Brandeis how indispensable businessmen are in the management of a war economy. What was wanted, he told Wilson, was a professional free lance, an out-and-out speculator independent of all the organized interests, who knew how to raid the vulnerable ones and to trade with the powerful ones. The description fitted Baruch, and Baruch had fitted the job.

Over the years Roosevelt had more or less grudgingly developed a lively appreciation of the man's sophistication and realism. As one professional politician to another, he acknowledged the high returns Baruch had consistently earned on his small investments in the primary campaigns of Southern Democrats who had a knack of accumulating seniority. As one expert on administration to another, he felt obliged to keep posted on Baruch's views of the problems of the

Presidency. And as one past master at public relations to another, he accepted the public's awed re-
appraisal of the once suspect speculator. Altogether,
therefore, Roosevelt had no doubt that Baruch was
a shrewd and rugged independent. In fact, his respect
for the gabby old sage was the measure of his mistrust.
When Baruch returned from Europe, late in 1938,
Washington assumed that he would be called upon to
take up the burden he had laid down after Armistice
Day. If the crisis had been more pressing, and if the
War Resources Board had been less flimsy, he might
have.

Now Baruch knew the times. "Dr. Facts," as Wilson
used to call him, realized that the Roosevelt Era was
as far to the left of the pale and by-gone time of Wilson's War Industries Board as was this new club for
respectable tycoons only, called the War Resources
Board, to the right of its venerable predecessor. And
he knew his man. F.D.R., Baruch was quick to concede, had a shrewder instinct for the complexities and
turbulence of the times than himself. The White
House, he therefore assumed, could not be taking this
Washington subsidiary of J. P. Morgan and Co. very
seriously. And though he wished to serve as a Presidential advisor, he also wanted to survive as a political
power.

Baruch saw through the President's strategy clearly
enough to elude that part of the maneuver which
threatened to add him to the list of Wall Street expendables. But at the same time, he was realist enough to
be aware that no man in his position could attack
President Roosevelt in public without getting hurt,

and Roosevelt knew that Baruch did not want to get hurt. The old man had learned how to win battles by staying above them, and he intended to cling to his pedestal.

This nice balance between Baruch's instinct for indispensability and his instinct for survival suggested the perfect formula for compromise—he would let himself be consulted. The ceremony of consultation would leave him free to advise the President in public; free, at the proper time, to agree with the President that Stettinius had failed: as free in fact as only an advisor who is a symbol but not a privy councilor can be. The joint announcement of the War and Navy Departments, accordingly, added a most unusual grace note. "One of the first activities of the new committee," it said, "will be to consult with the Chairman of the old War Industries Board, Mr. Bernard Baruch."

The Committee's other function, which it quickly fulfilled, was to get attacked. The businessmen Stettinius had recruited to deal with the national emergency were remarkably obliging—Gifford and General Wood did not turn up for the first meeting of the Committee. And Stettinius was obliging too. His first statement was a more devastating political indictment of his own Board than any critic would have dreamed of daring to level at it. It actually began: "We of the business community." None of the platitudes with which it continued could hide this gauche admission that the first effort to safeguard the national security had been conceived in the sin of class consciousness—by the wrong class.

New Deal opinion was demoralized. This mood

Secretary of the Interior Harold Ickes quickly converted into indignation. While the Henry Wallace of
those days was content to sit in his place at the Cabinet table, obedient and ambitious in the shadow of
Franklin Roosevelt, Ickes asserted himself as the one
ranking member of the Administration able and indeed anxious to defy the Boss. In this role, he was
privileged, for although Roosevelt usually resented
criticism, his affection for Ickes and reliance on him
literally fed on irritation with the old reformer's low
boiling point; on professional grounds, also, he admired
the Curmudgeon for having improvised both a political
career and an unimpeachable public standing out of
his unsubtlety. This was one Cabinet meeting at
which Ickes did not let his Chief down. "What goes
on?" he snarled.

The members of President Roosevelt's Cabinet were
not exactly independent jurors before whom the President was summoned each week to justify his conduct.
But for once he seemed defensive in their presence. He
liked Stettinius, he explained, and held him in very
high regard. But he too had been disturbed to learn of
Stettinius's choice of associates. They were chosen, he
assured the Cabinet, at a time when he himself happened to be away from Washington. Under the circumstances, he agreed, it was out of the question to
allow the Board to grow into the super-agency that
would eventually be needed to administer the executive powers of the Commander-in-Chief. But to dis-
solve it immediately was equally out of the question.
For the present, he suggested, the Administration
would do well to accept the War Resources Board at

face value and to use it as a kind of seminar for businessmen interested in familiarizing themselves with
the Army's plans for M-Day.

Lack of subtlety was not one of Roosevelt's failings
and platonic aloofness was not one of Ickes's virtues.
The Cabinet accepted Roosevelt's double talk as both
an explanation and a solution, but Ickes took it as
Presidential incitement to murder. Now, as Ickes and
the New Deal junta sharpened their knives to execute
what they insisted were Presidential orders, they found
themselves for once free to organize a blood purge as
an inside operation. For a strange ally, who commanded artillery powerful enough to cover their in-
fighting tactics, joined them.

This ally, General Hugh Johnson, was no friend of
the New Deal. But he was Baruch's spokesman. And
Baruch had a very urgent reason late in September for
wanting Johnson's syndicated column to trumpet forth
the word that "the new War Resources Board is going
to get the gate." Moreover, Baruch wanted there to
be no doubt why the Board had failed. Consequently,
the column continued,

Although the industrialists named are businessmen of the
very highest type and foremost leadership, they are all so
closely tied in with Morgan or Du Pont financial interests,
that it is a triple wonder that they accepted, that those
interests permitted them to accept, and that the President
appointed them.

This was blunt talk, even for "Old Ironpants"
Johnson. But the stakes were high, even for Baruch.
For when Roosevelt winked permission to Harold
Ickes to blitz the War Resources Board, he was mak-

ing Baruch a free gift of great power. And here was immediate and unarguable proof of the new mystique attaching to Baruch. Now while the invisible lines of communication that connect the Cabinet room with the country were still crackling with the news that Stettinius's group were to be thrown to the wolves, both the New Dealers and their enemies came rushing to the wily old sage for help. The men of whose class he was an official member pressed him to save them. The men of whose club he was becoming an honorary member pressed him to join in the slaughter. If this is not power, what is?

The shriven Wolf of Wall Street exploited his strategic advantage like a statesman. With all the dignity of one Government dispatching a plenipotentiary to another, he deputized his long-time associate, John Hancock of Lehman Brothers, to represent him on the War Resources Board. For this small favor the panic-stricken friends of the Board were as grateful to Baruch as were his strange fellow conspirators —the New Dealers—for his refusal to underwrite the Board by joining it himself. And then, to balance the account, Hugh Johnson deployed to the left. He echoed Secretary Ickes's warning that the Board to which Baruch's deputy had been added was "Morgan–Du Pont loaded." The New Dealers were convinced that they had been right to trust Baruch, and the Morgan interest was convinced of its recklessness in not having cleared such an historic project with him from the outset. Altogether, Baruch was established as the keeper of Wall Street's conscience. He had repaid the pompous element in the Gentlemen's Clubs

for a lifetime of slurs and snubs. The New Dealers
were in his debt, to their satisfaction and to his, and
he was more available than ever to advise with both
the President and the critics of the President.

For six weeks the fracas had raged on in the President's name. Then Roosevelt exploded a bombshell.
The War Resources Board would file a report, he told
his press conference, and disband. But its report would
not be published. For, Roosevelt explained, the United
States is not going to war and the public is not interested in plans for war.

Hitler was blitzing Poland. Yet, in one sense Roosevelt was justified in dismissing the offensive Board
whose existence in name only had created such a
political disturbance. For a long time before the Board
had assembled, Baruch and Assistant Secretary of
War Johnson had been working together in the closest
intimacy. The members of the Board, therefore, found
that their work had been done for them by Johnson's
staff before ever they came to Washington. Their only
contribution, in fact, was to sign the Report which
Hancock presented to them in October with the approval of Baruch and his collaborators in the War
Department.

The report served at once as the War Resources
Board's only official act, and as the justification for its
dismissal. It became a document of prime historical
importance. Locked up in the conspicuously secret
files of a handful of conspicuously public men—Roosevelt, who proposed to keep it locked up, and Johnson,
Stettinius, Baruch, and Hancock—this report during
the balance of Roosevelt's Presidency had a history

now bordering on mystery unresolved, now on scandal unexploded. Granting that the President intended to use the report, as in fact he did in 1942, its availability in 1939 justified his liquidation of the War Resources Board. There was considerable basis for arguing that, so long as the work of the War Department technicians was not interfered with, Baruch's advice could remain non-controversial and productive, and study of the defense problem might progress efficiently. In fact, it was in this very month, on October 21, that the most obscure of all Presidential agencies—the secret new Advisory Committee on Uranium—held its first meeting. It submitted eight proposals, and asked the Army-Navy Munitions Board for its first grant of $6,000.

There was, however, another consideration. In the practical sense—the sense in which Roosevelt was so uncanny and pitiless a judge—the inevitable humiliation of the War Resources Board could not help but be a staggering blow to Louis Johnson and his Army-Navy Munitions Board Staff, for Johnson's very prominence as an advocate of preparedness inescapably fastened on him the blame for this preparedness measure.

Causes and organizations rise and fall with the fortunes of the individuals who lead them. Inevitably, the cloud that now settled over the Assistant Secretary of War obscured the position of the War Department technicians. Whatever good had been accomplished in July by gearing the Office of the Assistant Secretary of War into the machinery of the White House was undone—within 90 days the first step forward had been followed by three steps backward. While Warsaw burned and the Maginot Line bristled, the Americans who were engaged in the routine business of planning how to coordinate and operate the apparatus of a War Economy came to seem as eccentric and irrelevant as the physicists fussing with their equations and their glassware.

Louis Johnson's distress was Harry Woodring's opportunity. At a Cabinet meeting, the Secretary called the President's attention to the fact that the Assistant Secretary had written a foreword to a book entitled *Adjusting Your Business to War*. No books on such subjects carry Administration approval, the country was promptly told, and 90 percent of them are written by people who know less than nothing about the problems involved. For a year Johnson had been the spokesman and confidential agent of the White House. Now the Presidential dunce cap, usually reserved for pundits, was sitting on his head. And Secretary Woodring, who had not known from week to week when he might be barred from his office, suddenly found himself speaking for the Administration. "We are not setting up any war boards or war machinery," he snorted, "and, as far as I am concerned, I hope we never will."

Time was on Johnson's side. But instead of waiting for Hitler to vindicate him, instead of maturing an opportunity for the President to swing back toward him and to move forward again on a sounder basis with their joint projects, the Assistant Secretary, controversial as ever, rushed forward into a major political blunder. What had made Johnson seem invulnerable was the reorganization that designated him the *ex officio* director of the formidable and irreplaceable machinery of mobilization. The further fact that this machinery under his personal control was manned by obscure and disciplined technicians, subject to the Commander-in-Chief, cemented the connection between the Office of the Assistant Secretary and that of the President. Johnson took the new power of the Assistant Secretaryship as a public promise of promotion to the Secretaryship. In addition, he happened to have a personal promise, but this hardly protected his option. The only guarantee Johnson had of promotion to the Secretaryship—at least during Roosevelt's Presidency—was his occupancy of the strategic foxhole into which the Assistant Secretaryship had been converted.

But before he could see whether his new administrative advantage over Secretary Woodring could be translated into the Secretaryship for himself, he rushed out into the political line of fire. He created a new emergency organization—the National Defense Power Committee—to cope with the electric power shortage he foresaw. This was wise. But—and this was politically reckless—he set it up as a partnership between himself and the most politically suspect barons of the business hierarchy, men whom the President hated and on whose hatred his power fed. He did it all with Roosevelt's permission, but then Roosevelt never forebade anyone to make a clay pigeon of himself.

In Europe the Sitzkreig had begun, but in Washington war was still a game, and utility politics was still war. "The young radicals and business-baiters of the White House circle," Arthur Krock had reported in the New York *Times* when the War Resources

Board was disbanded, "are giving out private 'victory' communiques and assuring the young band of Government employees for whom they have found places that 'Wall Street' has been routed and the President's heart is, as ever, in the right place." Now, as Louis Johnson followed his Resources Board and his Power Committee into eclipse, the President's supporters no longer felt obliged to whisper that his heart was really in the right place. To them, at least, the New Deal seemed more vigorous than ever. And indeed, Roosevelt himself had begun to exclaim, "If war does come, we will make it a New Deal war." This statement, so typical of Roosevelt, was designed to irritate the conservatives and their pundits. But it also served the broad purpose of stimulating F.D.R.'s army of followers and suggesting new combinations and experiments to himself. He went so far as to promise the Secretaryship of War to New York's famous stormy petrel, Fiorello La Guardia, which is proof positive that he was resolved to fight fire with fire by meeting trouble with trouble.

CHAPTER IV

THE LOST YEAR

"MY experience in two world wars, the aftermaths, and the endeavors to make a lasting peace," Bernard Baruch said in a speech before the Industrial College of the Armed Forces in 1947, "makes me marvel at the regularity with which errors are repeated. One of the errors that most frequently recurs is failure to study and understand the records of past experience. It seems as if my hearing aid is out of kilter—the voices and arguments are the same.

"At my first meeting with the then Under Secretary of War, Robert Patterson, he asked, 'Why is it that we don't start off where we finished in the last war? Why don't we adopt what was learned? Later, the Under Secretary of Navy and others propounded the same question.

"They may have had in mind, among other things, an outline of action that we drew up at the War Industries Board, covering America's participation in the first World War. I sent it to President Wilson, and he accepted it as the mandate for our existence. It is as true today as it was on November 10, 1918. . . . Time has tested the formula and found it good. It will be equally true of our next war, which the fates forbid. . . .

"The Armed Forces had an M-Day plan, which would have saved precious lives and the wasted wealth, but they were not permitted to put it into effect. We were told that this was a different kind of war and none of that 'old world war stuff' was wanted."

Arthur Krock, no friend of Roosevelt's but a great friend of Baruch's, took bitter delight in recalling the situation. Baruch had shown great restraint, Krock explained, in not revealing how, "when he offered his services in World War II, he heard echoed from the White House circle the remark that 'Bernie is too old, and this isn't his kind of war!'" But Baruch, nevertheless, refrained from telling a much more important story, tragic for the country and humiliating for himself.

Baruch had been the principal collaborator of Louis Johnson and the Army-Navy Munitions Board in preparing the 1939 revision of the Industrial Mobilization Plan. But the Plan was unacceptable to Roosevelt. Indeed, the Bureau of the Budget's history of the War Administration dismisses the plan as not having "merited the build-up it had been given; it was a document," says the Bureau's official history, "dealing only in generalities with the problem of governmental organization for war and it was formulated for conditions unlike those which actually arose. It presumed the existence of a state of war under which almost any power could be had from Congress for the asking and under which a full-fledged war organization would have to be created. Neither of these conditions prevailed, and until war came, progress could be made only as public opinion crystallized into decision.

Another crucial factor in the rejection of the 'M-Day' plan," this history continues,

was its provision for a single administrator with war powers over governmental organization and policy, far greater than those exercised by the Chairman of the War Industries Board in World War I. Delegation of such enormous powers would have made it difficult for the President to control the broad strategy of defense preparation and foreign economic policy during a most critical period. Such action would have constituted virtual abdication by the President and would have made him less able to meet his constitutional responsibilities. Moreover, the plan carried with it potentialities of far greater military influence in the management of governmental affairs than appeared either desirable or politic at the time. For these reasons, the plan seemed unattractive to the President. For the same reason, his political opponents held the plan in high esteem.

Robert Sherwood's wording is more imaginative, but his acceptance of this part of the record is as literal-minded:

There existed an Industrial Mobilization Plan, which, in the words of Bernard M. Baruch, its principal author, was designed to enable the country "to pass from a peace to a war status with a minimum of confusion, waste and loss." But—the thinking behind this and all other plans before 1940 was based on the assumption that a nation passed from a peace status to a war status as quickly and as decisively as one passes from one room to another. No provision whatever had been made for the maze of corridors, blind alleys and series of ante-chambers— labelled "Phony War", "cash and carry", "more than mere words", "Lend Lease", etc.—which the United States was compelled for the first time in its own or any other nation's history to traverse between September 1, 1939 and December 7, 1941.*

Secretary of Defense James Forrestal referred to this criticism in 1947. But he added a point that was genuinely valid because it applied not only to the Industrial Mobilization Plan of 1939, which was indeed vulnerable on the counts cited, but also to the suppressed Baruch-Hancock modification of it for Stettinius's War Resources Board. This modified version met the official Budget Bureau–Sherwood criticism. "The plan was deficient," Forrestal told a Senate Committee, "in the development of systems and procedures of control, such as The Controlled Materials Plan evolved during World War II for the allocation of steel, copper and aluminum." With characteristic perspicacity, he pointed to the very heart of the problem.

But in 1939 Roosevelt and Baruch had not yet locked horns over the operating problem. Rather, their disagreement over the Industrial Mobilization Plan had been on the policy level, and it had brought them closer to what both men loved—a bargain, in this case to take the form of a second Baruch Plan, which Roosevelt would agree in advance to accept. The legend is that Baruch stood his ground. But in fact, he was in no position to play the disinterested critic. He was beginning to bid for the job of administering whatever permanent organization he and Roosevelt could agree to form, although he was still wary of exposing his ambition. And so, he accommodated himself to

* Robert E. Sherwood, *Roosevelt and Hopkins* (New York, Harper & Brothers, 1948), p. 280.

Roosevelt's criticisms—the statesman traded himself down to the level of the politician. In this case, as Baruch apparently recognized, the politician was more statesmanlike than the statesman. For Baruch's second plan, the suppressed plan, was incomparably better than his first, the criticized plan. Thanks to Roosevelt's criticism, the second plan supplied a really workable blueprint of mobilization. But despite its merit, the plan was not put into operation, for in the confused months leading up to both the Blitz and the political conventions preparedness was not the best politics. Not until the summer would it become so, and meanwhile Roosevelt decided not to push the preparedness program. Accordingly, he suppressed the second Baruch plan, Roosevelt-inspired amendments and all.

THE tragedy of the failure to act on this second Baruch report lies in the fact that it was an excellent plan which successfully met all the major difficulties which the Industrial Mobilization Plan had failed to meet. First of all, the earlier plan had naively assumed that the only alternative to "Normalcy" is war. The suppressed Baruch plan, by contrast, specifically asserted, "We recognize that the plans made in advance to meet a wartime situation of an unknown character must retain a great degree of flexibility." Accordingly, it allowed for not one alternative to "Normalcy" but three. The first was the "paper" planning stage. The second was "the transition period when war seems imminent. In this stage, the previously made paper plans should be brought down to reality by the men

who are to be asked to execute any final program."
The third alternative was war.

The second weakness of the Industrial Mobilization
Plan was its recommendation that a "Super-agency"
be created under a wartime czar appointed by the
President but independent of him. Thus, while nomi-
nally conceding the President's constitutional and
legal responsibility for directing preparedness, the
Army's plan asserted that it was "obvious that the
magnitude and emergency nature of this task require
the services of an adequate organizational set-up to
which this responsibility may be delegated." Nothing
could have been less obvious to Roosevelt, and, on
this point, which the White House regarded as crucial,
the new Baruch plan accordingly reversed the original
Army plan. Exactly as if the Bureau of the Budget
and not Baruch were defining Roosevelt's role, the
Baruch plan said: "Final responsibility for policies
and for the coordination of the war program must be
vested in the President." Having thus reaffirmed the
principle of control by the President, it then proceeded to disavow the idea of a super-agency as the
instrument of coordination. Posing the alternatives of
(1) "a super-agency which would have under its direction a number of agencies each handling individual
powers" or (2) "the creation of a limited number of
agencies each exercising a delegated war power, but
with provision for their coordination among themselves, leaving to the President the problem of decision
only when they do not agree," the second report firmly
elected the latter alternative: "It is our considered
judgment that coordination offers the only effective

means of converting American industries to the purposes of war. . . . We . . . do not recommend cen-
tralization of power in a new super-agency."

The third essential weakness of the Industrial Mobilization Plan was that it might have lent itself to
militarism. Against this danger, the Baruch Plan provided elaborate safeguards. Instead of encouraging or
even tolerating any concentration of emergency power
in the War Department, it urged that "wartime powers
be vested in especially created wartime agencies which
will be automatically demobilized when war is over.
Should wartime powers be granted to existing executive . . . agencies of the government" (meaning the
War Department in particular), Baruch's report added,
in an unmistakable warning against administrative
militarism, "it will be next to impossible at the end
of the war to separate the wartime from the peacetime functions of the government."

Inherent in any mobilization program, Roosevelt
felt, were two threats to sane civilian government.
Militarism was one. The other he regarded as coming
from big business. How explosively the two threats
could combine into one had just been shown by the
feckless way in which the War Resources Board had
been recruited from the ranks of the tycoons. All the
more remarkable, therefore, was the outspoken warning to big business which Baruch wrote into his suppressed report to the War Resources Board. The discredited plan, the Army's Industrial Mobilization
Plan, had stated as a matter of course that "the personnel to fill positions of responsibility in the War Resources Administration should be obtained from the

patriotic business leaders of the Nation." But on this, as on so many other scores, Baruch's revised plan might have been written by Roosevelt himself.

No group in the body politic [it said] should hope to achieve in time of war a position which it has not been able to obtain under peace conditions. There should be no seeking for special advantage on the part of any groups. . . . It is not enough to secure the support of industry alone. It is also necessary to obtain the support of agriculture, transportation and labor and capital, and to control foreign trade, prices, credit and tax policies toward the single end [of] winning the war.

But of all this the Bureau of the Budget's official history says not a word. The fact is that in 1939 Roosevelt had his choice, not between adopting a bad Army plan or doing nothing, but between adopting a bad Army plan or a good Roosevelt-Baruch plan or doing nothing. The Budget Bureau history diverts attention from Roosevelt's decision to do nothing by concentrating its fire against the bad Army plan (in which of course Baruch had had a large hand), and continues the conspiracy of silence against the good plan prepared by Baruch and Hancock to satisfy Roosevelt—continues it to the point of omitting to explain that it finally was adopted in principle after Pearl Harbor.

Because the President had decided to do nothing, a year was to be lost. The story of this lost year is best told in terms of the suppressed Baruch plan which Roosevelt had first inspired and then discarded. In fact, the complications in which the President found himself involved a year later would have been avoided if he had followed the suppressed plan's simple recommendations.

To hindsight the story of the things left undone during the lost year of 1939–40 is unbelievable. What seems still more unbelievable is the behavior of responsible people who saw the danger, who were alert and indignant against isolationism and do-nothingness, who feared that America might follow the pattern in which the mood of Munich trapped Britain, but who nevertheless left these things undone. What is most unbelievable of all is the record of the administrators who were charged with doing the most important of these things and who left them undone.

ON one elementary point it had not been necessary for the second Baruch plan to reverse the first. This was the urgent need to stock-pile strategic materials normally imported. Under Louis Johnson's prodding, Roosevelt had invested considerable time and political expense in the spring of 1939 in squeezing a modest stock-pile appropriation past Andrew Jackson May's House Military Affairs Committee and through Congress. Yet, in May, 1940, instead of being in a position to press for a new and larger stock-pile fund as insurance against the greater danger threatening the country during the second year of emergency, the Administration's record amounted to an admission that Congressman May had been right and President Roosevelt wrong. If $100,000,000 had been needed to protect the national security against shortages of strategic materials, why had only $13,000,000 been earmarked or spent to implement the entire stock-pile program?

The four-year $100,000,000 stock-pile fund had become available July 1, 1939. Rubber was far and away the most important material to be inventoried. To expedite rubber imports, the Rubber Reserve Corporation was organized a year later, in July, 1940, as a partnership between the RFC and the rubber companies. This was intended to eliminate money as an obstacle to the solution of the rubber problem. Nevertheless, the problem was not solved. In peaceful years, American industry had consumed something less than 600,000 tons of rubber, annually. Conservative estimates for 1940 anticipated that defense needs would increase consumption to approximately 700,000 tons. By May, 1940, Hitler stood at the Channel and Japan was threatening the rubber routes from Southeastern Asia. Yet, of the appropriation voted by a reluctant Congress ten months earlier for the total stock-pile program, $87,000,000 remained unused; at the same time, our rubber reserve was pitifully inadequate to support a year's operations, at the peacetime rate. By the time of Pearl Harbor—one year and a half after the organization of the Rubber Reserve Corporation, and two years and a half after Roosevelt had wrung his first stock-pile appropriation from Congressman May—we had on hand only enough rubber to supply industry for a year at the normal peacetime rate.

Jesse Jones, the all-powerful "Czar" of the Federal lending agencies, had been using the Rubber Reserve Corporation's stock-pile fund for bargain-hunting in a war-inflated market that offered no bargains. Thus, in August, 1940, the Rubber Reserve Corporation set out to buy up to 150,000 tons of rubber desperately

needed at any price. The market was fluctuating between 18 and 20 cents a pound. But Jones was determined to hold back until the market came to him.
Meanwhile, Japan bid the price up to 20 cents. Jones
withdrew. While he played a waiting game, the Axis
got the rubber.

Why, when Pearl Harbor was in the making? Why,
when the Administration was attacking Congress as
isolationist, obstructionist, and unrealistic in its refusal
to heed Administration warning that a war crisis was
threatening America? Above all, when Congress had
voted money for a program demanded by the Administration, when for once the money had been voted in
time to fortify the country against a specific danger,
why had almost nothing been done?

Japan was coiled to snap at the life line through
which basic materials were pumped from Southeastern
Asia into America's factories. The German war machine was as powerful as its raw material supply was
adequate, and Japan was serving as its Asiatic purchasing agent. But on the eve of the great rubber
famine Jesse Jones did not regard rubber as a sound
investment at 20 cents. His private priority system put
dollars first and inspired one of the bitterest stories of
the bitter, frustrating months of the Pearl Harbor
period. At Fall River, Massachusetts, a warehouse
burned, destroying some 15,000 tons of rubber. "Good
thing we had it insured," Jones's critics mimicked him
as exclaiming. At the time of Pearl Harbor, the country's stock-pile amounted to only about 600,000 long
tons, with some 150,000 more on the ocean; less than
even a normal year's consumption.

As Secretary of Commerce and Chairman of the RFC, Jones was by far the most powerful member of the Administration. But for some months his work had consisted mainly of passing the word around that Roosevelt had to be restrained from involving America in a war that would bankrupt her without serving the national interest. To express such views was Jones's privilege, but not as a senior member of the Roosevelt Administration. However, Jones had no intention of resigning over a mere matter of political principle—certainly not at a time when, in spite of his "go slow" attitude toward defense problems, his position was becoming stronger daily. The third-term question having divided the Administration into rival cabals—one conspiring to make Roosevelt keep his promise not to run, the other to make him break it—Jones alone contrived to manipulate both plots as a leader of each. For in spite of his opposition to Roosevelt's politics and to the third term, he was an unashamed and a powerful aspirant to run with Roosevelt on the third term ticket, and he was astute enough to persuade Jim Farley that he was best qualified to replace their close friend Jack Garner as Vice President. It was to Roosevelt's interest, Jones argued, to appease business, the South, and Congress; on all three counts, Jones asserted, his opposition to the New Deal marked him out to stand with Roosevelt.

SCARCELY less urgent than the neglected stock-pile problem was that of foreign trade control; and to this the suppressed Baruch-Hancock report, by broadening the Army's Mobilization Plan, indicated a quick and practical solution. The State Department, preoccupied as ever with doctrine and diplomacy, had but one interest in the new economic and psychological facets of world politics: its insistence that all dealings with foreign governments be channeled through its anti-quated machinery. The world crisis found Hull's De-partment girded for relentless war against Macchia-velli, but in the original and not the twentieth-century edition. In the State Department's staid universe of texts and precedents, war was war and peace was peace.

The problem of foreign trade exposed at the outset two fallacies: the fallacy of peace-or-war and the fallacy of isolationism. The fallacy of peace-or-war, which was as deeply entrenched in the State Depart-ment as in the War Department, assumed that there was no intermediate ground between the impartial neutrality of peace and the armed conflict of war. The fallacy of isolationism, cutting far deeper than foreign policy, reflected a deep-rooted cultural resistance to the recognition of interrelationships. Thus, even when we abandoned isolation in diplomatic terms, we clung to it in economic terms in our approach to the question of mobilizing productive resources on a world basis; moreover, we adhered to an administrative segrega-tion which prevented coordination of Treasury and State Department action, though Britain had long since learned to subject all mobilization decisions to the double scrutiny of Foreign Office and Treasury. The Baruch Report proposed to coordinate mobiliza-tion, British-style, with both fiscal and foreign policy, and to meet the crisis with action in the markets of the world. It charged the administrators of the home front with the responsibility of coordinating the activities of the State and War Departments. This disposed of the fallacy of isolationism. At the same time, the report disposed of the false dilemma of peace-or-war by recommending exploration of "the possibility of making arrangements with the buying organizations of all foreign governments so that the Army and Navy Munitions Board would be kept currently informed as to the volume of all orders placed in this country, their character, the location of the plants involved, and the scheduled time of delivery."

Meanwhile, prepared or not, the American economy was rushing headlong into its first test of strength with the enemy. On September 20, 1939, Hancock wrote a memorandum for Assistant Secretary of War Johnson on two incidents that had occurred that week. The first, involving a French embargo on the export of graphite from Madagascar, was imposed, Hancock suggested, for the twin purpose of embarrassing France's enemies and of bringing pressure to bear upon neutrals—meaning the United States—to supply France with vital imports. The second concerned an inquiry by Amtorg for a large tonnage of strip brass of the grade, size, and gauge used in making cartridges, whether for Russia or for resale to Germany, Hancock was not sure. The Neutrality Act, Hancock emphasized, was working in reverse. Germany had plenty of cartridge-plant capacity. But she lacked raw materials for her machines to process. The Neutrality Act embargoed our exports of the finished munitions which Germany (unlike our Allies-to-be) was under no pressure to import, but invited her to buy the brass and other materials on which her war machine had to feed. More alarming still, Hancock pointed out, "There is no power in government for handling such matters, nor is there even a central agency for gathering the facts about them."

So unprepared was the Administration to regulate foreign trade that, at the very time when one agency of government was failing in its mission to import enough rubber to build a stock-pile, another was allowing the precious material already purchased to be siphoned out of the country into a war market dominated by Japanese bidders. Before a Presidential Order finally sealed our ports, we had lost thousands of tons to Japan. Meanwhile, friendly powers, anxious to exchange technical information with the United States on a *quid pro quo* basis, were finding the State Department lawyers vigilant. The British were negotiating with the War Department to exchange one Spitfire for one Bell. If we were to hold a line in Europe, it was clear that we had to prepare to send planes to our Allies by the thousands. In this particular case, moreover, American engineers would profit by the interchange, for the fighter models then adopted by our Air Corps later proved difficult to make and inadequate in combat, while the Spitfire was to be one of the brilliant successes of the war. But the State Department lawyers wanted to win the Battle of Washington. They had no power, they insisted, to stop shipments to countries which happened to be using imports from America to arm for war against America. But they did have the power to stop one unarmed, crated Spitfire from riding the rails to Wright Field, and this power they insisted on invoking.

A year later, the brilliant Roosevelt improvisation known as Lend-Lease showed how an emergency agency could coordinate State, War, and Treasury Department activities on the world economic front. Improvisation was necessary only because systematic preparation had been neglected. If the provision for foreign trade control in the suppressed Baruch Report had been adopted in time to anticipate the emergency, Roosevelt would not have had to pull the idea out of a hat at the eleventh hour.

On the problem of labor, as well, the suppressed Baruch Report correctly foresaw the mistakes to be avoided and the precautions that were needed. In this sphere of the economy, the report visualized three phases of governmental responsibility:

1. Correlation of labor problems with the emergency agencies, particularly the Selective Service Administration, the War Resources Administration and the Price Control Authority.
2. Direction of the flow of employment so as to assure adequate labor to essential industries.
3. Arrangement for mediation and conciliation to handle such labor disputes as may arise.

The recognition of these responsibilities required no great insight after the experience of Stettinius and his fraternity brothers on the War Resources Board, but Roosevelt's political realism was reflected in the procedure by which the Baruch report proposed to achieve these three objectives. The report suggested the creation of a War Labor Administration which would be parallel to a new war production agency (ultimately to be called the War Resources Administration). This agency, operating separately, was advocated "not only because of the varied character of the problems with which it would have to deal but also because of the possible danger of mistrust on the part of labor of an administration staffed largely with industrialists."

Here was a warning ready at hand for Roosevelt's use to advise the country that labor had an indispensable role in mobilizing the economy. Business and public opinion would have accepted such notice from Baruch as common sense: Roosevelt could have invited labor's contribution as a matter of course and without stirring up unnecessary and costly political controversy: and labor, freely granted responsibility, would have been eager to live up to it. Instead, labor spent the war in a state of sullen if prosperous resentment against being regarded as a necessary evil. And Roosevelt, instead of seizing this opportunity to correct the defects of the War Resources Board, dissolved the Board. This was the time to improve and solidify the preparedness effort. Instead, Roosevelt called it off.

Specifically, the long-term job of preparing to adjust the supply of manpower to the prospective war-economy demand was ignored. So was the immediate job of mediating labor disputes affecting arms production. But, meanwhile, as the stimulus of war in Europe spurred production in America, as prices and profits began to spiral upward, prosperity provoked strikes

as usual. Thus, at just about the time this second
Baruch report was being filed and forgotten, General
Arnold informed the Assistant Secretary of War that
a strike at the Bendix Company in South Bend, Indiana, was threatening to stop all airplane engine
production for lack of carburetors and to hold up landing gear for the B-24 bomber program. Unfortunately,
no procedure was available to keep production and
collective bargaining going at the same time. Assistant
Secretary Johnson's only recourse was a letter to John
L. Lewis, then President of the CIO, appealing to
Lewis to use his influence to settle the strike. The reaction was a complete shut-down of the Bohn Aluminum and Brass Company in Detroit, thereby depriv-
ing the airplane engines of bearings. The Bohn Company's attitude, as provocative as Lewis's, forced the
shocked Air Corps generals to the conclusion that the
company's management was more interested in using
the emergency to fight labor than to get on with the
aircraft program. By the same token, leaving the
delicate art of emergency labor relations to generals
was scarcely the way to help the generals function as
military men or to give labor a sense of participation,
or even security, in the job at hand.

On both counts this was a pattern-making error.
For the duration, the home front was to be hampered
by the diversion of ranking military personnel to
essentially civilian work; and production was denied
the unique impetus that American workingmen bring
to factories which challenge their initiative and in-
genuity and which welcome their participation in a
common enterprise. The miracle of American produc-

tion in World War II should not blind us to the greater miracle that the war could have produced if the crisis had forced upon the home front a sense of mass participation.

One incident tells the story from the earliest days of the aircraft program to V–J Day. A shop paper published by a United Auto Workers' local in Southern California complained about the quality of production. Army inspectors called in the union men and asked for proof. The men agreed to give the details to Army officials in confidence. But they were unable to meet with the Army inspectors except in the presence of company officials. "We're under production and behind schedule," the foremen finally snapped. "As long as the planes get by inspection, keep your mouths shut." Men who took the initiative in assuming responsibility for workmanship found themselves demoted. Time was the only thing that the people fighting on the home front were expected to put into production, and money was the only reward anyone could expect to get out of it. American production was to be a miracle. But it was not to be a measure of America's capacity to produce or of the power of the American people to achieve.

PROVIDENCE, as is well known, has a soft spot for the United States and Providence substituted once more for common sense. (Which does not prove that common sense might not have worked better.) Common sense on mobilization has come to be synonymous with the opinions of Baruch. The key to the problems of production was the idea of budgeting requirements.

In spite of Baruch's insight, few men whose business it was to understand the problem of modern industrial mobilization saw what had to be done. For example, General H. H. Arnold, in confessing to the Senate Military Affairs Committee his doubts as to Britain's ability ever to equal German aircraft production, had this revealing discussion with Senator Gerald P. Nye, a rabid and bigoted Congressional isolationist. "Does there not come a time," the Senator asked, "when there will be a breaking-point beyond which people cannot go?" "That, sir," admitted General Arnold, "is one of the mysteries that I have not been able to solve in connection with Germany. I do not understand how they can produce . . . as they have. I do not understand what kind of economic set-up she is able to put into effect that will enable her to build these tremendous research laboratories, these tremendous plants, keep all her personnel at work, and at the same time, apparently, pay all her bills. I do not understand it." "Well," Senator Nye pointed out, "an authority who appeared before this committee earlier in the session expressed the opinion that Germany might destroy herself before she had a chance to destroy anyone else." "It is highly probable," agreed the officer in command of the air force which was to blast German production to rubble six years later.

The German achievement was a mystery to Senator Nye and to General Arnold, but not to the authors of the suppressed War Resources Board Report, who viewed it with an understanding born of their designing the prototype of the same achievement a generation earlier. Hindenburg had recognized in his *Memoirs*

the superior effectiveness of the American program—
that is, the Baruch program—of production in World
War I: "Her brilliant, if pitiless, war industry," he
had written with more resentment than precision, "had
entered the service of patriotism and had not failed it.
Under the compulsion of military necessity a ruthless
autocracy was at work . . ., even in this land at the
portals of which the Statue of Liberty flashes its blind-
ing light across the seas. *They understood war.*"

Although Baruch was the self-proclaimed personification of the "Jewish speculator," the Nazis had not
hesitated to copy his ideas. With pardonable pride
Baruch wrote in 1941: "German military experts have
said, 'Except for a few minor changes, the German
economic mobilization system was conscientiously
built in imitation of the similar American system.'"
The American system was built on the proposition
that requirements must be budgeted. To be sure, our
own implementation of this truth was belated. And for
our failure to seize on this idea as the key to the problem in 1916–17, we had paid dearly in the first war.
Now, Baruch was urging us to use it as the Germans
had, in the formative stages of World War II.

A study should be made [he urged] as to national productive capacity in relation to war requirements. The World
War indicated, as nothing else could have done, the
significance of bottlenecks and weak or missing links in
the national economic mechanism. Aggregate production
was seriously restricted because of shortages in certain indispensable lines. If reasonably accurate knowledge of
the abilities of the various industries to expand output
were available at the outbreak of a war, the problem of
administrative coordinotion would be enormously aided.

Inside the War Resources Administration the new Baruch Report recommended the organization of a Raw Material and Manufacturers Division, its principal function being to coordinate requirements and productive capacity.

We have tried to provide . . . [Baruch and the experts assisting him explained] a central point of contact for a manufacturer of any given product and the WRA. [It] is our concept that each [industry] section have within itself a number of specialists. One of such specialists will be concerned with price matters, another with priorities, another with transportation. Thus, the specialist on prices within an industrial section would handle, subject to the direction of the chief of section, all relations with the Price Control Authority, and would inform all executives within the section about the decisions of the Price Control Authority.

To supplement the work of the Raw Material and Manufacturers Division, the Report proposed a Facilities Division. This, the Report warned,

should be concerned with the creation of new industrial facilities and the conversion of existing facilities where present capacity is inadequate to meet procurement needs. . . . All problems arising in connection with providing additional plants should be centralized within the Facilities Division. Thus, if the expansion of a plant creates a shortage of housing for industrial workers within a given area, the Facilities Division will not stop at the point of arranging for supplying only manufacturing space and equipment. Accordingly, the Facilities Division will have jurisdiction over the problem of necessary housing facilities for workers in those points where districts are congested and the housing is inadequate.

Since the expansion of industrial facilities will in many instances involve requirements for new and additional capital, it is our view that problems of such capital needs of industry should also be handled by the Facilities Division.

Prophetic of the continuous and uncontrolled imbalance between raw material supplies and production facilities, the Report went on to emphasize the indispensability of the following:

A continuous study of the supply of essential materials.

A continuous study of industrial facilities which may be converted to industrial needs.

Expansion of the educational orders program. A beginning has been made in giving plants experience in turning out essential munitions by means of so-called educational orders. A material expansion of this program would not only expedite production in the event of war, but would provide useful reserves of important munitions.

Development of plans for munitions plants where no counterparts capable of conversion to war work now exist.

Modernization of machinery in government munitions plants. Although existing manufacturing arsenals and depots are capable of producing less than ten per cent of total requirements in the case of a major war, they are of great significance in two ways:

a)   They help to fill the breach in the early months of the emergency before the large converted commercial plants can be converted; and

b)   They should serve in some instances as standards to develop and test methods and check costs in private establishments.

The accumulations of adequate reserves of munitions and special manufacturing equipment for munitions, quantity production of both requiring a long period.

In his Annual Message to Congress in January,

1940, Roosevelt had been careful to explain: "I am asking the Congress for Army and Navy increases which are based not on panic but on common sense. They are not as great as enthusiastic alarmists seek. They are not as small as unrealistic persons claiming superior private information would demand." By March, the Army had reduced this policy of the happy medium to budgeting terms. It asked the House for an appropriation to build 496 planes. The House was indignant, and not because so little had been demanded of it: it voted the Army 57 planes.

Again, the Army was sufficiently concerned over Japan's plans to ask $12,000,000 for Alaska. Unlike the famous dispute over the fortification of Guam, this was no question of foreign policy; the executive and legislative arms of Government had to assume responsibility for the defense of the North American Continent. But the House, instead of questioning whether $12,000,000 would be enough to hold a line at the Bering Straits, refused to vote a cent for the defense of continental America's most vulnerable frontier. A few weeks later, Baruch chided Assistant Secretary of War Johnson for the Army's failure to win Congressional backing for projects so urgently needed. "The Navy says how punk it is," he wrote, "and gets all the money. The Army says how good it is, or is going to be, and doesn't get much of a check." Johnson replied in kind: "You say: 'The Army says how good it is.' . . . Not me—I'm howling about the shortages." The shortage Johnson was reduced to fighting to make good in April, 1940, was in the first instance a nominal appropriation for the clothing and elementary equipment needed to bring the National Guard from 60 men per company to 200.

During the Sitzkrieg, in the spring of 1940, Roosevelt and the War Department persuaded Congress to allow the British and French to have 2,100 of the 5,500 planes budgeted for the Army Air Corps in 1941. In May, however, the Senate took alarm. If the situation was so explosive that England and France needed so many American planes, the Senators argued, it was explosive enough for America to provide herself with at least as many planes as it had intended to build for this new emergency. Roosevelt at this point was asking for $1,182,000,000. To this the Senate promptly added $364,221,468, no more and no less, mainly for planes. General Arnold and Admiral Towers of the Navy Bureau of Aeronautics, in turn, told the Senators that the services had no immediate need of so many planes. But by this time the Senate as a whole was aroused. It forced an extra $100,000,000 upon the Navy air arm, and an extra $103,000,000 upon the Army Air Corps, with the admonition that it expected the unwanted money to be spent promptly on American air power. Then, on May 16, Hitler spared the Army and Navy the embarrassment of further protest against Senatorial zealousness. He occupied Denmark and Norway. The President asked for another billion.

In preparing to mobilize the economy, nothing had been more important than the proposals advanced by the Army engineers and the Temporary National Economic Committee, at the instance of Senator Joseph O'Mahoney and Chairman W. O. Douglas of the Securities and Exchange Commission, to create a steel industry in the West. The trend of peacetime demand justified such a project. More pressing, the problem of western industrialization justified the great emphasis the suppressed Baruch Report had placed on the need for a constant three-way balance among materials, plant capacity, and manpower. Thanks to Roosevelt's decision to reject the Plan, more energy was to be wasted on the West Coast than in any other production sector of the home front. For some time it had been obvious that no other sector would generate as much new energy. Shipyards had mushroomed in the great port cities of the West during War I, which, after all, had been a purely Atlantic operation. By 1940 no one could doubt that the threatening war would have to be fought on both oceans and in the air as well as at sea. Inescapably, therefore, a West Coast arsenal-building boom was in the making. But where was the steel to come from? It could be hauled through the Panama Canal or shipped overland by rail, or it could be manufactured in the West from western raw materials. How vulnerable our coastal shipping lanes were to become to the submarine pack of 1942 very few people dared to imagine. But, by the same token, who dared to imagine that the Panama Canal was not vulnerable? Our thin rail tunnels through the mountains were also treacherous and highly vulnerable bottlenecks. Before the keels could go on the ways, millions of tons of steel had to pass through these East-West bottlenecks. Nevertheless, the engineers' blueprints, the economists' briefs and the pressures coming from the West were ignored.

"In the field of transportation," the suppressed Report had recommended, "a study should be made to determine definitely all weak points which might cause trouble in case of heavy war traffic, with a view to ascertaining where the bottlenecks would most likely be found. A program for the solution of any such problems should be developed. All facilities, including highway, waterway, and marine transportation should be analyzed." By 1942 the words transportation and bottleneck were to be inseparable.

The first transportation shortage demanding action was that of railroad equipment. Before ships could be built, freight had to be hauled; and the railroads were unable to carry freight as fast as American industry could produce it. Now, at last, mobilization was promising to bring a major recovery to the capital goods industries; and, therefore, it was threatening to cause a major dislocation between production and transportation. To this danger the White House economists were alert. Accordingly, the National Resources Planning Board retained Robert N. Janeway, of the Chrysler Corporation, to study the freight-car situation. The agency never found the courage to publish the Janeway Report. Here was yet another confidential document. Its findings were simple enough: In the 10 years, 1929–39, the supply of serviceable freight cars owned by the railroads had fallen 30 percent. Of those available, 20 percent were over 25 years old, and 40 percent over 20 years old. Merely to offset the annual shrinkage in the nation's car pool caused by obsolescence, the Report pointed out, 75,000 new cars would have to be put into service each year for five years. In other words, the construction of 100,000 freight cars in one year would add only 25,000 cars to the available car pool.

The Report went further. It calculated the burden that "full employment" would impose on the rail-roads, and concluded that 500,000 new cars would be needed to carry the freight. A volume of production heavy enough to keep 500,000 new freight cars rolling at capacity, Janeway warned, was likely to cause a steel shortage too. But no Governmental machinery existed for doing what the situation required, and in time. All that the White House economists could advise was that the railroads put their orders in before prices rose, before quality deteriorated, before produc-tion schedules filled up, before priorities suspended Business as Usual. Fear of isolationist sentiment prompted the White House to issue instructions that the Janeway Report be formulated in terms of pros-perity and not mobilization; and that, nevertheless, it be kept confidential. Budd's office allowed it to "leak" to the Association of American Railroads. "Irrespon-sible war-mongering" and "astronomical statisticians" were the answers called forth by this precise calcula-tion of the strain mobilization was about to place upon the economy at the weakest point. In the face of such outbursts from the isolationists and the railroad lobby, the Administration dropped the subject of freight cars and discontinued a parallel investigation of the need for new locomotives.

Within 30 days, the hysterical Premier of France was sobbing for American production to save Europe. Europe fell, and so did Neville Chamberlain. Six days after Winston Churchill took over in London, Roose-

velt announced the end of the lost year. He astounded
the world by calling for the production of 50,000 airplanes—he became an "astronomical statistician" himself. By May 28, the British began to evacuate Dunkirk, and the President had appointed the men who
were to manufacture the planes.

On that day, Roosevelt told William S. Knudsen,
President of General Motors, that, as Knudsen was
to testify a year later, "I was to be put in charge of
a production section of the Advisory Commission of
the Council on National Defense, I was to be one of
seven members, and I only had time to fly to New
York the next morning and tell my people, and the
following day I was in Washington. Without any previous conversation I called on the President, and in
15 minutes it was all over, I was working in Washington." The country assumed that Washington and industry were working under him and from a blueprint.

But, then, the country in 1940 was altogether unprepared for the age of crisis that had begun—unprepared politically, economically, and above all emotionally. It was a country still so inert, for all its
energy and achievement, that it wasted a third to half
of its manpower potential on and outside the marginal
fringes of its economy. It was a country whose people
were as unready to fight a war as its economy was to
win it. In the perspective of the waves of wartime
and postwar expansion and prosperity which have
since dimmed memories of depression, it was a country in which millions mattered and billions seemed
big, in which the masses had not yet accumulated

capital, and capital had not yet accumulated the costs of turning the masses into capitalists. It was a country, in short, in which the economy had not yet been mobilized for security, social or national.

CHAPTER V

PRESSURE FOR PRODUCTION

IN May, 1940, Senator Arthur Vandenberg, whom the Blitzkrieg had shocked out of his militant isolationism, made a bold bid for consideration by the approaching Republican Convention. He demanded on the Senate floor that Roosevelt make the suppressed Baruch-Hancock report of 1939 available to Congress. But, in June, the Blitzkrieg nominated Wendell Willkie. A few months later, Baruch, the advisor of Presidents—and of potential Presidents—briefed the Republican candidate on the causal connection between Roosevelt's failure to adopt the Baruch-Hancock report of 1939 and the failure of American preparedness in 1940. Willkie thereupon read several paragraphs of this same secret document to the newspapermen covering his campaign. Righteous in his wrath, he charged Roosevelt with responsibility for America's unpreparedness. Although Willkie had been careful to read only the most general passages, which merely endorsed cooperation between Government and business, Roosevelt reacted like a man hit on an exposed nerve. The Republican candidate had no right to divulge the contents of the Report, he snapped. The only reason why Willkie's conduct was not irresponsible, the President indicated, was that the information to which he attached such sensational meaning happened to be irrelevant. There was as much reason to dig up the Stettinius Board's report, he explained, as there was to make public a report on the Civil War.

"Surely the Government is not keeping the Civil War Reports confidential," Willkie retorted. "Again I urge that the Report be made public, as I am sure that it will show a much more effective method of operating our Defense than is being pursued by the Administration."

Willkie was right. He was effective as a candidate and he was constructive as an American when he sounded the alarm. During this campaign, first Roosevelt and then Willkie indulged in promises of peace to a people soon to be faced with war. But that war was won not by American foreign policy; it was won by American production. The fall of France had found the American economy unprepared even to become prepared. Overnight Hitler seemed to have won the war; nevertheless pressure originating nearer home than the English Channel was needed to jolt American production into motion. Americans should be everlastlingly grateful to their political system for supplying the initial jolt. Both Roosevelt and Willkie resorted to demagogic appeals in the name of peace. But however much politics tarnished our public morality on this score, it evened the balance at the practical level by spurring production. Republican gibes at munitions "on order" instead of in the Army's hands called forth not only hurried Presidential "inspection trips" to arsenals but Presidential action to speed production as well. In the summer of 1940, it was the challenge of political competition which forced

Roosevelt to make up for lost time on the home front.

The fact was that a year had been lost. Early in 1939, Roosevelt was in a much better position to mobilize the economy than in the early months of 1940. For one thing, war *in posse* after Munich was assumed to be immediate, blasting Blitzkrieg, while war *in esse* had turned out to be mere Sitzkrieg. For another, Roosevelt's personal political dilemma over a third term had not yet become pressing and public. The War Resources Board, as constituted, had, of course, been a mistake. But to have reconstituted the Board for efficient operation would have been a simple matter in 1939. By the middle of 1940—that is, by the beginning of the political campaign—any attempt to evoke the War Resources Board from the limbo where it had lain for so many months, any attempt to disavow the disavowals with which it had been buried, would have been infinitely embarrassing. It would have been politics, and bad politics at that.

Altogether, therefore, Willkie was right—and he was making votes for himself—when he asserted that the lost year could have been saved if Roosevelt had put preparedness ahead of politics and followed the plan he himself had helped Baruch to blueprint for the War Resources Board. Up to this point—before Willkie accused Roosevelt of responsibility for the crisis that had been a generation in the making—the case Willkie made was much more devastating than that usually leveled against Roosevelt as a poor administrator of popular objectives. For he was charging that preparedness had not been the President's objective.

ACTUALLY, to blame Roosevelt for the fact of our crisis in 1940 was as unfair as it had been to blame Lincoln in 1862 for the fact of slavery. The crisis was no outrage perpetrated by Presidential fiat. It was everybody's responsibility. The issue was how to cope with it—that is, under which man as President. The Republican candidate would have done better to admit what everyone felt: that great credit was due Franklin Roosevelt for anticipating the crisis; and what everyone knew: that isolationism and pacifism, like internationalism, were bipartisan. This admission would have focused attention on the President's handling of the defense problem. It would have dramatized Willkie's original contention that Roosevelt was playing politics with preparedness. Here good politics would have continued to serve the country, for it would have increased the pressures needed to speed the defense program.

Instead, both men failed to rise to the challenge of the great crisis of 1940. The measure of how they failed was that in the end neither candidate rested his case on the defense issue: Roosevelt was afraid of it and Willkie wandered from it. Both men regarded war as unavoidable. Nevertheless, Election Day found each posing as the peace candidate and outpromising the other as the guarantor of past prosperity and future security. Both candidacies were products of the emergency, and yet each was merchandising "Normalcy."

To be sure, Roosevelt's purpose was statesmanlike, and Willkie's indignation was sincere. Admittedly, war was unpopular in the summer of 1940. But preparedness was becoming both popular and profitable. The very fear of war was causing everyone to clutch at preparedness as the alternative to war, as the answer to fear and, incidentally, as the effective primer of the nation's economic pump. Now the 1940 campaign was a very close race, much closer than was ever quite apparent, because of Roosevelt's reputation for invincibility. For, over and above the third term issue, Roosevelt had first put himself on the defensive by his courageous stand against the aggressors; and then compromised himself by his unsatisfactory administration of defense. But Willkie threw away the advantage Roosevelt had given him when he diverted the debate from defense and insisted that Roosevelt and Roosevelt alone was the issue. Willkie had begun by denouncing Roosevelt as an isolationist; but he then shifted his ground and shouted that Roosevelt meant war; and, finally, his campaign isolationism harried Roosevelt in his turn into proffering the voters a matching offer of peace which was not so much insincere as it was sophistical. Like so many epic contests, the campaign between these unforgettable leaders unfolded as a comedy of errors.

On the merits, it was not by our sorry performance on the home front in World War I that Roosevelt's administration of it in World War II should be judged, but by his own criticism of our past mistakes, by his own insistence on avoiding any repetition of them. Newton Baker, in his polemic against the charge that Wilson led us into World War I, cites as evidence for his case the fact that, under the National Defense Act of 1916, "Our preparation for war was really based upon a 'five year plan.'" The consequences of this

Roosevelt had described in detail in his famous Defense Message of January, 1939. He then warned the nation:

Those of us who took part in the conduct of the World War will remember that in the preparation of the American armies for actual participation in battle, the United States, entering the war on April 6, 1917, took no part whatsoever in any major engagement until the end of May, 1918. In other words, while other armies were conducting the actual fighting, the United States had more than a year of absolute peace at home without any threat of attack on their continent, to train men, to produce new materials, to process them into munitions and supplies, and to forge the whole into fighting forces. It is even a matter of record that as late as the autumn of 1918, American armies at the front used almost exclusively French or British artillery and aircraft.

The 1939 Message had gone on to cite two additional reasons for speed in preparing for World War II: "We cannot guarantee a long period, free from attack, in which we could prepare"; and "There is new range and speed to offense." Nevertheless, after 19 crucial months—19 months during which "the United States had . . . absolute peace at home without any threat of attack on this continent"; during which Hitler had demonstrated (and, incidentally, expanded) the revolutionary "new range and speed" of offense at the expense of our Allies-to-be; during which the French, British, and other allied armies had been knocked out of combat on the Continent— our National Defense program was still "on order." During 19 months of danger, Roosevelt, the Administrator, had defied and thwarted Roosevelt, the

Prophet. In spite of his own insistence on speed, the administration of defense was proceeding at the Wilsonian pace, which was inadequate in Wilson's day. Inevitably, therefore, we were in danger as a country, and Roosevelt was in danger as a political candidate.

Roosevelt, for all his acute and sincere criticism of Wilson, nevertheless found himself risking a repetition of the great Wilsonian blunder—the blunder of forcing an irreconcilable split with the Senate over an issue of foreign policy. He should have known better. Certainly his experience of history should have told him that this was not the prudent thing to do at any time; and his judgment of the immediate situation should have told him that it was not necessary on the eve of the emergency. The issue on which he challenged the Senate was neutrality—specifically, he demanded repeal of the arms embargo. Now the arms embargo was mischievous and wrong-headed. It did not prevent the aggressors from feeding on the American economy, but it did restrain the United States from helping their victims. The arms embargo was powerless to stop war, and war was certain to force its repeal. But it was not the issue: no issue of foreign policy could be fundamental in a crisis that only productive power could resolve. In the absence of productive power, no foreign policy could avail—as was shown when France fell. To insist on repealing the arms embargo at a time when the economy was producing no arms for any purpose was to reach for the shadow and not the substance.

The substance was production. And here is the

irony: if it had been production that Roosevelt had
demanded of the Senate, he would have got it; if he
had asked for money for American ships and planes
and arsenals, as a form of insurance for American
security, the answer would have been yes. Congress
was confused and alarmed by the turn of events
abroad, and insurance was what it wanted. Preparedness was one historic synonym for American insurance. Neutrality was the other. Instinctively, the representative majority that blocked repeal of the Neutrality Act wanted to "wait and see." But nearly all
the members of that majority would have felt more
comfortable if America's strength had been mounting while they waited. If repeal was wise, preparedness was necessary. But how could repeal be urgent
and preparedness unnecessary, the puzzled members
of Congress asked as they tried to fathom Roosevelt's
purpose? The demand for repeal without preparedness
they received as nothing but an invitation to a political argument, and to this they responded as usual—
by arguing and not by acting. When finally the fall of
Warsaw forced repeal of the arms embargo, it was only
an empty gesture. Hull had won his argument with
Borah, but we had no arms to send. And when eight
months later, on the eve of the fall of Paris, Reynaud
appealed to Roosevelt for fighter planes, we were still
as far from being able to help as when Warsaw was
being sacked. Roosevelt had won his battle of dogma.
There was no arms embargo. But there were no arms.

Nor was this the end of the paradox. Although
Roosevelt did not have the votes for the program he
asked for—repeal of the Neutrality Act—he did

have the votes for the program he did not ask for—preparedness. The shibboleth of neutrality was almost sacred to Congress, and therefore Senate and House were determined to swing away from it as gradually as possible. Thus, when the impact of war caused Congress to repeal the arms embargo, it still clung to the cash-and-carry principle. When the fall of France forced it to abandon cash-and-carry in favor of Lend-Lease, it still forbade American merchantmen to enter belligerent waters. Not until American sailors were killed off Iceland—Roosevelt insisted it was the Western Atlantic—was this last restriction of the Neutrality Act removed. But while Congress held on tenaciously in these matters, it would certainly have voted for measures to increase production. Western members would have voted overwhelmingly for a program to prepare the area from the Wheat Belt to the Pacific Coast for its role in the potential emergency. While internationalists voted for such measures on emergency grounds, isolationists and pacifists would have supported them on liberal grounds, for, as Forrestal pointed out, they meant in any case that the country was going to get more aluminum, more copper, more electric power, more steel, more freight cars, more food, more of everything, which was wholly in accord with the New Deal's peacetime program of abundance.

Crafty old Senator McNary summed up the Congressional attitude towards Roosevelt's demand to repeal the Neutrality Act when he said: "The trouble is that people would think, if we repealed the whole Neutrality Act, that we were repealing our Neutral-

ity." What Roosevelt and Congress were really fighting about was not the action needed to meet an emergency, but the respect due a shibboleth. Roosevelt
wanted to defy the sacred slogan of neutrality and,
under cover of the resultant commotion, to fall back
upon the Congressional policy of wait and see. Congress on the whole agreed that war in Europe would
render our neutrality obsolete. But Congress was determined to violate the historic rule as gradually as
possible, and in fact only, not in name.

Fundamentally, while Congress wanted no responsibility for provoking the crisis, it wanted no responsibility for blocking the moves the President thought
necessary to protect American neutrality in the crisis.
Roosevelt, however, was so anxious to remain innocent of the charge of war-mongering that he refused
to evoke the industrial potential of Pittsburgh and
Detroit and Chicago which alone could wrest the
initiative from the Axis. "There is no thought," he
told a press conference following his Proclamation
of Limited Emergency, on September 8, 1939, "in any
shape, manner or form, of putting the Nation, either
in its defenses or in its internal economy, on a war
basis." Sherwood sadly calls these "probably the weakest words that Roosevelt ever uttered: he was out-
doing even Warren G. Harding by getting the country 'back to Normalcy' before the war had really
started." * Much more serious than anything Roosevelt said was the fact that, at the very time when
Congress was finally scrapping the arms embargo, he

* Robert E. Sherwood, *Roosevelt and Hopkins* (New York,
Harper & Brothers, 1948), p. 134.

was scrapping his own Industrial Mobilization Plan.

For Roosevelt's administrative myopia Sherwood offers two excuses, mutually contradictory. The first: that Roosevelt had to play the hypocrite in order to wheedle concessions like repeal of the arms embargo out of Congress. The other: that, until Hitler blitzed his way to the Channel, Roosevelt did not see how desperately American production was needed. Both assumptions cannot simultaneously be taken at face value. If, as Sherwood says, "Roosevelt did not have full comprehension of the real, paralyzing force of the Nazi fury, nor of the imminence of the danger to the United States," * he was not playing the hypocrite in compromising with neutrality. All he was doing, actually, was accepting the reality that America would not become a belligerent unless and until attacked. Sherwood contradicts his thesis that Roosevelt was at one and the same time Machiavellian and naive when he makes a point of emphasizing Roosevelt's sudden fear at one point late in 1941 that America might not be attacked: that, instead, Japan would continue to detour around America's Pacific possessions and entrench herself all through Southeastern Asia and the Middle East without provoking America to stop her. Roosevelt was honest enough with himself and with his intimates to admit that a military attack upon the United States could bring us into the war; and he was realistic enough to know that such an attack was coming.

On one point Roosevelt thought himself more realis-

* Ibid., p. 125.

tic than he was. Thus, while he was waiting for Japan's attack to catapult us into the war, he assumed that we would be free to fight primarily in Europe. We were. But because we failed to recognize the opportunistic implications for the future of fighting World War II as primarily a trans-Atlantic war, and because throughout we failed to budget requirements and allocate resources in terms of the two-ocean reality confronting us, we set in motion the forces which soon after World War II were to deprive us of our freedom to decide on which front and against which enemy—and when—to fight, or even to negotiate. History's judgment on the strategy which transformed our defensive war in the Pacific into essentially offensive war across the Atlantic was pronounced in 1949, when Soviet imperialism compelled us to begin fighting in the most unstrategic of circumstances across the Pacific while rearming across the Atlantic.

Meanwhile, Roosevelt waited for Japan's impending attack. He wanted no question about the identity of the aggressor. On one point, consequently, Roosevelt was the opposite of hypocritical in going along with the neutrality bloc: he, too, wanted to wait and see what the Axis would do. But there was a real difference between Roosevelt and the neutrality bloc. Its representative members wanted to prepare while they waited. Roosevelt, expecting attack, and distrusting the extent to which any peacetime planning could really prepare, was still ready to wait. He was well aware of the risk. But, then, Roosevelt in spite of his own contribution to mobilization planning, always gave risks a priority over plans. What he be-

lieved in, fundamentally, was the energy of the people
and his own skill at improvising leadership in a crisis.

OUR unpreparedness did not end with the fall of
France. But the time of waiting did. The catastrophe
forced action, as a reflex, as a token, and as a beginning. True, the beginnings of mobilization were confused and self-defeating, amateurish and inadequate.
But at least they were a beginning and, therefore, a
promise as well. For the moment at least, the fact
that a beginning had been made was more important
than the fact that it was an inadequate beginning.

Inadequate is a most generous description of the
organization William Knudsen had been drafted to
head. The Advisory Commission to the Council of
National Defense, which the President reestablished
on May 28, 1940, with a membership of eight "advisors," was not one of Roosevelt's casual yet inspired creations. In a crisis which called for a stroke
of genius, Roosevelt produced a throwback to the
Wilson Administration, a throwback which even the
Wilson Administration had discarded as unworkable.

At the time when Knudsen was called to Washington on a few hours' notice, the Defense Commission
awaiting his leadership was exactly four months and
thirteen days short of being twenty-four years old. It
had been less than a streamlined vehicle of power
when it was born. It was a rusty and decrepit antique
now. The harassed Wilson Administration had tolerated its inadequacies for little more than a year
before supplanting it with a modern form of organization. Roosevelt himself, as Assistant Secretary of the

Navy, had been one of the exasperated critics responsible for this improvement. For years no one had been more keenly aware of how impossible it is to mobilize with advisory committees. No one had a more practical grasp of the advantages a wartime President can gain by creating a strong and independent civilian command to direct the home front. In 1940, no one could have seen more clearly than Roosevelt did that this war was going to be won or lost on America's home front. Nevertheless, it was the decrepit antique of World War I which Roosevelt put to work; and as the Bureau of the Budget history says, "Decision to revive the Advisory Commission meant a rejection of the Army-Navy Industrial Mobilization Plan."

The President's action, the official historians admit, "drew no little criticism from both his friends and enemies." But, they explain, "his decision was dictated by judgments of what was feasible in the general political circumstances—and in political matters the opinion of the President had always been accorded respect. Reliance on existing legislation made it possible to avoid seeking action from Congress, action which might, and probably would, have resulted in administrative inflexibility at a time when the utmost flexibility was required. Moreover, other and more important issues, such as Selective Service, needed to be given priority by Congress without the distraction of additional urgent Presidential requests."

On both counts this argument is transparent sophistry. The first argument, that Congressional action would have been required to set up a more modern and effective organization, is contradicted by the blunt fact that the War Production Board was finally created in 1942 by an Executive Order, not by a statute; and all Congress did was applaud. The other argument, that Selective Service had to be given priority over the organization charged with arming a mass army, is disproved by Roosevelt himself. He is quoted in the Budget Bureau history as saying of his action in recreating the Advisory Commission that, "We are not talking at the present time about a draft system, either to draft money or men or women, or all three."

Roosevelt's own rationalization of this first faltering step forward is more revealing. "This is not complete, immediate national mobilization," he said. "We are trying to expand about a billion and a quarter dollars more than in the normal process. And in order to do that, it has seemed wise to put into effect what has been ready and planned for a long, long time, under an existing statute, without having to go and propose something entirely new in the way of legislation that would take weeks and months and a great deal of pro and con discussion, partisan and otherwise, and would probably end up in practically the same thing that we have on the statute books now."

At least Roosevelt was honest enough to admit that he was counting on money, and not on leadership, to prime the production pump.

It was the Army Appropriation Act of August 29, 1916, which provided for the creation of a Council of National Defense. Membership in the Council was restricted to six Cabinet members—the Secretaries of War, the Navy, the Interior, Agriculture, Commerce, and Labor. What an eloquent commentary on the insularity of the Wilsonian Era! Defense was a domestic problem, no business of the Secretary of State, and too small for the Secretary of the Treasury to be held responsible for helping to organize its solution. Ignored was the grim British rule: coordinate all decisions on defense with both foreign and fiscal policy.

Ignored, accordingly, were the two Cabinet figures (the two Service Secretaryships being in transition) most relevant to the task at hand—Morgenthau and Hull. In 1939 Roosevelt had made Morgenthau the key man in his rudimentary defense operation. In 1940 Morgenthau was still the key man in the organization of aid to the democracies. The Treasury technicians, notably Oscar Cox, were already at work on the plan which in little more than half a year was to crystallize into Lend-Lease. The Army and Navy, meanwhile, were beginning to operate in billions. Nothing was more urgent at this still formative stage of defense organization than to reconcile the requirements of our Allies with the requirements of our armed forces, and to budget for defense production sufficient to satisfy the combined schedule. But Morgenthau was nevertheless left out. As the entire history of the war years was to show, either we would learn to coordinate defense decisions with foreign and fiscal policy at the beginning or not at all; and, if not at all, the magnitude and the inevitable opportunism of the defense decisions about to be forced upon the administrators of foreign and fiscal policy would first com-

promise and then confuse and finally defeat any idea
of national policy.

Hull's claim to inclusion in the defense Cabinet was
also unassailable. He was the senior member of the
Cabinet. The prestige he enjoyed with Congress and
with the country was unique. During those very weeks
Roosevelt was pressing him to run for Vice-President.
If Roosevelt had not been by way of running for a
third term, Hull would have been the Democratic
nominee for President; and, unhandicapped by the
third term issue, he would probably have had an
easier time winning than Roosevelt. Willkie conceded
Hull's strength with the country when, during the
last week of the campaign, he punctuated his promise
not to send American boys overseas with the assurance that, if elected, he would keep Hull on as Secretary of State. But over and above Hull's integrity and
experience, the fact was that both the broad policies
and the actual administrative and business arrangements incidental to the prosecution of global warfare
had to be cleared through him and in many cases to
be negotiated or directed by him. To assume that he
did not have a major role to play in the home front
High Command was to be guilty of isolationism at
the administrative level as naive as Borah's at the
policy level.

Roosevelt had not planned to exclude Hull and
Morgenthau from his new Cabinet Committee. Indeed, the predicament in which he was now involved
left him little opportunity to plan any of his moves.
He had felt obliged to reach desperately for an existing
statute, and to reach for it as a complete package.

Not until he had opened the package did he have a chance to examine what it gave him to work with.

The most important members of the Council of National Defense were the Secretaries of War and the Navy and, at the moment, Roosevelt had neither a Secretary of War nor a Secretary of the Navy. He did have a Secretary of the Interior. But Ickes was the first to recognize that he was bigger than his job. He was pressing for the vacancy in the War Department. To appease him, to employ his tremendous talents and energies, and, incidentally, to check the men to whom the major war economy jobs were given, Roosevelt endowed first the Interior Department and then Ickes personally with endless powers unconnected with the responsibilities of "Normalcy." Alongside the regular structure of the Interior Department, he erected an emergency organization for the control, among other things, of oil and coal. Thanks to this dual organization, Ickes enjoyed the status of both a Cabinet member and a wartime czar.

So did Jesse Jones. He was Chairman of the Reconstruction Finance Corporation, which meant that he would soon emerge as czar of the Federal lending agencies. He was also negotiating with Harry Hopkins. Frustrated in his campaign for the Vice-Presidency, he was to be Hopkins's successor in the Commerce Department while retaining his control over the powerful Reconstruction Finance Corporation. Hopkins was close enough to Roosevelt to name his successor to the Cabinet, and in an act of political irresponsibility on a par with his getting Nelson appointed production czar after Pearl Harbor, he named

Jones. Sherwood publishes Hopkins's letter of resignation as Secretary of Commerce, dated August 22,
1940, in which Hopkins wrote to Roosevelt: "The only
questions at this time are with regard to the character, pace and magnitude of our defense effort. We
must build armaments, and because of your own foresight and determination, this is being done. We must
marshal our complete economic strength for the task
of defense." Sherwood also quotes Hopkins as telling
him at one of the early October meetings that cemented the bond between them, "There is absolutely
nothing important in the world today but to beat
Hitler."

What Sherwood does not record was that Hopkins
bought a political alliance with Jones by supporting
Jones for the Secretaryship of Commerce and, with it,
membership on the Cabinet Defense Committee. Jones
had assets to trade that Hopkins needed, especially
on Capitol Hill and in London: and so, Hopkins, being
a cold-blooded politician, paid Jones's price. He knew
perfectly well that Jones did not feel any need to
"marshal our complete economic strength for the
task of defense," and he had no illusions about the
number of objectives Jones considered more important than beating Hitler. This does not mean that
Hopkins did not want to win the war. He did. But,
as Boss Murphy used to say of his nominees in the
great days of Tammany Hall, he wanted to win the
war with "men he knew well."

Jones's entrance into the Cabinet created one additional complication in the relations between the normal and the emergency agencies of Government, and

Henry Wallace's exit created still another. Agriculture had been excluded from the Stettinius Board, and it had to be represented on the Defense Commission. Unlike the Interior and Commerce Departments, the Department of Agriculture was equipped to control a major sector of the war economy. But the perversity which placed strong Secretaries in these marginal Departments now left Roosevelt no alternative but to put a weak Secretary—Claude Wickard—into the more important Department. A strong Secretary of Agriculture would have dominated the Defense Commission's farm work, but no farm member of the Defense Commission could possibly have used his position to control the strategic political and economic machinery lodged in the Department of Agriculture. On the farm front, accordingly, Roosevelt subordinated Cabinet to emergency agency leadership; on the labor front, where the Secretary had long since been by-passed, Roosevelt lodged the controls in the emergency setup.

To man the production pump Roosevelt had brought Knudsen to Washington and put him in charge of an advisory committee subordinate to an inactive and non-representative Cabinet advisory committee subordinate to the President and modeled after Wilson's original advisory committee which had failed and which Roosevelt had helped to supplant in 1917. But what Roosevelt wanted from Bill Knudsen was not advice and what he expected was not success.

KNUDSEN was, of course, the most important member of the new Commission. Production was to be his responsibility. His six fellow advisors were:

Edward Stettinius, Jr., Commissioner responsible for raw materials

Ralph Budd, Commissioner of Transportation

Sidney Hillman, Commissioner in charge of labor problems and manpower utilization

Chester Davis, Commissioner delegated to coordinate agriculture and food problems with war needs

Leon Henderson, Commissioner assigned to control the prices of the materials and foodstuffs whose production Commissioners Stettinius and Davis were assigned to expand

Harriet Elliott, Commissioner whose presence was intended to advertise the importance of women in a war economy and to remind producers that they are also consumers

It was an ingenious combination, worthy in its way of Roosevelt the politician who had created it. Each pressure group enjoyed conspicuous representation, but, as the Bureau of the Budget history says, "the impression collectively was that no single group enjoyed special advantages." This time he had given big business three votes out of seven. He had, moreover, created a situation in which the voters were bound to spend the summer doubting Willkie's charge that Roosevelt and business could not work together. No less effective was Roosevelt's gesture in giving a place to organized agriculture's favorite son: in the Midwestern farm areas, the appointment of Chester Davis neutralized the fact of Sidney Hillman's presence at the council table and suggested that conservatism might boast a majority of four. The Hillman appointment was as striking as anything Roosevelt had ever done, and as shrewd: it dramatized much and risked nothing. The presence of Henderson advertised Roosevelt's desire to make the coming holocaust one war that would not nullify reform—and broadcast the more immediate fact that billions for defense meant guns for the future and butter for the present.

Said Roosevelt, to a press conference at the time:

I think people should realize that we are not going to upset, any more than we have to, a great many of the normal processes of life. There is one of the ladies, in the room, for instance, who is going to ask that question, and wants to know whether we are not only going to have new automobiles next year, new models, but whether it means a lot of other things that could be put into the luxury class would have to be foregone by the population—I am not looking at anybody; I am looking at the ceiling—the answer is that this delightful young lady will not have to forego cosmetics, lipsticks, ice cream sodas and—(Laughter). Thank you, Mr. President (Laughter). (President again): All right . . . that does it. In other words, we do not want to upset the normal trend of things any more than we possibly can help.

Finally, the Board included Stettinius, as ever, earnest, available and anxious. Sooner or later, he had to be given some assignment. He had been badly exploited in 1939; he was the head of the Steel Corporation; he had broken a stubborn tradition in signing with the CIO; he had preached and practiced price competition; he was anxious to sever his corporate connections and become a bureaucrat. Moreover, not to have called him back in 1940 would have been to

admit error in using him in 1939. At the public relations level, Stettinius could have been used to good
advantage and without risk. But, on the other hand,
public relations never posed a problem for Roosevelt,
whereas finding men of ability did. And the raw materials problem was the first major obstacle confronting the entire program. Failure to solve it was bound
to bedevil, delay, distort, even jeopardize the program
for the duration. Roosevelt was calling for 50,000
planes, and Lindbergh and Dewey were able to document their derision by asking where the raw materials
were coming from. To answer this question, Roosevelt
needed the very best man to be found. But though
Roosevelt knew at first hand how much Stettinius's
abilities fell short of this standard, he appointed Stettinius to the most crucial position of all.

CHAPTER VI

THE CABINET OF NATIONAL UNITY

Now that the defense effort was at last launched, Secretaries had to be found for the War and Navy Departments. How much the impending Republican Convention had to do with the choice of Republicans for the posts was a matter of spirited discussion at the time. But the politics of the moment passed. The symbolism of national unity endured and served.

Three political maneuvers prepared the pattern of national unity. In each a ranking member of the New Deal family was the victim.

The redoubtable Fiorello La Guardia was the first of this triumvirate. He had a genius for punching his way into the headlines, but he was a quarrelsome administrator, and when Roosevelt began to speak of him for the Secretaryship, poor La Guardia did not realize that he was being used as a stalking horse. In due time he learned not only that the post was not for him, but that the appointee was a man who would force Roosevelt to break a second promise—of a generalship—and this after the bouncy little mayor had had himself fitted for a uniform.

Ickes was the second potential Secretary. Roosevelt had been doing so much off-the-record talking about the necessity of avoiding Wilson's mistakes and "making this a New Deal War," that, logically enough, his New Deal intimates pointed out how appropriate it would be for him to appoint his most effective New Deal administrator to a ranking post in the War Cabinet. "Harold would bark orders at the brass hats and he'd whack the five percenters' snouts every time they tried to dip their straws into the punch bowl," it was agreed inside the White House. "Besides, he would be for the kind of war we must fight."

Perhaps the last point irritated Roosevelt. The glamor of the war years has obscured the fact that by 1940 people had begun to grow tired of Roosevelt. His problem was to shock the public out of this feeling by finding a respectable symbol alongside whom he would seem more dynamic and progressive than ever. Harold Ickes, armed with the wartime powers of a Secretary of War, would inevitably have prevented this by sharing in the role that Roosevelt was determined to monopolize. Nevertheless, while Roosevelt set about looking for a man whose appeal would contrast with the liberalism and the masterful realism which it was given only to the Commander-in-Chief to personify, he made Ickes one of his famous promises, which was enough to put the enraged Curmudgeon on notice that someone else was to have the place Roosevelt had promised Louis Johnson.

It was Johnson himself who was the third victim. He, having been promised the Secretaryship, instead lost his post as Assistant Secretary. The War Department, after all, was the new center of power, and Johnson had become the conspicuous symbol of Roosevelt's personal control over it. This was the fact which disqualified Johnson for the Secretaryship and it was also the fact which prevented Roosevelt from shuffling him back into the Administration on another deal: by appointing Johnson to another important place, Roosevelt would inevitably have set him up as a rival to any new Secretary. But the most important reason why Johnson had become an expendable is that the trial balloons floated for La Guardia and Ickes had convinced Roosevelt that he wanted his new Secretary to be neither a Democrat, nor a New Dealer, nor even an independent, but a ranking Republican.

The Cabinet Departments enjoy no Constitutional status apart from their use by the Chief Executive as instruments of the Executive arm of Government financed by the Legislative arm; and of all the Departments, the War Department was the Commander-in-Chief's special province. This fundamental Presidential preserve Roosevelt determined to renounce— that is, he determined to renounce it for the Democratic Party and the New Deal on the theory that a third term for himself was worth the price to them. He had no intention of sharing his powers with anyone, much less of diluting the war Presidency into a coalition of which he would be a kind of chairman. On the contrary, he was looking for a new platform on which to stand while he operated the war powers. To help him build the platform, he proposed to draft his political opponents or, more precisely, the political opponents of his supporters. On the eve of the 1940 Republican National Convention, he decided to surrender the War and Navy Departments to the nominees of the 1936 Republican National Convention. The decision, taken as it was in the mood of crisis following Dunkirk, enabled him to move to the political counter-offensive.

ALFRED M. LANDON was a man of limited capacities but unlimited integrity, which is as much as can be said for anyone. He made a religion of Republicanism, and nevertheless once took a walk. In 1924, resenting Coolidge's cagy reluctance to speak out against the Ku Klux Klan's intrusion into Republican politics, he voted for La Follette. Roosevelt wanted him to take another walk in 1940, but reckoned without his provincial independence.

Landon's story of Roosevelt's maneuverings for national unity goes back to the outbreak of World War II. He says:

In September, 1939, Frank Knox and I were invited . . . to participate in a White House Conference. . . .

When I reached Washington, some of the . . . reporters . . . said to me, "Of course, you know you are being considered for a Cabinet position." Says I, "Oh, that is Washington . . . gossip." "No," they replied, "there is more to it than that."

A few days later, in New York, I called on the President to bring on national harmony, by taking himself out of the third term race. . . .

Mr. Roosevelt had gone to Hyde Park. The reporters there caught him in an automobile with his mother, and asked him about my statement. The President made no comment, but the AP reported Mrs. Roosevelt as saying, "Why don't you, Franklin?"

A few weeks later Frank Knox was offered a place in the Cabinet. He replied—according to the word he sent me at the time through L. C. Haynes of the Kansas City

Star, which he subsequently personally confirmed—that he would be in a position of being a traitor to the Republican Party if he went in the Cabinet alone, and that the President would have to get me.

The conversations went on between the President and Mr. Knox in the winter of '39 and '40.

On May 13, 1940, Frank Altschul, . . . brother-in-law of Governor Lehman, called me. He asked if I knew of the job they were talking about for me in Washington. I replied that I thought I did. Mr. Altschul asked me if I would go down to talk to the President about it if he would invite me to lunch. I replied, "I would be glad to talk to the President on any subject that he desired to talk to me about." Altschul then said, "Governor Lehman is going over to Washington tonight. Can he take that message?" "Yes," says I.

Tuesday, May 14, I received a telegram from General Watson inviting me to have lunch with the President on Wednesday, May 22. I called the General immediately and informed him that I would be delighted to have lunch with the President. I also informed the General that I was making a speech in Warrensburg, Missouri, on Friday, May 17, on foreign policy; and that, naturally, I would be glad to have the publicity for my speech which the luncheon engagement would give me, but they might not like to have me have it. I also thought I ought to tell him that I was taking some "pokes" at the President, and that I would air mail him my first release . . . that afternoon. If the President still wanted me to come after reading my Warrensburg speech, I would be very happy to do so.

Wednesday, May 15, Frank Knox called me from Washington and said, "Alf, you are going to ruin yourself and your party." "Why?" says I. "This is no time to criticize the President," replied Frank. "Have I said anything below the belt?" I asked. "No," replied Frank, "Everything you said is perfectly justified. . . ."

Sunday, May 19, Barney Kilgore, of the *Wall Street Journal,* Roscoe Drummond, of the *Christian Science*

Monitor, and Turner Catledge, of the New York *Times,* had dinner with me. They said, "We don't know whether you know it or not, but the Republican Party is facing a debacle." The night before, Governor Ratner, of Kansas, had called me and said, "Alf, what are we going to do? I was at a Republican picnic in Riley County yesterday, and three of our best women workers asked me if we should not let the election go by default."

That was when Dorothy Thompson and Kaltenborn were on the air urging that the Republicans should not contest the re-election of President Roosevelt.

After dinner, I worked out a statement with the three Washington correspondents in which I spoke of the necessity of holding an election in order to carry out our democratic processes.

When I finished my statement, the three newspapermen said, "Of course, you know this means you will not be offered the Cabinet position." "Yes," I said, "I know it, and that's the way I want it. I will only take it under one condition. I don't think the President will meet that condition. Therefore, I want to save the President the embarrassment of offering me the Cabinet position, and myself the embarrassment of refusing it. . . ."

I left Monday Noon, May 20, for Washington. . . . When I reached Chicago . . . New York was calling . . . Frank Altschul was put on the phone.

Mr. Altschul said, "General Watson called me, and asked me to get hold of you and have you cancel your engagement with the President for lunch. . . ."

"What reason did the General give?" I asked Altschul. "He said, in view of your Warrensburg speech and your statement in this morning's papers . . . it did not seem to serve any useful purpose." "What did the General suggest that I say?" I asked. Altschul replied, "He suggested that you could say you had a sudden attack of illness or a bad cold, and that you were returning home but would come down later on." "I won't say any such damn thing," I replied.

I then . . . fixed a press conference at 10:00 [the next morning, Tuesday, May 21].

At that press conference, I just finished reading a statement . . . when the telephone rang. I said, "I can't be interrupted now." . . . [But] it [was] the White House. I said to the press crowd of some twenty reporters, "Hold everything, I don't know what this means."

When I answered the phone, the President was put on. He said, "Alf, between Watson and Altschul, they got us all balled up. I didn't mean to cancel our luncheon. I wanted them to see if we could postpone it until Thursday. I have been wanting to see [James] Wadsworth and a Committee, but I find I can see him this afternoon so you come on. We won't have any trouble understanding ourselves when we get our feet under the table." I replied, "Thank you Mr. President, I will be there." I returned to the press conference and canceled my statement. . . .

The explanation given out by Stephen Early at the White House for the off-again-on-again luncheon business was that the President wanted to see Wadsworth. The newspapermen called Representative Wadsworth's office —found he wasn't in town—hadn't been in town for two or three days—and didn't expect to be in town the rest of the week.

Frank Knox and I sat down to lunch together in my room. He started talking about the horrible prospect of Nazi victory and what it meant to the kind of civilization we believed in and the security of our country. I said, "Yes, I know, Frank. . . . But I think a third successive term for any President is as great a threat to our institutions as anything from the outside. If we go into the Cabinet we might as well call off the election. . . .

Knox replied, "Alf, he can't run again if he wants to. He is in terrible shape physically. The President said to me last week, 'Look at me, Frank. I couldn't run for a third term if I wanted to.'" And Frank held out his trembling hands to illustrate how the President had held out his hands to him.

"Yes, I know," I replied. "But I don't trust him."

Frank then said, "Couldn't we each take a note from him to the effect that he would not be a candidate for the third term?" I replied, "Frank, what kind of position would we be in, asking the President to give us that note? He has told you that he is not in a physical condition to run for a third term if he wanted to, and yet—on the eve of going into his Cabinet—tell him we don't trust his words?" Frank replied, "I guess you are right. Tell him you speak for me." I replied, "You ought to tell him that yourself, Frank." He replied, "All right, I will. I will send him a telegram as soon as I go to the office." I then said, "It ought to be a letter, in your own handwriting, on your own letterhead. I tell you what. Wire Paul Leach [Chicago *Daily News* correspondent in Washington] to meet me at the train. Send me the note when you get back to the office. I reach Washington at 8:30 on the Pennsylvania. Leach can take the note to the White House, and it will be there before I get there." Frank Knox agreed, and brought the note to me at the train himself. . . .

I had a delightful visit with the President for two hours. He reminisced about the maneuverings that went on to get Mr. Hoover to say whether he was a Republican or a Democrat in the winter of 1919–20. He expressed his opinion as to the characteristics and abilities of the . . . candidates for the Republican nomination. We discussed the foreign situation. The President said, "In about an hour I am going to talk to Bill Bullitt. I am going to tell him to tell Reynaud to take the 450,000 French soldiers guarding the Italian line and use them in a flank attack on the Germans. . . ."

The nearest the President got to discussing the Cabinet was . . . "Now, Alf, don't believe everything you read in the newspapers. If you will just call me I will be glad to set you straight. Ickes has been wanting me for a year to dedicate some national parks in the West. As soon as I announced my trip the newspapers said it was a political swing around the circle." (I had used that phrase in my

Warrensburg speech. After the White House had received my release the President announced the cancellation of his trip. The only change I made in the text of my talk was the reference to that cancellation.)

The President said, "I have to make some new Cabinet appointments and the newspapermen immediately started talking about a coalition. When Edison told me he was going to run for Governor of New Jersey, I told him if he got the nomination he would have to resign as Secretary of the Navy. The situation in the War Department is intolerable, and I have to get a new Secretary of War. Secretary Perkins shows the mistake of naming a woman to high office, and I have got to get a new Secretary of Labor. I am thinking of thirty or forty men for these places. I don't know whether they are Republicans or Democrats." I said, "Then you didn't agree with Frank Knox to get another Republican to go with him in the Cabinet?" The President said, "No."

[The point of Landon's statement, which Knox was to have echoed, was that Roosevelt could achieve national unity at once by renouncing a third term.]

I left the White House luncheon at 2:00. That automatically fixed my press conference at 3:00. . . .

I called Frank Knox and told him that the President had not mentioned the Cabinet position to me, and read him my statement. When I got through, Knox said, "That is bully, that is grand, tell him you speak for me." I hesitated a second (Frank had been a great fellow to work with in '36 and in politics you have to think of your friends). Frank caught the hesitation and said, "Don't you think so?" I replied, "I am thinking of your own prestige and your own position of party leadership. It would be better for you to make your own statement instead of a 'me too' statement." Frank said, "All right, I will, I will put it on the wire in an hour." He wired Paul Leach. Paul Leach put it on the Washington news ticker that Knox's statement would be out at 4:00. . . . But it never came. Several years later Edgar Mowrer told me

Knox had shown him his telegram, but Mowrer persuaded Knox that he owed it to the President to talk to him personally.

"The President regrets," the White House replied, "that he has no time just now to give to . . . political statements."

And, indeed, nothing he might have told the newspapers could have given them a better political story that day than what he said to Frank Knox over the telephone.

ALTHOUGH this episode frustrated Roosevelt's first attempt to find a Secretary of War, it provided him with a potential Navy Secretary, for it satisfied him that Knox could be handled. No scrutiny was needed of Knox's political credentials: they were perfect. Knox had been a hero with President Roosevelt's cousin Theodore and was given to sporting his ancient sombrero with a pair of bullet holes in it as a reminder of San Juan Hill. He had been Chairman of the Republican Party in Michigan, and he had followed Theodore Roosevelt into the Bull Moose movement. "He is just our type," Theodore Roosevelt had written in introducing Knox to the young Henry Stimson, and, as if proof were needed, Knox, duly established as the leading publisher in New Hampshire, had kicked downstairs an emissary of the Ku Klux Klan who had come with an offer of support of Knox's candidacy for the governership of New Hampshire. As Vice-Presidential nominee of the Republican Party in 1936, Knox was the ranking Republican in Illinois, and he was as outspoken an internationalist as Colonel Robert McCormick was an isolationist.

Few pleasures and few prerogatives were as important to Roosevelt as his feud with the nation's opinion-makers. Of all his critics the publishers were the most apoplectic and the most high-minded; and of all his practical jokes none promised to be more devastating than his appointing their distinguished colleague, the proprietor of the Chicago *Daily News*, to his new National Unity Cabinet. Among the publishers nothing could have provoked more private fury or inspired more public praise.

Lincoln lore treasures the story of the protest of an Illinois political friend against the inclusion of Salmon P. Chase in Lincoln's new Cabinet. "[Chase] thinks he is a great deal bigger than you are," the friend warned. "Do you know of any other men who think they are bigger than I am?" was Lincoln's reply. "I cannot say that I do," his friend answered. "But why do you ask me that?" "Because," Lincoln told him, "I want to put them all in my Cabinet." Whatever Lincoln and Roosevelt had in common, they did not share this attitude, which explains why, in spite of the great temptation to appoint Knox, Roosevelt hesitated. He wanted to be sure that behind the man's bluff and hearty exterior there lurked no Cassius. A Secretary of the Navy capable of forcing or manipulating his way into the councils of war was just the kind of formidable politico Roosevelt did not want to add to his problem list. But a Secretary who could be trusted to fight vigorously and incessantly to keep his

name within earshot of the public was not likely to
interfere with Roosevelt's determination to continue
running the Navy his own way.

In order to render the neutralization of the Secretary certain, Roosevelt had to find an inside man, able,
unobtrusive, devoted, and politician enough to survive
the hazards of working for the President inside the
Navy Department. Such a man Roosevelt was bound
to scrutinize for esoteric marks of the virtuoso qualities which he never tired of admiring in himself—
qualities by which he explained his own successful
apprenticeship to power as the young man who had
run the Navy Department while Josephus Daniels
quarreled with everybody. The difficulty was that any
remotely plausible candidate for second place in the
Navy Department was bound to arouse suspicion in
Roosevelt. Only a man satisfying Roosevelt as to both
his usability and his harmlessness had a chance of
qualifying to serve in this most exacting and intimate
of all places. It was the one place, in fact, in which
Roosevelt felt obliged to put a man unusual enough
to operate as he himself had operated as a young man.
It was the one place in which he could not tolerate
anyone remotely capable of applying such rare talents
outside the restricted area of Navy procurement and
Navy politics.

James Forrestal was a Wall Street banker. This in
Roosevelt's eyes made him safe. Forrestal had been
born a Catholic but had left the Church. This on both
counts insured the risk. On the other hand, he was a
second-generation Dutchess County Democrat, which
made him seem intriguing. Forrestal, on his part, was

intrigued. For all his purposive preoccupation with work—or, perhaps, because of it—he was a deeply divided person: he was at once fascinated by politicians and defiant of politics; alternately tempted to become a politician and to remain an intellectual; and in both moods a lone wolf, foredoomed, perhaps, to frustration and despair. As a young man he had been one of the Navy's pioneer flying aces, and he looked like a welterweight in fighting trim. This made him a plausible figure to be presented to the Admirals. But the most impressive fact about Forrestal was his sponsorship. For Forrestal was recommended to Roosevelt by the man against whom he had had to bargain in the New Deal days—Justice W. O. Douglas. Of all the men Roosevelt appointed on the home front, Forrestal was by far the ablest, and his contribution to the permanent problem of mobilization was the most enduring. With these qualifications, he completed the formula and permitted the President to act, by naming Knox to head the Navy Department and Forrestal to run it for him.

All of Forrestal's talents were needed for the job at hand. For in the summer of 1940 we had no way of knowing whether we would have to fight on both oceans at once or on which we would have to fight first. In the final analysis, Roosevelt's campaign promise to keep America out of war and to keep war out of America hinged on the Navy. But the Navy at that point was too weak either to break the first half of the promise or to honor the second half. For it lacked the strength to ferry an Army across even one ocean, and, as Pearl Harbor was to show a year later, it was not prepared to withstand attack on the front on which it was best prepared. When responsibility for Navy procurement and production was thrust upon Forrestal, the great question facing the Army, the economy, and the country was: How much time dare we hope for?

This question the Navy had to answer. How much time the country was going to have, first to prepare and then to fight, would depend on how quickly the Navy could manage to put fire power to sea. The leverage on America's entire war effort, accordingly, had to be swung by the Navy, and had to be swung from inside the Navy Department. Hence Roosevelt's fear of a Secretary capable of directing the Department; hence his need of an Under-Secretary who could. Of the four national unity appointees in the War and Navy Departments, it is significant that only the man picked for the inside job in the Navy was not a Republican.

In the grand perspective of the war, the salient fact —the fact which explains not only why Pearl Harbor happened but when it did—is America's dependence upon the Navy. After the war, the Navy temporarily became one of the casualties caused by the atomic bomb. But so long as dictatorships rely upon the unpreparedness of democracies, it will remain axiomatic that the American Navy's first mission must be to buy for the economy behind it the time to make up for lost time. If further proof were needed, the Korean crisis of 1950 supplied it.

Thus, the decision of the Axis to attack our Navy in 1941 was predetermined by the intensive program which the Navy had launched in 1940, under Forrestal's direction, to equip a naval force designed to screen the economy during the period of tooling for conversion to war production. The Axis, in other words, had to strike at the Navy's main base before the program put on the drawing boards in 1940 could begin to come off the production lines in 1942. Moreover, after 1942, the country had to fight its way into the war behind the Navy. But during the dismal months of 1942, when the submarine pack was blockading America and not only the war of shot and shell but the war of nerves was rising to a sickening crescendo, the crisis of morale expressed itself as a bitter question: "Where's the Navy?"

Sinkings mounted. Dirty oil, water-soaked planks, and worse, were washed up on the beaches along our blacked-out coasts. The Navy had counted on the Army to equip its vessels with anti-aircraft guns, and the Army had forgotten. But the Navy did have plenty of aluminum furniture. Why didn't it have what was needed to drive the U-boats out to sea and sink them? The answer was that the Navy was being rebuilt. Forrestal earned a secure place in American history during the long months from June, 1940, to June, 1942, when he was living by the calendar and praying for his 1942 and 1943 and 1944 crops of fire power. Until they were harvested, until our new Navy had fought its way into the war, neither production nor manpower could be carried to the overseas fronts.

BEFORE Roosevelt could move the Knox-Forrestal team into the Navy Department, he had to fill the most conspicuous vacancy of all—the Secretaryship of War. The most obvious Republican having refused to let the job seek him, the way was now open for plausible Republicans to seek the job. None was better equipped than Henry L. Stimson, and none had a more energetic and resourceful manager to represent him in the White House. It was at the suggestion of the Talleyrand of the times, Justice Felix Frankfurter, that Roosevelt named Colonel Stimson as Secretary of War.

No American has ever been more thoroughly misunderstood than Frankfurter. He was widely regarded as an aloof intellectual, and he reinforced this popular impression by parading certain concepts—such as the English Common Law, States' Rights, and the Holmes-Brandeis tradition (which is, in fact, two traditions) —for which he claimed a kind of personal custody. But the Professor's real preoccupation was with power, and, unlike those dedicated ideologues who seek to control the masses by manipulating abstractions, he gloried in a power which was personal and was exercised over the elite at close quarters. By 1940, he had long since become the proprietor of an organization for filling government positions of every kind from a Cabinet post to a clerkship. When the prospective employer suspected him of boring from within, he was always ready with plausible intermediaries plausibly briefed to act as brokers. No ward heeler ever patrolled the neighborhood saloons as energetically and with as business-like a sense of detail as Frankfurter did the nation's salons. He was, in fact, a kind of alderman-at-large for the better element. As a consummate practitioner of the politics of principle in sponsoring Stimson, Frankfurter not only scored a brilliant political coup but performed a public service as well. The following paragraph quoted from Stimson's autobiography *On Active Service* (written in the third person) is revealing:

No discussion of Stimson's relationship to the Administration would be complete without one further name, that of Mr. Justice Frankfurter. Without the least deviation from his fastidious devotion to the high traditions of the Supreme Court, Felix Frankfurter made himself a continual source of comfort and help to Stimson. Although he never heard a word of it from Frankfurter, Stimson believed that his own presence in Washington was in some degree the result of Frankfurter's close relationship to the President. In any event, he found Frankfurter always the most devoted of friends and the most zealous of private helpers, and the Justice's long and intimate knowledge of the Roosevelt administration was placed entirely at his disposal. Time after time, when critical issues developed, Stimson turned to Frankfurther; sometimes [eloquent understatement] he heard from Frankfurter even before he had turned. It is not fitting that the activities of a Justice still serving on the Court should be discussed in detail, and Mr. Justice Frankfurter will not be mentioned again; there was in his relationship with Stimson nothing, of course, that even remotely touched upon his duties as a Justice, while there was much that added to the country's debt to a distinguished American.*

In supporting Stimson, Frankfurter had thrown his influence behind a man of unusual capacity and unassailable credentials. No one on the home front was to prove a more incisive administrator. From the

* Henry L. Stimson, *On Active Service* (New York, Harper & Brothers, 1948), p. 334.

standpoint of the formal record, Stimson had been Republican nominee for Governor of New York; also, he had served as Secretary of War and Secretary of State; and he was one of New York's leading corporation lawyers. The Republican Party could not disown Stimson as Roosevelt's Secretary of War, and the press could not question Roosevelt's motives in appointing him.

But first Johnson had to be dismissed. And Frankfurter's formula gave Roosevelt a pretext for engineering this, too. The ceremony required an appreciative audience and an unassailable witness. Who but Baruch could play both roles at once? Who but Baruch, with his passion for playing the insider ex officio with everybody and his wariness of becoming identified with anybody? Baruch had grasped at the chance to become Johnson's official mentor, a dignity which enabled him to maintain a private pipeline into the White House and at the same time to be as critical as he pleased of its occupant. It was this penchant of the Elder Statesman for playing the part of the fox instead of the wolf that explained why Roosevelt resented but did not fear him. In this transaction Baruch was not so much a necessary evil as a willing accessory. It was from his protégé that Roosevelt was about to withdraw the famous promise of the Secretaryship of War.

Roosevelt was never more plausible, never more likable, never more frank, never more considerate than when he was explaining to the men whose turn it came to be taken into his confidence why he was about to hire someone else in their place. Just as a condemned man is sent to his fate with a hearty meal and a solemn prayer, so the ritual Roosevelt observed in sacrificing the faithful always gave them a good confidential story to tell and sent them out of office with a warm and intimate glow, hopeful that the higher strategy agreed upon in the White House had put them into partnership with history. The decision to transcend the option Johnson held on the Secretaryship had been dictated by urgent and unimpeachable intelligence from the political front. "Felix" (meaning the Justice), Roosevelt explained, nodding at the attending Elder Statesman, "has assured Bernie that if I make Stimson Secretary of War the Republicans will call off their Philadelphia Convention."

FRANKFURTER had timed his operation perfectly. On June 17, Stimson addressed the Yale Alumni at Commencement and came out for compulsory military training. On June 18, he addressed the nation on the radio, repeating his demand for compulsory military training, urging all aid short of immediate war to England and France, and calling for the defeat of Germany. "Short of a direct declaration of war," Stimson says in his memoirs, "it would have been hard to frame a more complete program of resistance to the Nazis. And a declaration of war, then and for months thereafter, was not in Stimson's mind. It could not be, because in years of dealing with foreign affairs he had learned the necessity for pitching policy to opinion.

"As it was, he had stepped well out in front of the

President and most other leaders in the debate—at least ahead of their published opinions. In the newspapers the next morning he found himself on the one hand a hero and on the other a villain. But he did not have much time to consider these reactions, for on the afternoon of June 19 he received a telephone call from the White House."

Stimson was above guile, disingenuousness, or false modesty. His account tells the story.

I was called up by the President [he says, lapsing into the first person singular] who offered me the position of Secretary of War. He told me that Knox had already agreed to accept the position of Secretary of the Navy . . . To say that Stimson was surprised [he continues, reverting to the third person] would be putting it mildly. Some weeks before, he had heard from Grenville Clark [a leading New York lawyer who was prominent in the Aid the Allies movement and whom Frankfurter admired] that his [Stimson's] name had been suggested for the job. Clark had coupled it with that of Judge Robert P. Patterson as Assistant Secretary. He [Stimson] knew, too, that this suggestion had reached the President. But that the President should have listened to it, and acted on it, was astonishing. His first reaction was to point out that he was approaching his seventy-third birthday. The President said he already knew that, and added that Stimson would be free to appoint his own Assistant Secretary. Patterson's name was mentioned and approved by both men.*

Like Stimson, Patterson was a good and a high-minded man, forceful and zealous, but guileless to the point of naïveté. In combination with Forrestal, whose introversion found a sympathetic and hearty outlet in

* Henry L. Stimson, *On Active Service* (New York, Harper & Brothers, 1948), p. 323.

Patterson's literal-minded profanity, he was effective. But in the hands of the Washington brass Patterson was a blunt instrument, to be used against the civilians. To each new complication his answer was, "We've got to win the war," as if anyone wanted to lose it and as if slogans, orthodoxy, and character were enough to avert the danger that we might lose it.

But Frankfurter had been shrewd in seizing on Roosevelt's interest in Stimson to include the Under-Secretaryship in the arrangement. Since the pattern-making preliminaries to mobilization had already insured War Department control over the home front, and since the Departmental apparatus for administering mobilization was the Office of the Under-Secretary, the Patterson appointment gave Frankfurter strategic access to mobilization headquarters, now staffed by his friends. It put the civilians about to emerge as powers on the home front in the position of having to deal with Patterson in order to deal with the War Department. It gave Frankfurter political power out of all proportion to the patronage he could manipulate inside the White House. The first to recognize this was Harry Hopkins. Hopkins was as aggressively low-brow as Frankfurter was ostentatiously high-brow. Nevertheless, swallowing his irritation, Hopkins, too, made an alliance with the Justice which enabled him to work with the Republicans in the new war administration. Meanwhile, as the crisis deepened, the country at large was reassured by its belief that the President had waived partisan advantage and yielded some of his own power in order to build a Cabinet on the principle of national unity.

CHAPTER VII

THE WAR BOOM

By the beginning of 1940, the economy was in transition and in confusion. When Hitler invaded Poland, almost everyone expected the war to pick the economy up exactly where 1919 had dropped it. There was a sinister excitement in the autumn air of that first Second World War year, and it set grocers and tycoons to muttering "War Boom" under their breath. The price of steel and the production rate of steel surged upward together. Copper companies and the manufacturers of ladies' handkerchiefs put on new help. The stock market sky-rocketed. America prepared to handle European orders.

The boom materialized. Industry after industry began to operate at capacity. And still the orders poured in; but they were American, not Allied, orders. In anticipation of a 1916-style export rush, and in fear of mounting commodity prices (wheat, lard, and rubber climbed 30 percent in two weeks), American industry spurred American industry to new heights. Businessmen followed prices. Speculators in spite of themselves, they bought all the way along, literally in self-defense, wanting only protection against a goods famine. Notices went out to domestic customers to lay in stocks for future use at once to guard against the coming export scramble. Expecting enormous export

orders themselves, the companies thus warned signed
every order blank in sight. When the British actually
did try to place a moderate order for steel, the companies, working feverishly to satisfy American customers, ignored them.

Producers remote from the war-goods market were
affected. Although the manufacturers of cotton textiles
received fewer export inquiries than even the steel
industry, they sold more than at any time since the
peak of the 1920 inflation. Into warehouses, like nuts
into squirrels' holes, went sheets of steel and percale
alike. The rush to cache merchandise which had not
the slightest chance of being exported soon overloaded
the railroads, which reacted by ordering thousands of
new cars (now at boom prices!) and rushing others to
repair shops. No munitions orders had been placed.
But overnight American production shot up past the
1929 rate.

And then it was over. By the time of delivery of
freight cars ordered in September, 1939, trainfuls of
empties were on the sidings, waiting to carry 1939's
new surpluses to the ultimate consumer. But the ultimate consumer, even the sugar-hoarding housewife,
had stopped buying. The short-lived production boom
had failed to stimulate a consumption boom. Meanwhile, exports, the hope of which had set off the production boom, failed to materialize. Instead, exports
failed to recover to the 1937 level. It was not until the
first quarter of 1940, by which time business had
slowed down to its pre-war rate of activity, that export
trade began to show signs of a serious increase.

So did the activity of the German army. May, 1940,

turned the war into a terrifying and potent catalyst of nightmare. On the economic plane the immediate result to America of the transition from Sitzkrieg to Blitzkrieg was the loss of the expanding European market. Indeed, such export business as the Sitzkrieg phase of the war stimulated was altogether different from the business the economy needed. In the commercial sector, industry after industry was stagnating for lack of a 20–50 percent increase in volume. Without exception, war exports were concentrated in the munitions industries, which, by the summer of 1940, stood in least need of exports.

Most conspicuous of the new war growths was the aircraft industry, whose shipments abroad more than doubled in the first quarter of 1940. Between the beginning of the war and mid-May, America managed to send 2,300 planes to the Allies alone. By July the industry was working against an order backlog of $1,200,000,000. Individual manufacturers who had pioneered in sheds, and who called their skilled mechanics by their first names, now struggled between stock promotions to finance a staggering flood of commitments. They found themselves measuring their plants in miles, their work forces in tens of thousands, and their bookkeeping in hundreds of millions. Traditionally, the manufacturers had been rich in ideas but poor in cash. By the summer of 1940, they were casual about cash, but desperately short of organizing ability and tooling. But the machine tool industry, meanwhile, was also rushing from famine to feast. It had been one of the beneficiaries of the brief export boom —exports to the Allies increased four times over the

1938 rate and, thanks to the added impact of Russian and Japanese orders, exports accounted for about half the industry's sales and production lagged behind demand.

The export situation was a study in contrasts. The brass companies were working 24 hours a day, but were as far behind their backlogs as the aircraft industry. Late in May, the president of one of the companies was quoted as saying that a full year would be needed to enlarge copper-fabricating facilities sufficiently to meet the expected ordnance requirements of the new American defense program.

In contrast to this almost embarrassing boom in the heavy industries, agriculture, the one sector then still dependent upon exports, was depressed. The shooting in Poland had reminded some farmers of the first war boom—they started a land boom. This did not climb very high or last very long. For the first six months of 1940, farm exports (excluding cotton, which benefited temporarily from an export subsidy) were off 21 percent. Cotton exports began to fall in a straight line in February, when the subsidy stopped. Then, in May, the most crushing blow of all fell on the cotton market: the British, by far our largest customers, having taken advantage of the subsidy's bargain price to stock up, prohibited further imports except under license. In June, while inventories of every major crop from cotton to fruits accumulated, prices collapsed. The war did not profit the American farmer in the beginning.

The farmer is the one factor in the American economy in chronic need of relief through exports. To help solve the farm problem, export subsidies, bad investments in themselves, had been fired at Europe between the two wars. To no avail. During World War I and its aftermath, our export subsidies took the form of private lending abroad. This was the period, as Judge Jerome Frank put it, of Wall Street's private PWA. The loans of that era served a general pump-priming purpose as long as they lasted, but as soon as they stopped the great depression began.

By the time repudiation stopped foreign lending, agriculture was in acute crisis. Proceeding on the traditional assumption that farm recovery had to follow from a general export recovery in which agriculture could hope to participate, we invented a new method of pump-priming: we began to buy gold from all comers, paying $35 an ounce for this metaphysical mirage of "permanent and universal" money. By mid-1940 the United States Treasury had accumulated a dental reservoir of $19,000,000,000 in buried treasure at Fort Knox, of which only $7,300,000,000 came from domestic holdings and production. The balance, plus an additional billion of only slightly less permanent and universal money in the form of silver, came from abroad. What the United States got back from this $13,000,000,000 investment in gold and silver during the six years and five months from January, 1934, to the fall of France was an export trade balance of $3,545,240,000—roughly 25¢ on each dollar of subsidy. When France fell, we had to stop the subsidy on pain of financing Hitler, who by that time held Europe's gold.

But the idea had long since been discredited. As early as November, 1939, the gold import rush was overshadowing the hoped for war export boom. This fact, proof positive that the war was not profiting us, prompted the *Wall Street Journal* to break an editorial lance against "those who still believed it is the Heaven-given right of the United States to sell abroad every-thing it chooses to ship and to buy there only what it cannot produce at home, and those who think of large export balances as the only 'favorable' foreign trade results." To the latter group, the *Journal* pointed out that the $3,100,000,000 of gold we imported between January and November, 1939, came to "more than four times [our] export balance."

But the exports which materialized were confined to airplanes and other war necessities for which there was a fierce and solvent demand anyhow. The farm products, for which we so badly needed an export outlet, were passed over. Congress, unreconciled to reality, voted export subsidies for each major crop. In the case of cotton, the subsidy during the 1939–40 crop year amounted to some $60,000,000, and left the cotton crisis exactly where it was. Moreover, the cotton export subsidy soon came into direct conflict with our foreign policy. For the export subsidy netted Japan, who hardly claimed first call on our charity, a saving of some $4,000,000, no mean sum to her. And Spain, passive partner of the Axis, against whom we were presently to wage economic warfare, received from the Export-Import Bank 80 percent of a $13,-750,000 cotton credit.

The wheat-export subsidy was shorter-lived—it was

canceled at the end of 1939—and equally fruitless. Between August, 1938, and December, 1939, the United States dumped 128,200,000 bushels, at a cost of about $33,000,000. At one point in the summer of 1939, the world price was so far below the domestic cost of production that 50¢ was lost on every bushel dumped. The most unfortunate part of this episode was that it involved us in a dispute with Argentina. We were ill-advised enough to carry our wheat offensive into her bailiwick by proposing to dump 50,000,-000 bushels in the Brazilian market, which in the depression year of 1938 had absorbed the entire Argentinian surplus. All that was involved for America in this adventure was $23,000,000, which meant very little to us but a great deal to Argentina.

In May, 1940, another short-sighted campaign was undertaken to dump 20,000,000 bushels of another sick crop—corn—our exports having suffered from a 30¢ differential in favor of Argentinian corn. The subsidy fund was only $6,000,000, not nearly enough to ease the pressure of the huge surplus. But it quickly provoked—and substantiated—Argentinian charges in that tense situation that we were violating the Good Neighbor policy.

These intermittent crop export subsidies failed to scratch the surface of the farm problem. At best, they served as very temporary palliatives: at worst, they brought us into open conflict with our hemispheric neighbors, the latter being countries with nothing but crops to sell and no place but Europe and other Latin American countries to sell them. Within two years, we were anxiously wondering if we could depend on the loyalty of our Good Neighbors.

Crops were not American agriculture's only surplus. Marginal families constituted an even more uneconomic waste crying even more desperately to be absorbed into the war economy's stream of productive energy. As W. L. Clayton, later Assistant Secretary of State and then head of Anderson, Clayton and Company, the world's largest cotton firm, said: "We have in the United States a surplus of at least 2,000,-000 farm families and 75,000,000 to 100,000,000 acres of farm land."

The new Defense Commissioner for Agriculture, Chester Davis, agreed wholeheartedly with Clayton. Some 30,000,000 people were living on farms in the United States. In November, 1940, Davis proposed that no less than 5,000,000 low-income, single cash-crop farm people leave the land and go into defense industries.

You remember the slogan of 1917 [he said], "Food will win the war." Then we strained ourselves to limit domestic consumption and expand production to provide food for our armies and our Allies. Now you might say the situation is reversed. We have an abundance of food and fiber to meet normal civilian requirements and any military demand that may arise. On top of that, the surpluses are piling up which would have gone into export had there been no war in Europe. . . . The big job is to keep our farms in healthy production and at the same time prevent American farmers from becoming the first American casualty of this new world war.

For the moment, at any rate, Davis's argument was

unanswerable. But on the farm front, the danger was always present that we might fight so hard to win the last war that we might lose the one confronting us. Milo Perkins, Secretary Wallace's most forceful aide, saw this danger clearly and warned that what he called "the Farm Bureau Federation attitude" would make food shortages an issue again before the war ended. In 1941 he laid it down that "food would win the Peace." Perkins was prophetic, but Davis was not impractical. Nothing could have been more uneconomic and devitalizing than to continue freezing a couple of million marginal families on marginal land. They were urgently needed in war plants, where machinery and organization were certain to multiply immeasurably the productivity of their malnourished muscles and their ignorant methods. If greater food production was needed, the efficient way to get it was by increasing the yields of the nation's economic farms —a brace of wars could be won or lost in the time needed to modernize the ways of these marginal farmers and make their output a factor in world politics. Meanwhile, once relocated in plants, this reserve of unskilled, marginal labor could (and did) produce farm equipment for mechanized farms faster than they could produce food for others to eat. And if only they could be prevented from streaming back to the farms after the war, as they did during the 1920's, their addition to the nonagricultural population would present postwar agriculture with a new market bigger and steadier than exports had ever been.

Here were drawn the lines for one of the bitter and basic battles on the home front. Organized agriculture began by grasping at speculative opportunities suggested by memories of World War I. Quickly disillusioned, it reacted by seeking insurance against any repetition of that war's deflationary aftermath. But throughout, it saw the war not as an immediate urgency forcing action on its own terms for the sake of survival, but rather as a manipulation in political economics—exactly as Roosevelt did. What Roosevelt wanted was to win the war. His objective was as simple as his methods were complicated; and he pursued it as an end in itself subject to only one qualification—to win it with as little fighting as possible by Americans. But organized agriculture spent most of the war agreeing with organized business and organized labor that Roosevelt was trying to win the war for the New Deal blueprint of social reform by which all three groups agreed he worked. And articulate farm opinion was constantly on the alert to uncover evidence that the war was being won for this fancied postwar economic program of Roosevelt's. But the farm organizations insisted that the war be won for their own postwar economic security. They counted its victories and its defeats in threats of surpluses and hopes of shortages. This is not to say that the war did not come close to American agriculture. On the contrary, it is the measure of how close the war did come.

THE beginnings of organized defense production were inchoate but hopeful. By October, 1941, the American Army was to comprise some 1,600,000 men. What passed for the initial program envisioned orders sufficient to equip an American army of 2,000,000 men.

But the whole framework was impractical: either the production schedule had to be revised to provide for adequate shipments to such Allies as might survive the Blitz or, if none did, an army of 2,000,000 men would be useless to us. The initial program—guessing would be a kinder and no doubt a more accurate word —was plagued by the same unrealism which dogged its successors. It failed to budget for the combined needs of our Allies' fighting forces and our own.

Chaos and crisis were inherent in the scheme of things. On the one hand, the Defense Commission was working with the Army and Navy to equip a prospective force of 2,000,000 Americans. On the other, top priority had to go to the Allied forces fighting to remain in being. To maintain this division of labor, it was necessary to allocate productive capacity, raw materials, transportation, and manpower for export account. But no one had the authority to schedule production for overseas shipment, or even to pay for it. The country looked to poor, harassed, well-meaning Knudsen to settle all production problems. But when the British, not knowing whether they would manage to hold Hitler off from month to month, proposed to place an order calling for delivery of 3,000 planes a month in 1941 and 1942, Knudsen threw up his hands and said he was "just an adding machine." He sent them to Morgenthau, not realizing apparently that his own coming to Washington had superseded Morgenthau's original power of initiative. Now this British order would have required the construction of no less than 38 new plants. In spite of the pressure of time against which they were fighting, the British were perfectly realistic in trying to operate on this scale. The Blitz had beaten them into seeing that, if they were not going to be knocked out of the war, they would have to fight their way back into it on just such a scale. By contrast, our combined domestic and export August schedule called for the delivery of 895 combat and transport planes—of which 396 went to our Army and Navy and 236 to the British Government.

Before the Defense Commission could budget production requirements, it had to allocate manpower, and this posed the most delicate and complicated of all the problems of home front administration. To add the number of Allied troops to our own Army and Navy, and to say that our home front had to equip not merely 2,000,000 Americans but 3,000,000 or more Allies, was not the answer. The equation of material to manpower was not a simple one. The manpower component had to be broken down into three parts: Allied manpower, American manpower in uniform, and American manpower in overalls. What complicated the calculation was the fact that varying values had to be assigned to each group of mobilized Americans. Nor could each American in uniform count equally with each Ally in uniform. All calculations had to allow for the leverage factor exerted by the Americans in overalls. How many Allies could each American in overalls supply? And how many Americans in uniform? How many Americans were needed in overalls to begin supplying 2,000,000 Americans and 3,000,000 Allies? How many to bring our armed forces to 5,000,-000 and to supply 10,000,000 Allies? How many to

bring our armed forces to the 1944 goal of 12,000,000?
And to supply them and our Allies defensively? Offen-
sively? Across one ocean? Across both oceans?

Thus, all questions about the size of the combined
Allied forces reduced themselves to one fundamental
question about America's home front: how predict-
ably would it use manpower? Not how efficiently, but
how measurably. The number of Americans needed in
uniform depended upon the number of Allied troops
on the various fronts; the fewer they had, the more
we had to have. Their fighting effectiveness depended
upon our productive efficiency, and our productive
efficiency depended in turn upon the size of our work
force.

But how these factors geared in together was lost
on Knudsen; this was not the kind of gearing he knew
about. His conception of his job was as simple as an
infantry private's. "You bring it to the shop door," he
told Stettinius, who was responsible for raw material
supplies, "and I'll cut it up." Far from considering
how to schedule British and American orders for the
benefit of the combined program, he resolved not to
let British orders interfere with the new American
program. His job was to supply 2,000,000 American
soldiers, and he was going about it as single-mindedly
as in his day he had turned 2,000,000 Chevrolets off
the line. Literally, his approach to his Washington responsibility was a throwback from his General Motors
responsibilities to his apprenticeship at Chevrolet.
When asked, as he repeatedly was, whether he could
do more with more authority, he always replied, "I
don't want any more."

In September, 1940, Knudsen predicted that we would have 33,000 planes of all types by April, 1942. This seemed like so many that he felt justified in saying: "Don't let us get an inferiority complex and beat our chests and tear our hair." Inspecting aircraft plants in the West with General Arnold the same month, he predicted that, by the spring of 1941, production of planes would be so great that he would begin worrying about the second-hand market. His report to the Army Ordnance Association in October was more realistic. Plane production was lagging behind expectations, he explained (as if he were talking about what someone else was doing), because the plants were concentrating on expansion rather than on delivery. Contracts for the Army program were 70 percent drawn, he continued, but quantity production was at least 15 months away. Tool designing was still a serious bottleneck, but this major problem was overshadowed by the appearance of the first shortage. It was a shortage of powder plants! After War I, the powder industry had been liquidated and, in 1940, as Knudsen said, we were "awfully late in getting started."

In the middle of May, 1940, the President, reacting to the Blitzkrieg, asked Congress to make immediate appropriations of $896,000,000, and to permit him in addition to sign contract obligations for a total of $286,000,000. Congress acted favorably on this request a month later, in mid-June. By that time it was obvious that much larger sums would be needed. The fall of France and the evacuation of the British forces from Dunkirk led Roosevelt to ask and Congress to grant new sums of money; about one and three-quarter billions being authorized before June ended. But even this was far from enough. Roosevelt on July 16 requested of Congress approximately five billions more, and in due course—with barely a memory of the forgotten issue of economy—Congress acquiesced in the Act of September 9, 1940. Meanwhile, on June 27, the Council of National Defense had taken Donald M. Nelson from the Treasury buying job which brought him to Washington, and made him its Coordinator of National Defense Purchases. As contracts were signed, money was set in motion and, after money, manpower. By August, 80,000 new workers—almost all of them unskilled—had been drawn into the mushrooming shipyards. The aircraft plants had already absorbed 50,000. Through the more selective bottlenecks of the machine-tool industry passed 18,000 skilled operatives. Another 80,000 had been recruited into the defense plant training program which Sidney Hillman's Division of the Defense Commission had organized. But the threat of a manpower shortage still lay in the future. The war effort found gainful employment for over 64,000,000 Americans, but in 1939 only 49,000,000 had been employed. The Defense Commission's immediate problem, accordingly, was how to deal with unemployment.

From June 1, 1940, to the end of the year, contracts were awarded at the rate of $1,500,000,000 a month. Nevertheless, as late as August 31, 1940, the Commission found itself obliged to assure the country that the defense program would be used to "reduce unemployment." One of its suggestions was, of course, the observance of the 40-hour week in war work, with over-time being paid "in accordance with the local recognized practices." Resting on a dictum dug up out of the archives of World War I—the Army Chief of Ordnance had declared in 1917 that safeguards designed to protect labor should be retained during emergencies as measures of efficiency—Hillman and the Administration persuaded the Defense Commission to instruct manufacturers receiving defense contracts to comply with the Wagner Act and the statutes protecting labor employed on Government projects. This was fair enough. After all, defense contracts were Government projects. The Commission actually went a step further than Roosevelt had been able to lead Congress. It went on record against racial discrimination. By November, Hillman had forestalled several major strikes in defense industries—on the West Coast waterfront, in the copper mines, in the aluminum industry, at Boeing in Seattle. And he had been denounced by Representative Cox of Georgia for having immigrated to the United States "from the Baltic provinces of Russia."

The fairest progress report of the year was provided by *Factory Management and Maintenance,* a McGraw-Hill publication. "We are miles ahead of 1916–17 in some ways," it said, "and miles behind in others."

We have not even begun a real defense effort as such things are understood in Europe. . . . The whole defense job cries for strong, central leadership. . . . The very existence of N.D.A.C. is perhaps the most encouraging feature of all. But the Commission is . . . an advisory board, and nothing more . . . many of the Commission members feel it would be better if they had a boss of their own who would in turn report directly to the White House.

By that time any report on the opinion of the N.D.A.C. tended to approximate a *Fortune* Poll of Executive Opinion. The N.D.A.C.—which, after all, was not an administrative entity, but merely an advisory committee of seven individuals—had been transformed into a monstrosity of executive elephantiasis. It boasted between 400 and 500 $1 and $9,000 a year factota, and, racing to keep pace with the spending-and-production trend, it was setting its sights on the creation of a team of 700 top bracket tycoons by Election Day. It had flowered into a Trade Association Secretary's Paradise.

OUTSIDE Washington, meanwhile, the economy was astir. Contracts processed inside the Defense Commission were so many pieces of paper until industry could find the facilities to produce what they called for; which is to say, production contracts had to be construction contracts before anything could be produced. In the past, shot-and-shell items were produced in arsenals outside the main stream of economic life. Arsenals were still needed, but they could no longer be operated autonomously. On the contrary, the quickest and cheapest way to provide modern arsenals was not to build new plants, but simply to expand existing facilities.

This posed a problem: How would the facilities thus expanded be paid for? The Government could own such new capital assets and lease them to the companies using them to fill contracts, the rent being calculated as part of the cost of production. But what would happen to these productive resources after the war? How would the Government divest itself of ownership? And to whom? To its wartime tenants? To their competitors? By auction? Or by negotiation? None of these questions were answered during World War I and, when it was over, the Government filed suit after suit to recover funds advanced to expand the facilities of companies having war contracts. This was obviously unfair to such companies. By the same token, the procedure improvised before the Defense Commission took over—to include the cost of constructing new facilities in the production contract, and to pass title to the companies on completion of their contracts—was unfair to the Government.

This dilemma produced a stalemate. As Nelson says, "Companies which had been asked to expand wouldn't or couldn't do so until they knew how this expansion would be financed." * The famous "five-year amortization plan," formulated for the Defense Commission by Henderson and Nelson, in collaboration with William C. Potter of the Guaranty Trust Co. and Floyd B. Odlum, solved the problem. The formula was simple and workable. It provided that all assets of commercial value would be owned free and clear by the contracting companies at the end of five years, during which they would be allowed to write installation costs off their tax returns at the rate of 20 percent a year. This gave corporate managements and investors a

* Donald M. Nelson, *Arsenal of Democracy* (New York, Harcourt, Brace and Company, Inc., 1946), p. 106.

double advantage: it enabled corporations to deflate their taxable earnings, while increasing their earning facilities. Clearly, the assets written off on tax returns as if they were to be scrapped in five years were in fact good for twenty years or more of normal productive use. But the annual depreciation charge against assets usable over a twenty-year span is 5 percent, not 20 percent. The difference between the earnings artificially depressed for tax purposes and the real earnings accruing to the stockholders' equity was a bonanza for business.

Leon Henderson was at this point emerging as an almost semi-official spokesman for the New Deal. But in spite of his coauthorship of the new plan, it ran into fierce and stubborn opposition. Labor charged that business was exploiting the emergency not only to win new privileges for itself, but to restrict labor's new rights. Actually, defense expansion had been stalemated by confusion resulting from administrative unpreparedness. But labor seized on this situation as a Heaven-sent opportunity to settle a few scores with business. Since labor's critics were calling for a moratorium on strikes, labor and its allies now taunted business for having organized a "strike of capital."

No more mischievous slogan than National Unity could have been devised for the propagation of national disunity. Why conduct business as usual for the usual stakes when it was better business for any lobby to show that every rival lobby was conspiring to destroy National Unity? As the Bureau of the Budget history wryly observes, "Everybody was clamoring for the Government to knock heads together; i.e. other

people's heads." Fortunately, our system works better when the incentives of disunity check and balance
one another than when any dominant group contrives
to impose its notion of National Unity upon everyone
else. Genuine National Unity could be achieved only
by coping with the crisis. But the only practical way
to cope with the crisis was to reward every group
needed to cope with it. Thus, the way to secure unity
was by rewarding the forces of disunity. This is exactly
what Roosevelt did. To appease business, he gave it
the 5-year amortization plan. To appease its critics,
he forced it to accept the excess profits tax.

And with the excess profits tax, he gave business
and the economy an insurance policy. The excess
profits tax rate was very high indeed. But the excess
profits tax that business paid was not given up—as
ordinary tax money is given up—irretrievably: this
money was being put on wartime deposit with the
Treasury. On the inevitable day of postwar readjust-
ment, losses could be "carried back" as claims for re-
funds of these excess profits tax payments. Thus was
created the biggest and most resilient cushion in the
history of public finance. Common sense called for
exactly such a cushion, and common sense made it
work automatically. Money that neither companies
nor their stockholders could have used wisely at the
time went to the Treasury when it was most needed
there. But when peace put the Treasury into the
black, companies in the red could redeem the wartime
"deposits" they had put into the Treasury as taxes.

It was too simple for organized business and its organized critics to grasp. Not for six years did any of

the pressure groups realize that Roosevelt had in this way avoided one of the major Wilsonian failures (and, incidentally, frustrated one of the major Marxist prophesies). Before World War II had begun, he had prevented the postwar depression. Organized business predicted socialism, and professional liberals warned of crisis. But with this one stroke Roosevelt set in motion the process which refuted both forecasts.

But this was far from the only trick the Roosevelt Revolution played on Marx. Its borrowing program made everyone a creditor of the Government, and its taxing-and-spending program made the Government a partner in everything. The Roosevelt Revolution was no excursion into socialism: it was an invasion of socialism and, like all invasions, it assimilated and was assimilated. Its socializing impact launched the greatest boom in the history of capitalism; and along every new frontier capitalism expanded by making socialism its partner and, no less profitable, its customer. Capitalism flourished in a moral sense, and democracy flourished in a practical sense—on both counts this made history. The Roosevelt Revolution crystallized the idea of the welfare state. But the beneficiaries of the welfare state, far from being proletarianized, began to accumulate their own funds of capital. On the one hand, millions of working people joined the class of small investors while, on the other, capital went back to work. Management, meanwhile, was being transformed into a special class of big labor, and agriculture into big business—the difference being that the tax laws permitted farmers to accumulate capital but prevented management from doing so.

Reflecting these changes in the economic status of the principal producing groups, far-reaching regional metamorphoses occurred. The Roosevelt Revolution brought industrialization to the West, modernization to the South, internationalism to the midwest, and vitality to New England. It saw Negroes move about in their own Cadillacs, farmers in their own airplanes, hill-billies in their own shoes, and the rich in their own kitchens.

Marx in his day had boasted that he stood Hegel on his head. Roosevelt, if he had been interested in such by-play, might well have claimed that his Revolution promised to turn Marx into a patient of Freud's. For it led neither to socialism nor to crisis, but back to the *status quo*—within the meaning of what the Red Queen told Alice, "A slow sort of country! Now, here, you see, it takes all the running you can do to keep in the same place." For being able to see so far through this particular looking-glass, Roosevelt deserves to be forgiven much.

THIS wisdom at the highest policy level was supplemented at the working level. On June 25, 1940, the Reconstruction Finance Corporation was given statutory power to finance the creation of defense production facilities and the stocking of strategic materials by private corporations or Government agencies. Three days later, the Rubber Reserve Company and the Metals Reserve Company came into existence as RFC subsidiaries. Late in August, the RFC also created the Defense Supplies Corporation and the Defense Plant Corporation. Chairman Jones indicated that he was organizing both units at the suggestion of the Defense Commission. The immediate mission of the Defense Supplies Corporation was indicated by the shortage of aviation gasoline. But, the New York *Times* reported, "Jones's statement did not explain the purpose for which the Defense Plant Corporation was formed, nor have details progressed far enough for him to announce the extent of the funds which it will employ."

The reason behind Jones's vagueness was simple enough. The Defense Plant Corporation had been a functioning entity for some time before he announced its creation, and in December he himself was still trying to find out what it had done and how much of "his money" it had committed. From the beginning he had prided himself on running the RFC as a dictatorship; and, in fact, it had grown into a one-man empire. For years, one of the standing jokes around Washington was that, except for "the Chairman," no one knew who sat on its Board. Requests for loans he scrutinized as "business propositions," impatient of talk during the peace years about their social purpose and, as the emergency developed, about their validity as security projects. The only security he had eyes for was the collateral he could see pledged against his loans. Before he would negotiate a loan in the national interest, he demanded enough collateral to satisfy a country bank. And he negotiated each loan like a country banker, sharp-shooting for each point in slow motion, dragging out the bargaining to exploit the borrower's need for cash, literally carrying his various deals around in his pockets.

One of the risks Jones ran by confiding in no one

in his organization was that no one in it talked to him. While everyone said, "The RFC is Jesse Jones and Jesse Jones is the RFC," a striking collection of tough-minded younger men had been attached to its staff. Emil Schram, the future head of the New York Stock Exchange, was one. John Snyder, the future Secretary of the Treasury and Truman's closest intimate, was another. Clifford Durr, brother-in-law of Justice Hugo Black and a future Federal Communications Commissioner, was still another. Alfred Hobson, Secretary of the RFC and a genuinely nonpartisan personality, worked with this group. And Tommy Corcoran, whose official designation during his period of power was Special Counsel to the RFC, functioned as the group's catalytic agent and liaison with the White House, with his intimates—Assistant Secretaries Patterson and Forrestal—and with his friend and nominal boss, Jesse Jones. The simple premise of every member of this group was that the RFC, instead of imitating the nation's country banks, should do the emergency job that the country banks could not do. While Uncle Jesse bargained and procrastinated, they resolved to use "his money" to buy the time the country needed.

The War Department, by this time, was literally machine-gunning requests for money at the RFC. The cases were identical in principle. Nevertheless, Jones insisted on sniffing personally at each as if it were a rare and risky banking deal. His subordinates saw that the situation called not for negotiation but for administration. The applications, after all, were being made by but not for private companies: the real applicant in each case was another Executive Department of the United States Government; the real security behind the requested loans was the credit of the United States Government and its power to appropriate funds to honor the contracts it was signing with the corporate applicants for RFC loans (the contracts in every case making provision for repayment to the RFC).

Jones, determined to scrutinize each case on its separate merits, had become a one-man bottleneck obstructing the efforts of the Government to pass money between one administrative pocket and another. His team of subordinates did not buck him directly, but instead ran around his end. Each morning, the War Department would telephone its latest applications to Durr; Durr would process them for Snyder; Snyder would approve them for the lawyers; the legal staff would begin reducing the daily batch to contract form before lunch; the papers would be ready for transmission to the War Department by the end of the day; and the company with the contract would have its construction-and-tooling-up money the next day. No team of administrators, before or since, has achieved as much. It was a model of Governmental efficiency.

This conspiracy of administrative efficiency—it was nothing less than a conspiracy—was three months old before Jones discovered what had been going on inside his empire while he was looking at balance sheets. The revelation stung him into action, not behind his men but against them. Out went Schram to the New York Stock Exchange. Out went Snyder to the First National Bank of St. Louis. Out of effective action went the DPC, though the organization remained. Jones could not liquidate it, and he would not operate it. By the time he had slowed it—and the expansion program—down, he found himself as busy looking at the loans that had been made for him as at the new loans he was being pressed to make.

Curtiss-Wright owed him $58,500,000 that he knew about, General Motors was manufacturing engines with another $32,000,000 of his money, Studebaker had been given another $50,000,000, and this was just the beginning. The list of loans was endless and, worse still, he—the Government's banker—had been reduced to a check-writing robot. He set out to reassert his bargaining power and his nuisance value with the Defense Program's corporate clients just as the expansion movement was swinging into its second phase—the phase of industrial expansion to match the arsenal expansion of the first phase. To put the arsenals under construction into production, new raw material supplies and new equipment were needed. In bookkeeping terms, to insure a return of DPC's first round of investments, a second round was needed, and it was needed fast enough to supply the assembly lines being planned and to employ the work forces being assembled.

Congress, sensitive to any suggestion that it was holding up defense progress, gladly authorized Jones to multiply his commitments, and told him to come back for more as soon as he had to. The War and Navy Departments and the Defense Commission, sensitive in their turn to Jones's legendary influence with Congress, were no less willing to pass the buck to him. To his cost—and to the country's—he grasped eagerly at the responsibility thus offered him.

By autumn shortages were inevitable, thanks first of all to the beginnings of Selective Service. Building materials and equipment were needed for cantonments. So were roads and utilities. So were uniforms, food, fuel, and ordnance for the draftees. So was transportation, so was storage, so was paper work. The impact of this cumulative demand hit the country's markets, moreover, at a time when at least a couple of million able-bodied men were being withdrawn from the pool of employable manpower. By the same token, most of the draftees were bound to be drawn from the lower strata of the economy, which meant that with each uniform there was also issued a draft upon the nation's productive plant for more and better goods and services for the consumer wearing it. And since the cantonments had to be spread around in noncongested areas, especially in the South and West, most of this new consuming load was bound to fall upon regional markets not equipped to supply the goods and services demanded. With shortages, accordingly, came dislocations.

Soon people began to follow money into motion. At Charlestown, in southern Indiana, du Pont went to work on a major powder plant project. Attracted by the atmosphere of boom, swarms of unskilled labor swelled the population from 800 to 5,000, to 15,000, to a mass of unabsorbed and unhoused workers spread over all the neighboring towns. In Hartford, workers complained, "You can't get a rent anywhere." In Detroit, rents rose as much as 40 percent. At Portsmouth, Virginia, the Navy Yard admitted losing 100 workers a day because of intolerable housing. The Navy Department clamped a censorship on all housing news at its stations around the country. Seattle settled down to a siege of defense workers sleeping in the streets. San Diego absorbed 30,000 defense workers in six months, and pointed to 6,000 "housing units" set up in auto courts. At Bremerton, on Puget Sound, 600 new housing units were finally offered, but 4,900 workers applied. Up and down the country, hamlets mushroomed into towns, and towns into cities, while cities flowed over into metropolitan areas. Soon every community with a contract was fighting to hold off at arm's length the invading horde of "Hoosiers" which, from Seattle to St. Louis, became the generic word for war workers from the hills.

Wherever the incentives of the war boom attracted masses of marginal workers, it attracted them regardless of race, creed, or color. The exception was those unfortunate Americans of Japanese descent who were interned en masse in camps after Pearl Harbor.

Wherever Negroes and Mexicans came to contribute to the production effort, they carried with them the burning controversy over Democracy's future. Everywhere the bitter dilemmas bared the issues: "Don't you want to win the War?" vs. "What are you fighting for?" and "You can't change people's minds by passing laws" vs. "You can't change people's minds without passing laws." The Negro's progress toward equality was epochal (nowhere, thanks to Forrestal's effective and enlightened patriotism, more than in that traditional stronghold of the South—the Navy). And, because aspirations feed on achievements, the Negro's frustration intensified apace. But the impact of the war economy once and for all jolted the Negro into possession of employment opportunity, skill, and security; into possession of money and its perquisites; into possession of the wherewithal to force redemption of the old promise that education would win opportunity; into possession of the political and legal claim on Government for unlimited opportunity. Most important of all, the Negroes showed that they were compromising with segregation and discrimination— by communities, by employers, by other working people, by the Army, by public administrators—in order more effectively to discredit the principle of segregation.

In every community swelled by the floating army of war workers, health had to be safeguarded and housing provided. The conservative New York *Journal of Commerce* agreed with the Administration that a minimum of 200,000 dwellings had to be built; and $3,500 per unit seemed a realistic estimate. But it pointed out that the Defense Housing Coordinator had even less authority than the Defense Commission. In December, 1940, it called for a law to provide housing. Six months later, *Business Week* reported that only 13,000 units had been completed, while some 67,000 more were under construction and nearly 100,000 were allocated. But twelve separate agencies, including the Army and Navy, were distracting themselves with squabbles over the housing crisis, and no agency was bringing it under control. Nevertheless, as *Business*

Week conceded, Roosevelt had already outperformed Wilson: "Prior to the Armistice in 1918, not one government-financed dwelling had been completed." Not until February, 1942, did Roosevelt consolidate the agencies concerned with housing—by then, there were 16—into the National Housing Agency. And then, every fresh demand for housing (and supplemental utilities) had to be weighed against gas, rubber, and man-hours wasted by commuting and turnover.

The reality of shortages in the making, however, was obscured all through 1940 by the Great Debate. In August, between seasons for political fisticuffs, General Marshall had pleaded for Selective Service as "urgently necessary." Nevertheless, the War Department's inveterate critic, Senator Clark of Missouri, had accused the Administration of conniving to delay the draft of men between the ages of 21 and 31 until after the election. Marshall denied the charge, but not even his sincere and vigorous reassertion that, election or no election, the draft was needed immediately, was enough to dispel the widespread suspicion voiced by Clark and his fellow isolationists that Roosevelt meant to talk peace until Election Day and to make war afterwards. Only action could dispel this feeling.

Roosevelt provided it. The public was going on the assumption that, whether or not General Marshall was right, Selective Service would be political poison during the political campaign; and, therefore, it credited Roosevelt with enough political acumen to let General Marshall testify but to do nothing. But Roosevelt was more realistic than the realists. While everyone expected him to play smart politics, therefore, he recognized that the smartest politics he could play so far as the draft was concerned was no politics at all. Defying conventional political advice, accordingly, he first charged that Willkie was trying to put the draft issue into politics; and then timed the draft to begin with the campaign. On September 16, 1940, he signed the Burke-Wadsworth Bill, and set October 16—the very climax of the campaign—as the day on which 16,500,000 eligible men would have to register. He also announced that the first 400,000 draftees, or "trainees," as they were called in the beginning, would be called by January 1, and the second 400,000 by the spring. It was a political master stroke.

Public opinion approved. The polls, for what they were worth—and they were worth more in 1940 than in 1948, if only because the pollsters were less presumptuous—showed a dramatic and decisive drift towards Roosevelt's position, from 39 percent in October, 1939, to 50 per cent early in June, 1940, to 67 percent in July. But, then, Roosevelt's position on the draft was more moderate than either his opponents charged or the future assumed. He wanted as much as he could get, and he hoped this would be more than enough. It was precisely this mixture of realism and unrealism which made his position so representative.

For although the war situation was beginning to come to a head, what two-thirds of opinion—and Roosevelt—agreed upon was nothing more militaristic, to use the shibboleth of the period, than a one-year draft. This was mobilization on the installment plan. And yet, who can criticize Roosevelt for handling this problem as he liked to say, "in two bites"? Granted that a one-year draft was a contradiction in terms, it was nevertheless a contradiction which made practical sense: it set mobilization in motion.

What would have happened if Roosevelt had been guided by logic instead of by sense, if at the outset he had demanded the unlimited draft which the situation demanded? The answer is suggested by what did happen the following August, when the draft's allotted year was running out. By that time, Hitler's juggernaut was rolling over Russia, and Japan was openly preparing to commit the Axis to a two-ocean war. As the danger grew that Germany and Japan would effect a junction of forces on the other side of the world, the familiar meaning of isolationism began to change. In this grim situation, when Roosevelt's prestige was enhanced by the record of his predictions and when his power was renewed by his victory over the third-term tradition, he asked Congress for the right to continue the inductees of 1940 in service and to induct new trainees. This was the new Congress that had been elected with him. His Administration had billions at its disposal, and, even if war could be averted, it was clearly going to have many billions more to spend. He personally had a full term of patronage to trade for votes on the floor. And, as he quickly discovered, he needed every last piece of bait his floor leaders could offer. His bill to renew Selective Service passed the Senate by only 15 votes (a switch of only 8 would have beaten it!), and it passed the House by exactly one vote. Without Speaker Rayburn's classic labors, the draft renewal fight would have been lost by many more votes than one.

But the one-year limitation was not the only reason why Congress had been willing to go along with Roosevelt on the draft in 1940. As a guarantee to the lower income groups that no war profiteers' orgy was in prospect, he had also asked for the power to draft industry. This reassured the sections of opinion on whose confidence Roosevelt's position rested; but it shocked Senator Taft who, in a memorable statement, declared:

This is a most extraordinary provision for the confiscation, or at least the appropriation, of property. It modifies every concept of American law we have ever had, as does the draft law. If it were absolutely necessary in time of war, I should be in favor of it, but I do not believe the emergency is one which justifies the drafting of men. I shall refuse to vote for any measure to draft men, and I do not propose to vote for any measure to draft property.

It was an able and honest lawyer's brief submitted as a postscript to a case which was not being tried in Court. If it were, Taft would have lost it there too. For no group of judges would presume to set their judgment of what constituted an emergency or how to cope with it above the President's *at the time;* and, indeed, not even Congress was willing to continue doing so. Roosevelt's Bill did not modify "every concept of American law we have ever had," as Taft charged. But the situation had long since modified every concept of American security we had ever had. Congress and the President have the power to modify law and the concept of law. Taft's stand dramatized Roosevelt's argument that the time had come to use this power.

THE time had also come to use the power of priorities. The new program was uncovering shortages because it was producing traffic; and the traffic was either going to be regulated or it was going to jam. The problem was recognized from the beginning. On June 27, 1940, the Army-Navy Munitions Board created its own Priorities Committee. This move anticipated by a day the passage of a bill by Congress authorizing the President to give Army and Navy contracts and orders priority over all work for private account or for export. Much more important, it also anticipated the apparatus the Defense Commission was bound to create to do the same job; and, therefore, it put the civilian administrators in the position of being interlopers the moment they tried to meet their obvious responsibilities.

While the pattern of administrative competition was being set, the need for administrative regulation was making itself felt. At the top of the list of dislocated industries was steel—the bellwether of the economy. For some years the proportion of scrap to pig iron in steel-making had been rising. A great deal of scrap was also being exported, particularly to Japan. So long as the steel rate was closer to 50 per cent than to 100 per cent of capacity, this did not interfere with production. But as soon as the production rate began to approximate capacity, the supply of scrap determined capacity. By the same token, the bidding for scrap began to inflate the cost of production. Roughly, half the scrap needed originated at the mills themselves; the other half they had to buy. The administrative problem, therefore, was twofold: the steel mills had to be encouraged or directed to use their own "captive" scrap for production, claiming defense priority; and scrap bought in the commercial market had to be channeled—by regulation and not by auction—into defense production. Time and materials, equipment and labor were needed to build new blast furnaces to expand the supply of pig iron. But the scrap reservoir was a ready resource constantly being replenished. It wanted only to be regulated.

So, by this time, did the entire economy. Manufacturers were being swamped with contracts; the Government was underwriting elaborate expansion programs; and businessmen, understandably enough, were fighting to service their regular customers. The pressure of anticipating combined Government and commercial demand put a growing premium on free raw material supplies, on free machine time, on free warehousing. In every sector of the economy customers began to buy for longer periods of time into the future. Human nature prompted every businessman to expand his commercial operations every time he signed a new defense contract. And simple arithmetic dictated that the piling of a defense program upon even a moderately expanding business boom called for either regulation or a prodigious expansion of raw material supplies and basic facilities—or for both.

Instead, neither regulation nor expansion was attempted. The machine-tool industry was hopelessly log-jammed. Inevitably the by-product of each new defense contract was a new batch of machine-tool orders. But shipments were going to Japan, and work

was in progress on new tooling for the auto plants.
On the other hand, work was not going forward on
defense contracts held by the auto manufacturers—
they were unable to get new tooling! The coming
aluminum crisis was being forecast by Raw Materials
Commissioner Stettinius's solemn assurances that "the
fellows at the Aluminum Company say the aluminum
situation is O.K." More shocking still, the shortage
of railroad equipment was in the making.

Commissioner Stettinius was mainly to be criticized
for taking responsibilities outweighing his capabilities.
But Commissioner Ralph Budd knew better than to
act as he did. His record as a railroad President, pioneering the advantages of modern equipment, justified Roosevelt's appointment of him. His mischievous
failure as Transportation Commissioner was due to
his insistence on catering to the prejudices and the
ignorance of the railroad presidents whose performance contrasted with his own. They viewed the emergency as a New Deal plot to have the Government
take over the railroads; and their characteristic way
of asserting their faith in private ownership before
Pearl Harbor was to insist that no new equipment was
needed.

As recently as the previous fall, the normal surplus
of freight cars had still been in evidence. But as defense production took form as solid reality instead
of a premature fever dream, the question became not
whether but *when* the railroad equipment shortage
would be felt. Nevertheless, Budd allowed himself to
be quoted soon after coming to Washington as worrying about an excess of facilities. True, by July he

acknowledged that the railroads had reached a state of precarious dependence upon cars withdrawn from the official car supply and earmarked for repair: he sent word to the railroads to limit the ratio of bad-order cars in service to 6 percent. Nevertheless, when he was asked to pass on the Administration's recommendation that 100,000 freight cars be ordered in anticipation of a 1941 car shortage and steel rush, he refused to "interfere" with railroad management. Indeed, as Transportation Commissioner, he acted not like the Government official responsible for telling the railroads what to do, but like the railroad spokesman telling the Government what the railroads would not do.

Budd's directives were geared to the press releases issued by the Association of American Railroads against Janeway and other "astronomical statisticians." Budd used his order limiting bad-order cars to 6 per cent as the occasion for repeating his prediction that the roads were equipped to handle any volume of traffic in sight. But the AAR soon compromised—or thought it did—with Janeway's calculation that 100,-000 new cars were needed. As if its office and not Budd's were directing Defense Transportation, AAR recommended to its members that they increase new car orders to 100,000. Nothing could have revealed more vividly the cumulative unrealism of railroad management. Its spokesmen made no allowance for the difference between gross and net additions to the car supply. In the 15 months ending March 15, 1941, 84,000 new freight cars were installed, but the net car supply rose by only 6,000—scrapping that could be deferred no longer canceled out no fewer than 78,000 of the new cars put into service.

The obstinacy of the railroads in 1940 limited their 1941 carrying capacity to a peak of 900,000 cars a week. In fact, by September, 1941, Budd admitted that carloadings were rising above the 875,000 level and beginning to interfere with operations. He pleaded with shippers not to hold freight cars on their sidings for storage, and with the Government to build more warehouses. The *Wall Street Journal* reported that the 1941 crop could not be moved because the West had been drained of freight cars. An emergency pressure campaign rushed 25,000 cars back to the West, but regulations were soon lifted and maldistribution recurred.

Actually, the first responsible spokesman to face the facts was neither Budd nor the AAR, but Averill Harriman, a representative of financial rather than of operating management. In February, 1941, when he was still a high official of the Office of Production Management, he made a speech to the Traffic Club of Washington which the *Wall Street Journal* reported as "the first official admission that a tight situation might develop." By October, 1941, the National Association of Manufacturers was blaming the lag in defense production on the inadequate freight car program—the fight for free enterprise had ceased to be a fight against modernizing the railroads! Finally, in the month of Pearl Harbor, from their ivory tower the railroad presidents demanded that the administration stop restricting orders for new railroad equipment. They had come to doubt that the equipment

they had would be enough. As usual, they accused
the Government of responsibility for their own shortsightedness. Admittedly, the reason for the freight
jam was the Government's defense program, and as
usual, therefore, they looked to the Government for
relief.

Budd himself never was equal to issuing the most
elementary order of all—restricting the use of less-
than-carload freight. LCL freight was almost uni-
formly non-defense; and, in recommending that it be
restricted, the Janeway Report had estimated that it
tied up at least 100,000 cars in very marginal operations. Not until May 1, 1942, after Budd had been
superseded by the Office of Defense Transportation,
was this waste eliminated.

CHAPTER VIII

GUNS AND BUTTER

BY the time industrial mobilization had begun to make headway, the differences of opinion between Roosevelt and Baruch had come to be taken for granted. As these differences reached their full development, it was ironical that Baruch, rather than Roosevelt, took the radical view. And a very radical view it was. "In modern war," Baruch had laid it down, "administrative control *must* replace the law of supply and demand." He proposed to upset the economy with a vengeance, suspending competition and freezing prices, profits, and wages.

Roosevelt's dissent from the principles of mobilization according to Baruch was effectively stated by Donald Nelson: "Knudsen had been told off," he says, "to perform this magic [of tooling] without upsetting the civilian economy." Having given this assignment, Roosevelt had the satisfaction of siding not merely with the CIO, which was normal, but with Senator Taft, the American Farm Bureau Federation, and the National Association of Manufacturers, which was not. He was the symbol of the controlled economy. But in this situation he was content to let the momentum of unplanned defense spending substitute for the over-all controls of total mobilization. Not that he balked at upsetting the economy—but events were beginning to upset the economy without benefit of policy and Roosevelt's problem was to move with events. His way of moving with events, no faster and no slower, was to be for guns *and* butter. He was for labor—as gunmaker and as butter-consumer; and, therefore, he refused to go along with Baruch's demand to freeze wages. Refusing to freeze wages, he found himself obliged by the principle of compensating pressures to refuse to freeze prices or profits. Thus, being for the working man enabled him to be for the farmer and the businessman, too.

On the merits, Roosevelt may well have been wrong, but on the actual record about to be made he was right. The course Baruch advocated would have been economic from the administrative standpoint, but costly to Roosevelt's strategy of appeasing the pressure groups and appealing to their incentives. Baruch's disagreement with Roosevelt arose from his preoccupation with the administrative rather than the political question and from his strong conviction that competition has no place in a war economy. Said Baruch:

In war . . . the Government must assume control of the whole supply and ration and apportion it—not to the longest purse but to the most necessitous use . . . the distinguishing characteristic of peacetime economic operation is *competition,* and basic prices are largely determined thereby. . . . Under war conditions the entire process is reversed. There is more business than all of the facilities of the country can handle. Competitors must become cooperators in order to meet the very minimum demand for shortage items. Control of this cooperation rests in Government. Thus, both because Governmental

determination (*and not price*) controls demand, and because only complete cooperation (*and not competition*)
can produce supply in sufficient quantity, the law of supply and demand adjourns itself.

Baruch was a practical man of affairs, yet here he
was advocating, as dogmatically as one of Roosevelt's
professors, the adoption of a theory *in toto*. Roosevelt was willing to experiment with this theory of Baruch's, as one of a number of theories, but not as
dogma and certainly not as a political commitment.
Just because he was so receptive to all theories, he
never let any of them make his political commitments
or plan his political timing for him. On the contrary,
he managed again and again to be simultaneously receptive to mutually contradictory theories.

This he did now. His counterweight to Baruch's
theory was the anti-trust dogma of that colorful New
Deal professor and formidable practical politician,
Assistant Attorney-General Thurman Arnold. Arnold,
furiously attacking Baruch as the master strategist
of the trusts, won such popularity for his dogma that
Willkie, the Wall Street candidate, bracketed him
and Hull as the two statesmen he would continue in
office if elected.

As defense production was impeded by shortages
of railroad equipment, of aluminum, of electric power,
and of aviation gasoline, Arnold, like a poker player
putting down one ace after another, alternated his
highly publicized anti-trust drives against the Pullman
Co., the Aluminum Co., General Electric, and 22 oil
companies. As fast as a corporation took a defense
contract, Arnold proposed to investigate it for abuses

of the anti-trust laws. Although businessmen in the defense program, backed by the military, were pressing for suspension of the anti-trust laws for the duration, Arnold insisted that indictment and trial for such violations was the most efficient way to spur big business into speedier defense production.

To dramatize his case, he was able to cite hair-raising episodes of economic warfare by Germany's Nazified cartels against the American economy. Over the years America's biggest and, presumably, most shrewdly managed corporations—Standard Oil of New Jersey and General Electric among them—had entered into patent and marketing agreements with their opposite numbers in Germany, not realizing that German big business pursued profit by pursuing power for the Reich. With little awareness of America's technological unpreparedness, ranking American businessmen and their lawyers had allowed themselves to be gulled by the political manipulators of the German corporations and the economic strategists of the German Government. Many of these arrangements had been known and approved by the State and War Departments, which accordingly also came under attack by the trust-busters. The German cartels had perfected processes for manufacturing synthetic rubber, synthetic oil, magnesium, optical instruments, tungsten carbide, and the like; supposedly these were to be developed on a commercial scale by their American associates. But, though their American partners had in every case lived up to their business obligations, the promised reciprocity had not developed. And no American corporations outside the cartel orbit had felt free or able to undertake competitive research projects.

It was not a pretty story, and Arnold told it well and often. It strengthened the popular impression that the average American businessman could be trusted only with production and with buying and selling at the working level, but not with responsibility for regulating even his own business at the social or political or security level.

Public opinion sided with Arnold for still another reason: although he was a New Dealer, and a spokesman and a deputy for Roosevelt, he was as quick to condemn big labor as big business for conspiracies in restraint of trade. Moreover, as Arnold pressed his argument against the policy advocated by Baruch, the country was becoming aware of the extent to which the defense program was being run for and by big business. Defense Agriculture Commissioner Davis, a farm conservative, opposed by Wallace and suspect to Roosevelt, complained to the Southern Governors' Conference in March, 1941: "Defense contracts are being absorbed by a small handful of concerns. The very smallness of the number threatens to be a serious bottleneck on the full use of our industrial and human resources. It is a bottleneck and it must be broken."

Davis was expressing not only an aroused farm opinion, but also the resentment mounting among that most representative of all Americans—the small businessman. One reason why the small businessman is so powerful in America is that no one quite knows who he is. Statistically, the small business group is elusive, but sociologically and politically it is ubiquitous. As Carl Becker once said of Kansas, small business is a state of mind—it is *the* state of mind of the average American, rich or poor. At this point small business was beginning to suspect and resent the men running the defense program. Not that it disapproved of their policy of guns and butter—it just wanted the butter spread around more. Chester Davis spoke for this cross-section of opinion as well as for the farm community when, in a subsequent speech, he said: "In the first stages of the Defense program, I must frankly say important opportunities have been missed."

The farm, labor, and small business groups lacked confidence in big business. They doubted that the suspension of the anti-trust laws would be enough to spur big business to band together and make up for lost time. Moreover, the more intelligent members of the big business group were themselves aware that their public relations depended upon keeping the anti-trust laws operative. But the problem was not whether any proposed industry-wide committees of business would understand how to exploit a moratorium on the anti-trust laws in the public interest. It was that the Defense Commission could not begin to show them how to work in the public interest, for it had been carefully designed to serve as a battleground for competing pressures. It assumed that labor would be for labor, agriculture for agriculture, business for business, and businessmen for themselves.

Baruch's proposal rested on an altogether different assumption: that the Commission should be an organ of leadership; and that any industry-wide committees it organized could be trusted to ignore the anti-trust laws in the public interest because the Defense Commission could be trusted to direct its agencies in the public interest. At this point, policy passed over into politics. However right or unavoidable Baruch's theory might have been in a desperate emergency—in the event of invasion, for example—in this situation it amounted to a demand on Roosevelt to let him take up where he had left off under Wilson. And this reduced his theory to political absurdity.

But not to irrelevance: or no more to irrelevance than Thurman Arnold's dictum that the Sherman Act, properly enforced—that is, enforced by him—was our best defense against Hitler. Roosevelt, certainly, recognized as clearly as Baruch that for the duration the anti-trust laws would have to be honored mainly in the breach. But he could not say so. For the assumption that he could and would enforce the anti-trust laws was one of his most useful political assets. The threat was enough to force the corporations to deal with him: the promise was enough to free him to deal with the corporations without alienating his followers. Again paradox set the pattern of logic. Only by rejecting Baruch's theory and sympathizing with Arnold's exposés could he hope to frustrate the offensive planned by Arnold and solve the problem described by Baruch.

The story of his success is told not only by the election returns but by the index of wartime prices. Unlike Wilson, he avoided inflation. And, unlike Wilson, he kept his freedom of action.

FROM one strategic industry competition was absent, not because the Government had waived the antitrust laws but because it had never succeeded in applying them. This was aluminum, where one company—Alcoa—was the industry. Alcoa's arrogance and Stettinius's shortsightedness quickly combined to make aluminum a test case of industry's capacity to produce for defense and for prosperity at the same time. In July, 1940, Stettinius announced at a press conference that the country would soon have on hand adequate supplies of all critical and strategic materials. In September, publicizing what he called "an unpublicized job of pessimistic charting" of defense demand for and supplies of strategic materials, he faced his worst fears and still promised that supplies would be more or less adequate. During these months of his stubborn retreat from reality, aluminum had become the key item in the industrial markets: if no aluminum shortage developed, no signficant shortages were to be expected elsewhere; if an aluminum shortage did develop, shortages were to be expected everywhere.

In December, Stettinius reaffirmed his conviction that no serious aluminum shortage was in sight. But, by that time, foresight was no longer needed to discover the aluminum shortage; hindsight was enough. For the initial impact of the aluminum shortage, and of the companion shortages developing with it, had forced Roosevelt first to prepare the Defense Commission for a receivership; and, then, to create one. In mid-October, he told the press that he hoped to avoid using the power Congress had given him in June to establish a system of priorities. But a week later, at the climax of the political campaign, he found it expedient to reverse himself. On October 22, he issued an Executive Order subjecting orders placed with private industry to priority control.

This order stated that the Council for National Defense had established a Priorities Board consisting of three of the members of its own Advisory Commission—the Advisor on Industrial Production as Chairman, and the Advisors on Industrial Materials and on Price Stabilization. It further stated that the Board had designated Donald M. Nelson as Administrator of Priorities. After giving Presidential approval to both of these steps, the Order then authorized Nelson to require Army and Navy contractors to give priority to delivery on defense orders, over all private or export orders. The Order was amateurishly drawn in that it was applied to the secondary, or manufacturing, level, and failed to reach the primary, or basic materials, level. As Chairman of the Priorities Board, Advisor on Industrial Production Knudsen was in effect made Receiver-Designate. As a member of the new Board, Advisor on Industrial Materials Stettinius was given immunity. As the driving force behind the new regime, the team of Henderson and Nelson was given an opportunity.

If Roosevelt had done less, his candidacy would have remained exposed to Willkie's savage and often justified criticism. If he had done more—if, for example, he had purged Stettinius—he would have entered a plea of guilty to Willkie's indictment. More than that, he would have made Willkie a free gift of this symbolic hostage. Instead, he diverted attention from both his record and Willkie's exposé of it by pointing with pride to progress. Although the wherewithal to defend America was, as Willkie and Mrs. Luce charged, "on order," Roosevelt insisted that meant it was on the way. And although the business leaders he had brought to Washington had been empowered only to advise him, he could now insist that he was giving them power to implement this advice; and indeed he was giving them power to use Presidential authority to assign defense orders priority over civilian work. By this bold counterattack he transformed an ominous liability into an impressive asset. Admittedly, his performance subordinated efficiency to politics. But Willkie himself admitted that Roosevelt's strategy took the preparedness issue away from him. "This result arose largely from the fact," Arthur Krock later recalled Willkie saying, "that the late W. S. Knudsen and Edward R. Stettinius, then in charge of major sections of the preparedness program, not only failed to support his charges but left the people with the impression Mr. Roosevelt gave them in the famous 'on-order' speech—that great military power and industrial mobilization existed when it did not."

It did not exist, and Roosevelt's new Executive Order brought it no nearer to birth. Nelson announced immediately that he had no intention of imposing a system of mandatory priorities upon the economy. Instead he compounded the confusion he was appointed to bring under control. He delegated the Presidential power vested in him over military priorities to the Army-Navy Munitions Board, which he resented and opposed. The power, as originally granted, would have enabled him to remain above the growing civilian-military competition for priorities and to exercise civilian control over the military from what Baruch liked to call the "synchronizing" level. But Nelson defaulted upon this power before he could use it, inviting the military to regulate themselves and to raid the civilian economy in the process.

The military's use of this power quickly demonstrated their own need of civilian control. They issued priorities on a scale which soon left nothing for civilian supply or for foreign aid or, for that matter, even for military programs commanding less than top priority (the forgotten landing-craft program was to emerge as the definitive military casualty of the loss of civilian control). Within the military orbit, claimants for priorities as a matter of course became hoarders, and hoarders bargainers. Every piecemeal allocation, whether of steel for farm implements or of shipping for Britain, inevitably precipitated a new chain reaction of administrative crises, policy disputes, and Congressional threats. Worse still, all grants tended to be made—and to be modified and unmade—on a piecemeal basis, from crisis to crisis and deal to deal, as pressures intensified and relaxed and as claimants accumulated and used bargaining power. Altogether, the direct result of this pattern-making default of Nelson's at the outset of his career in the coordinating role was the imbalance at the operating level which was to jam the production lines in 1942, when the first invasion Army was ready to move.

The enormity of this initial blunder of Nelson's is magnified by his own insistence that he understood he was committing it. This admission, which under-scores his deficiencies as a policy-maker, is strikingly evident in his account of his relationship with Bernard Baruch. For he conceded that his career in Washington consisted of learning Baruch's ideas, agreeing with them—and fighting against Baruch's attempts to apply them. In Nelson's book, he asserts that when he first joined the Defense Commission as Coordinator of Purchases, his three major objectives were: "(1) the coordination of purchases to avoid competition between Federal agencies, (2) compilation of combined Federal requirements, and (3) the organization of priorities and allocations." * He also expresses, as a disciple to his master, his indebtedness to Baruch for demonstrating to him the indispensable value of priorities:

Shortly after I joined the Commission as Coordinator of Defense Purchases there was a meeting with Bernard M. Baruch. . . . Perhaps the high point of Mr. Baruch's counsel concerned priorities, which he considered the "synchronizing force" of any war production program. This lesson, too, we were to learn, although not as soon, perhaps, as we should have done. He talked at great length about price control, and declared that the big production program toward which we were heading could easily run away from us unless we arranged for price-control mechanisms. It is my opinion that hundreds of millions, perhaps billions, of dollars could have been saved and many headaches avoided if this recommendation had been adopted from the start.†

* Donald M. Nelson, *Arsenal of Democracy* (New York, Harcourt, Brace and Company, Inc., 1946), p. 84.

† *Ibid.*, p. 90.

In the role of the dutiful schoolboy, Nelson agrees with everything the master says, even with his prophecy of the inflation which, in fact, Roosevelt avoided. He discusses it all in a tone more-of-sorrow-than-of-anger, as if describing not his own failure, but the failure of others. Thus, he blandly goes on, Baruch

knew what he was talking about when he expounded the ticklish subject of requirements and declared that they should be centralized in one agency so that each morning the agency could know just what had been ordered out of the nation's economy. Later on, when I was made head of WPB, I tried persistently to do this, but it was then too late. The program had grown so big that it was completely beyond control.*

Very true. But where was Nelson during this crucial time when, by his own admission, Baruch was giving the Defense Commissioners such practical advice? He was Director of Purchases for the Defense Commission, and he was fighting against Baruch. From the beginning Nelson was at war with the Army-Navy Munitions Board, and from the beginning Baruch was the Board's constant mentor and collaborator. The Army-Navy Munitions Board was the apparatus of the Under-Secretaries of War and the Navy; it was the apparatus of civilian control of the Army and Navy. From the beginning Nelson attacked Patterson and Forrestal, and their staffs, as "militarists," and from the beginning Baruch worked with them to insure civilian control of the War Economy and civilian control of Army-Navy contact with it. From the beginning the ability of civilian administrators to control

* *Ibid.*, p. 90–91.

hinged upon their ability and their determination
to schedule requirements and priorities. But when
Baruch's associates attempted to face up to this responsibility, Nelson branded them as "militarists"
planning to "take over" the economy, and at the same
time he lacked the resolution to undertake the one job
that had to be done to prevent control over inflated
requirements and competing priorities from passing to
the military by default.

Other critics and political opponents of the Army-
Navy Munitions Board, recognizing Baruch's affiliation with it, attacked him as a "militarist." This was
logical. But Nelson was not free to let logic write his
book for him, for he was the prisoner of his own
opportunism. On the one hand, his early exposure to
Baruch's advice put him in the position of having to
claim that the mentor of the Army-Navy Munitions
Board was *his* mentor. On the other hand, his account
of his crowning political triumph in 1943, when he
frustrated the efforts of the "militarists" to purge him,
forces him to admit—without comment!—that the
candidate put forward by the "militarists" to replace
him as Production Czar was *their* mentor, Baruch
(hence Nelson's victory in the White House). But
though Nelson defeated the "militarists" politically,
he was in turn defeated by the administrative responsibilities he won. With each new political victory and
each corresponding administrative failure, he gave up
a new hostage to Baruch. When Roosevelt finally sent
him flying off on the political equivalent of a slow
boat to China, the only line left for Nelson to take
was to revere Baruch and to revile the "militarists"

who fought by Baruch's side to force him to adopt Baruch's policies. It was a hopeless web of contradiction, and Nelson made a career of it.

ADMINISTRATIVELY, the Baruch approach assumed that "the essence of all control—commandeering [that is, allocations], priority and price-fixing"—would be "centered" in one agency. Roosevelt, on the other hand, was determined to keep power over production separate and distinct from power over prices. Accordingly, the reorganization of the bankrupt Defense Commission immediately after the 1940 election substituted two centers of power for seven circuits of conversation. The Office of Production Management established a personally cordial but sociologically unstable partnership between Knudsen and Hillman; and, to supervise the prosperity being spread by gun production, the Office of Price Administration and Civilian Supply (OPACS) established Leon Henderson as the key figure in the war economy.

Stettinius's War Resources Board had tried to give control over defense planning to big business and, therefore, it had promptly collapsed. The memory of the WRB taxed the Defense Commission with the burden of proving itself independent. Accordingly, it was an elaborate essay in checks and balances—the business and non-business groups checking each other, and the New Deal group holding the balance of power. Politically, the arithmetic of Commissioner representation was effective but, administratively, the Commission was not. In reorganizing NDAC into OPM and OPACS, Roosevelt proposed to continue the system of checks and balances—Knudsen and Hillman checking one another's pressure groups and Henderson holding the balance. But, in addition, Roosevelt was anxious to make it function plausibly enough to quiet his critics until the program "on order" could begin to materialize.

Meanwhile, as the Bureau of the Budget history says:

The issue in large measure was who was going to run the Defense program. Given the strength of special interests in American society and the shortage of leaders generally regarded as attached to the national interest, the issue of who was to control was posed sharply by the demand for the appointment of a single defense czar. . . . As it became clear that there would be a reorganization— and that there was at least a chance for a Defense "czar" —a desperate struggle for position got underway. Industrial and financial groups sought to gain control of the Defense program. The War and Navy Departments in the main were allied with them. Other groups, with equal zeal, fought to retain their gains of the preceding years and to prevent domination of the Government by industrial and financial interests. Mr. Knudsen . . . and Mr. Hillman . . . came to be regarded as spearheads of the industrial and labor groups respectively. Personally they were quite willing to accept whatever role the President assigned to them, but others energetically promoted their candidacy for a dominant role.

The broad issues were pointed up in a plan which Mr. Knudsen proposed to the President at his request late in November, 1940. . . . The plan was built on the idea that the advisor on Industrial Production should become a Director of Industrial Mobilization, vested with power to supervise and direct almost the entire home front effort. In its essentials it restated the Army-Navy Industrial Mobilization Plan, a scheme already rejected by the

President. It would have placed in the hands of the proposed Director of Industrial Mobilization the functions which eventually came to be performed by the War Production Board, the Office of Price Administration, the War Manpower Commission, the Foreign Economic Administration, and other agencies as well.

Typical of the bias in the Budget Bureau's history is the assumption that, because the President had "already rejected" the Army-Navy Industrial Mobilization Plan, the "scheme" was not worthy of his reconsideration. And typical of its distortion of history is its failure to admit that this "scheme," already discredited and now dismissed as unworthy of reconsideration, was in substance adopted as the plan of home front reorganization when Pearl Harbor called an abrupt halt to administrative hocus-pocus. The only way in which the Budget Bureau history attempts to justify the next episode is to argue that control by no one was to be preferred to control by "some class, group or interest."

Control by no one was the plan and the result during the year that culminated in Pearl Harbor. The outcome of the struggle to control the reorganized defense setup was, as the Budget Bureau history says, "a clear-cut victory for no single group. The President decided," it continued, "that the new agency—the Office of Production Management . . . should concern itself only with production."

This, on the President's own premises, passed the death sentence on the new agency at birth. For production was the one vital job that did not have to be done in Washington and, indeed, that could not be done in Washington—either the economy could be trusted to produce or the war was lost before it began. The job that had to be done in Washington and that could be done nowhere else was that of coordinating the resources of the home front with the needs of the shooting fronts. This problem Roosevelt's first reorganization ignored.

Instead, as the Budget Bureau history notes with smug disregard of Roosevelt's subsequent reorganizations, "Again the concept of the Army-Navy Industrial Mobilization Plan of a home-front 'czar' with extremely broad powers was rejected." Reiteration of the snub inspired Roosevelt to sparkle through one of his most effective press conferences. Never was he more magnetic, more sarcastic, or more sincere than on the memorable day, fifty weeks before Pearl Harbor, when he ridiculed the notion that the country's security depended upon his empowering any one man to be a combination "czar," "Poohbah," or "Akhoond of Swat." When thirteen months later, after the country's security was imperiled, Roosevelt reversed himself, he made sure that the czar he appointed was an authentic "Poohbah."

Both Knudsen and Hillman suffered from obvious limitations. But each was more formidable than Nelson and commanded more respect than he from those pressing for commitments from the defense program. The trouble with OPM was not Knudsen or Hillman, or both, but the idea behind it. Neither man was qualified to play the part of Assistant President, which is what the commanding place on the home front had to be and finally came to be. No man had a chance to function, much less to survive, in any lesser role.

Roosevelt's experiment divided the defense management problem into three parts. First, there was the customer—the armed forces. Then, there was management. Finally, there was labor. To represent these three factors, he designated four men. For the war economy's customer, he provided not one but two representatives, the Secretary of War and the Secretary of the Navy. The new Director of OPM was to speak for management, and Associate Director Hillman was to speak for labor.

It was logical but limited. Whereas Roosevelt had appointed two spokesmen to protect one customer, the fact was that the war economy was serving two altogether distinct and often competing customers—our own armed forces and those of our Allies. The effect of limiting OPM's customer relationship to America's armed forces was to pervert the principle of civilian control over production into an endless and pointless polemic over control of American military strategy. As the Budget Bureau history admits, even in 1942 "the relation of military operations to war production was not understood."

OPM never proved equal to the task of scheduling requirements, American or inter-Allied. When its harassed and bewildered officials demanded that production be geared to military strategy, their customer— the Army and Navy—told them to mind their own business. "Many a priority argument was closed by junior officers," the Budget Bureau history recalls,

"with hints of strategy consideration which could not
be disclosed." So preoccupied were the civilians at
OPM with their running feud with the military that
they failed to realize that the Joint Chiefs of Staff had
little more reliable current information about strategy
calculations than Nelson and his staff. That the war
on the home front between the civilians and the military was fought in a vacuum all through 1942 and
halfway through 1943, General Marshall himself finally
revealed in his definitive Report of June 30, 1945,
which states that discussions about grand strategy
were not translated into "firm commitments" until
May, 1943. Until then, consequently, we were mass-
producing munitions not for scheduled operations but
blindly, as the Budget Bureau history concedes, "for
the shelf." This was the McClellan phase, during
which the military demanded more and bigger shelves
to fill.

OPM should have been the coordinating agency between the American armed forces and those of our
Allies, allocating resources and scheduling production
to meet their combined requirements. Only America's
home front high command could have performed this
function. But when OPM's codirectors took over as
nothing but the partners and suppliers of the home
front's American customer, they were chopped down
at the outset from the level of high command to that
of conspicuous expendables.

The old saying about the Prussian Militarists, "They
are either at your throat or at your feet," applies to
the relations between the civilian and the military in
all countries. In rejecting the Army-Navy Munitions

Board (and the Baruch) approach, Roosevelt first separated power over prices from power over production, and then refused to give power over production to OPM Director Knudsen or to the Knudsen-Hillman partnership. Instead, he divided responsibility for production, purchasing, and priorities between Knudsen and Hillman on the civilian side and Stimson and Knox on the military side. Because Knudsen and Hillman were not in authority in what was left of their proper sphere of influence, they soon found themselves on the defensive, caught between the military fighting "to fill their shelves" and the pressure groups fighting to fill their pockets.

Meanwhile, Roosevelt's ingenious formula distracted attention from the question of who was going to produce results and focused it instead on his point that no one was going to have power. He described this anomaly himself in the catch-as-catch-can of his January 7, 1941, press conference:

I suppose the easiest way to put it is that these four people—the Office of Production Management, Knudsen, Hillman and the two Secretaries—fix the policy and then Knudsen and Hillman carry it out, just like a law firm that has a case; say there are two partners; and they carry it out as a law firm. Anybody that knows anything about management will realize that is the practical way to handle that kind of a matter, just like a law firm with two main partners.

Q: Are they equals?

The President: That's not the point; they're a firm. Is a firm equals? I don't know. See what I mean? Roosevelt and O'Connor were a law firm in New York; there were just two partners. I don't know whether we were equals or not. . . .

Q: Why is it you don't want a single, responsible head?

The President: I have a single, responsible head; his name is Knudsen and Hillman.

Q: Two heads.

The President: No, that's one head. In other words, aren't you looking for trouble? Would you rather come to one law firm, or two?

Q: I don't think that's comparable.

The President: Just the same thing, exactly. Wait until you run into trouble.

Q: I would rather avoid trouble.

The President: I think they will. They think they will —that's an interesting thing.

That the two immigrant Horatio Alger heroes avoided trouble with one another is an everlasting tribute to the sense of fair play and the authentic democratic integrity of each of them. But if they avoided trouble with one another, they did not avoid trouble. Nor did they produce results. On the other hand, they did not have power. Nevertheless, results were produced—the country began to sell what the Government wanted to buy. Unchallengeably, therefore, Roosevelt protected his position and irrefutably the country proved his point.

WITH OPM operating in an orbit smaller than that of the armed forces, and the armed forces operating in an orbit smaller than that of the war, Roosevelt needed liaison with the war. This was Harry Hopkins's opportunity, and it came at a time when he needed one. For Hopkins had been responsible for the irresponsible decision to thrust Wallace into the Presidential succession in 1940—even though, as Robert Sherwood admits, months after the political campaign, in the midst of the Lend-Lease fight, Wallace was barely beginning to realize that "the President's foreign policy . . . involved something more than a mere surrender to 'British imperialism.' " * Hopkins's motives, far from being those of a victory-intoxicated soldier, were those of a typical political manager pushing a candidate more anxious than able.

Eleanor Roosevelt herself admits that, before the political campaign was over, Wallace's vulnerability had spread panic among Democrats, who held Hopkins responsible for his nomination. When finally the political season was out of the way, Hopkins had good reason to sigh with relief. This was his opportunity to seek a new, non-political avenue to intimacy with Roosevelt. Fortunately for him, the war was opening exactly such an opportunity. Hopkins was shrewd enough to seize on Roosevelt's need of personal liaison with Churchill as a new chance to stabilize his own intimacy with Roosevelt on a working—a durable—basis. The way to go on living in the White House was to be constantly on the verge of leaving for London. The way to return to Roosevelt was to confer with Churchill.

Sherwood's account leaves no doubt that Hopkins, compromised by his performance as a political manager, had to press and manipulate and trade in order to be allowed a new chance as Roosevelt's personal representative.

* Robert E. Sherwood, *Roosevelt and Hopkins* (New York, Harper & Brothers, 1948), p. 229.

"A lot of this," Roosevelt remarked around Christmas, 1940, "could be settled if Churchill and I could just sit down together for a while."

"What's stopping you?", Hopkins asked.

"Well—it couldn't be arranged right now. They have no Ambassador here—we have none over there."

The gleam of high adventure came into Hopkins' sharp eyes. "How about me going over, Mr. President?"

Roosevelt turned that suggestion down cold . . . . [He] refused to hear of such a proposal. However, Hopkins now had an idea that seemed to him eminently sound, and certainly intensely exciting, and he would not let go of it. He enlisted the aid of Missy Le Hand and of Justice Felix Frankfurter who [Sherwood adds, with well-tutored naïveté] seldom offered any advice to Roosevelt after his elevation to the Supreme Court.*

Sherwood assumes that it was Roosevelt's dependence on Hopkins which made him "obdurate" against Hopkins's proposal. But Roosevelt was dependent only on those who happened to be around—and unexpended—at the moment. Hopkins was well on the way to being expended, and Sherwood quotes him as saying so. "I'll be no use to you in that fight," said Hopkins, referring to Lend-Lease. "They'd never pay any attention to my views, except to vote the other way. But —if I had been in England and seen it with my own eyes, then I might be of some help." * If out of consideration for Roosevelt's need of his intimate of the moment, Hopkins had stayed on, as Roosevelt wanted him to, he would have been used incessantly for a time and then not at all. He would have gone the way of Tugwell and Corcoran before him. By reaching instead, and to Roosevelt's annoyance, for the new

* *Ibid.*, p. 230.

franchise on communication with London, he promoted himself above the running fight inside the Presidential circle that no political intimate could survive indefinitely; and he established himself as Roosevelt's personal representative on the level transcending that on which passing Presidential intimates had to fight.

OPM had gone to work on a level too low to permit it to coordinate America's economic capacities with combined Anglo-American requirements. And now Hopkins was bidding for control of combined Anglo-American operations on a level so high that it left no room for any successor of Knudsen-Hillman to administer this off-shore phase of the home front as one of its two phases. By establishing undisputed control of the off-shore phase at the White House–Whitehall level, at a time when no one was taking control of the domestic phase at any level, Hopkins acquired a vested interest in preventing any strong successor to Knudsen-Hillman from coordinating the two jobs into supplementary aspects of one job. Thanks to his alliance with Frankfurter in his rear, and with Churchill and Beaverbrook on the fighting front, he managed to keep control after Pearl Harbor had intensified the need for coordination of these two jobs. This did not mean that he did not want to win the war, or that he did not want to serve Roosevelt. It means merely that he wanted to win it and to serve him with "men he knew." He did, and this was as close to coordination as the home front high command was allowed to come.

CHAPTER IX

THE ADMINISTRATION OF ANARCHY

"Now, what I am trying to do is eliminate the dollar sign. That is something brand new in the thoughts of everybody in this room, I think—get rid of the silly, foolish, old dollar sign." Thus Roosevelt to his press conference December 17, 1940. Like so much historic phrase-making, this was a half truth; and even as a half truth, it was probably irrelevant. It did not apply to what Roosevelt was trying to do on the domestic sector of the home front: far from getting rid of the dollar sign, he was relying on it to do the work public opinion was expecting his coordinators to do. And it was irrelevant because, on the off-shore sector of the home front, Britain's bankruptcy was getting rid of the dollar sign for him, without initiative on his part.

Until Lend-Lease began in March, 1941, the British used their dollar assets to finance their purchases; and the Treasury acted as their purchasing agent. In this role, Secretary Morgenthau and his aides had done an effective job of finding the exact equipment the British wanted. At that point, supplies and British funds were still abundant enough to permit the Treasury to shop and to specify independently of the Army, the Navy, and the Defense Commission. What Lend-Lease finally eliminated was not the dollar sign as a symbol, but the Treasury as the purchasing agent of the Allies. It concentrated the contracting power in the Army and Navy.

This crystallized OPM's responsibility, which was to coordinate the domestic and the off-shore sectors of the home front. Knudsen-Hillman did not propose to interfere with the contract-making functions of the War and Navy Departments. Roosevelt had not authorized it, and Baruch, with good reason, had cautioned against it: any civilians negotiating defense contracts would immediately have found themselves embarrassed by one or another kind of business affiliation, whereas contracting officers in uniform could be assumed to fill a relatively priestly function in a well-regulated hierarchy. Not contracts but creation was the responsibility of the civilian command. And creation meant creative engineering. The War Department did not have it and did not know where to look for it. The question was whether OPM would provide it.

In creating OPM, Roosevelt had described America's armed forces as the war economy's "customer." The description was apt: customer was indeed the noun, and big and amateurish were the adjectives that went with it. Our peacetime army had almost no equipment adequate enough for the realities of Dunkirk. Neither had the British. But the British suffered the cruel blessing of Dunkirk, which freed them from their obsolete equipment and forced them to make a fresh start. The American Army, on the other hand, kept right on growing, innocent of the awakening in store for its engineers who designed tanks able to shoot in only one direction. By the time the British were insolvent enough to be serviced by the War Department instead of by the Treasury, they knew what they needed; and they knew that the equipment the War Department was designing for its own use would not do.

First among OPM's responsibilities was this problem of getting the War Department to give the British— and, incidentally, our own troops—equipment specified by combat experience. Now OPM was sold to the country, effectively, if briefly, as an attempt to bring business methods and businessmen to Government. But every large business organization depends upon engineering. When Knudsen and his associates came to Washington, however, they left their engineers behind. OPM had no engineering division. The military controlled engineering research and design.

OPM needed an executive engineering apparatus to stop two sources of immediate waste and future tragedy. The first originated with the manufacturers specializing in War and Navy Department work, the second with the more representative groups of businessmen who regarded defense contracts as a distraction. As a class, the manufacturers of war equipment had no conception of standardization (or, therefore, of volume). They had developed vested interests in their individualistic methods and models, which they defended fiercely. OPM found no less than 55 different types of planes on order. The number of parts and accessories and fire-power models was much greater. Little wonder that skepticism greeted all assertions that mass production methods could revolutionize airplane and ordnance manufacturing.

Yet this was what they soon began to do. Typical was the case of General Motors' Saginaw Steering Gear Division, which undertook to hammer out 25,000 Browning Machine Guns. Deferentially, the General Motors production people made a pilgrimage to the gunmaker's shrine at Colt's in Hartford, where only a portion of the plant was tooled for line production. Parts were still passed from artisan to artisan, wrapped in sheets of paper with rubber bands around them, for machining by touch and by squint. The Saginaw unit agreed to mechanize the job, speed up schedules, and slash costs.

A dim view of the project was taken by the high priests at Colt's. The contract was signed in June, 1940. Auto production was booming, and it continued to boom. Experimental work began in a warehouse, and production was delayed until a new arsenal could be built. Without disturbing the priorities commanded by auto parts schedules, the Saginaw Division blue-printed the job by September. The arsenal site, not chosen until November, was in production by April. The contract, based on conventional gunmaking assumptions, called for production of the first gun in 18 months. It was delivered in 11 months. The contract projected a production curve of 40 in the 19th month, of 80 in the 20th, of 160 in the 21st, and of as many as possible thereafter until the full quota of 25,000 was reached. By the 21st month, which happened to be March, 1942, Saginaw had delivered not 280 Brownings, but 28,728. The War Department was astonished, executives of the Colt plant were confused, and more important, the Japanese were confounded. And yet it was all very simple—as simple as the story of America at peace. It also paid a dividend at the usual peacetime rate. The contract, based on the tempo of production by hand, calculated that the cost would be $667 per gun. Nelson reports that this rate of production cut the unit price to $141.44.

At the divisional level, the engineering personnel of the mass-producing corporations were stimulated by the new problems thrown at them. But at the corporate level, top managements and their legal and public relations advisors were wary, and understandably so. Individually, none of them wanted to be diverted from markets left open to competitors. Collectively, all of them shied away from responsibility for what they assumed to be a military problem. "Tell us what you want us to make," was their attitude, "and we'll make it."

It was an honest attitude, at once shrewd and naive. Shrewd because big business had been denounced so often and so eloquently for war profiteering; naive because it took the military at face value as expert designers of war matériel. Thus the masters of mass production, whose industrial contribution the military so desperately needed, deferred to the officers assigned to the home front. They approached their new assignments less as entrepreneurs or as manufacturers or as creative engineers than as mere contractors. The military, in turn, deferred to the least efficient of all American manufacturers—the specialists in defense production, who had many vested interests in notions and projects for which they wanted acceptance, and underwriting.

OPM's problem was to teach the defense specialists to produce; and to direct the production specialists to defense problems. Knudsen was the perfect man for the first job, which he tackled with vigor and imagination, as a teacher. But the second job called for executive initiative, and this was beyond him. All he knew was that the President had conferred this tremendous honor and responsibility upon him—an immigrant. He was proud, if bewildered, and he was determined to do his duty, which, as he saw it, was to get industry to produce what the Army and the Navy wanted produced. Who was he to tell the Generals and the Admirals what they wanted?

No case points the twin moral of production miracle and engineering default more vividly than that of Chrysler's $35,500,000 order to build 1,000 medium tanks. Tank leadership was a major opportunity, and the country noted with satisfaction that Knudsen offered it to the Chrysler Corporation, his former employer's competitor. He called President K. T. Keller and "over the long-distance phone," says Nelson, "they made arrangements to meet, and at this meeting they drew up plans for a tank arsenal with the latest and most improved machinery." * But they did not ask whether the tank to be made was "the latest and most improved" model. Knudsen assumed that the question of "how" set the limit of civilian responsibility; and Nelson did not argue with the assumption that answering the question of "what" was a military function. He notes the criticisms against the first mass-

* Donald M. Nelson, *Arsenal of Democracy* (New York, Harcourt, Brace and Company, Inc., 1946), p. 123.

production tank model, but dismisses them with the dictum that in the end we won the war—the standard retort of the typical Brass Hat in or out of uniform.

As a matter of fact, the War Department itself finally admitted that its first production tank was merely a hasty improvement upon the model that happened to be on hand at the time the pressure developed following the Battle of Flanders. The armor plate had been thickened and weight had been added in recognition of the offensive power of the Reichswehr. But the engineers had not been told to make the design of tanks in particular or war material in general their responsibility; and, before effective equipment could be manufactured at the production level it had to be designed at the engineering level. The War Department's failure to recognize the need for engineering was jeopardizing other programs as well. Thus, bomber production was falling further and further behind schedule. Production was beginning to flow out of the plants as fast as aluminum was flowing into them. And, then, suddenly, in plant after plant, production stopped. At high altitudes, oil froze. Except under completely dry ground conditions and on ideal fields rarely available in combat areas, lurching and skidding endangered take-offs. These were routine problems, and they were solved as such as soon as they were raised. But the pressure of equipment failures was required to raise them.

Even more elementary were the errors of omission in engineering which hindered the tank program. The first tanks were powered by air-cooled engines of four different designs. This was wasteful of tooling, of time, of materials, and of fuel. By definition, air-cooled engines rely on cool air to keep them cool. But tanks are notoriously hotter than Hades, even when not deployed in the desert. Again, the treads used on the first tank models were ideally suited to concrete highways, but unable to provide maneuverability in muddy ditches. Nevertheless, OPM, Chrysler and all the suppliers, builders, and technicians involved in the project went to work designing the machinery and setting up the production line as if the questions which were just beginning to be asked had already been resolved.

Thus, on the assumption that every specification served a professional, and probably a secret purpose, the Chrysler engineers came to grips with the particularly knotty problem presented by the spring drawings, which called for the use of flat steel. They had never seen such springs before, and they were at a loss to devise ways and means of testing their stresses preparatory to putting them into mass production. Alert to the fact that tanks pound their springs harder than any other vehicles and, accordingly, confident that endless man-hours of specialized research had gone into this ultramodern development, they searched the field for clues. Finally, as they were about to give up, one unusually erudite engineer found the answer in an out-of-date railroad manual. The spring specified by the War Department for its new mass-production tank in 1941, known in its day as the "volute" type, had long since been discarded by the railroads as obsolete for freight cars!

The War Department was two generations behind

the railroads. Nevertheless, progressive engineering organizations like Chrysler were deferring to its know-how. Worse still, OPM, instead of subjecting War Department designs to competent professional scrutiny, was hiring the most efficient and dynamic managements in the country as mere War Department contractors. Even more wasteful, vast new arsenals were committing precious machinery and materials and manpower and time to the production of ordnance that was farcically obsolete before it went onto the drawing boards. Many months and arguments later when, Nelson to the contrary notwithstanding, the War Department admitted that its tank was not good enough, Chrysler designed not merely an adequate new tank spring but a more than adequate new tank.

But sometimes the War Department avoided such waste. Under the tortuous division of Army-Navy labor in force before the Forrestal-Patterson regime, "the Army," as Forrestal laconically put it, "was supposed to buy the Navy's anti-aircraft guns but forgot." As late as June, 1941, only a fraction of the anti-aircraft guns we had promised the British had been ordered. After Pearl Harbor, Roosevelt called for the production of 20,000.

WHILE capacities were thus being meted out, shortages were developing. On March 22, 1941, OPM's Division of Priorities, headed by the optimistic Stettinius, was compelled to issue its first priority order— M–1. This order required producers of aluminum to put defense orders ahead of civilian commitments, and listed the order of priority in which non-defense work could be handled. In quick succession similar priorities had to be issued for copper, iron and steel, cork, chemicals, nickel, rayon, rubber, silk—in short, throughout the economy.

Shortages created inflationary pressures. Accordingly, on April 11, 1941, the President by Executive Order created the Office of Price Administration and Civilian Supply—OPACS—and put former Defense Price Commissioner Leon Henderson in charge. The ability of OPACS to hold the price line depended upon its power to allocate supplies; and this, in turn, depended upon how sternly supplies would be siphoned out of the civilian and into the war economy. This OPM was not doing. But OPACS, whose ostensible mission was to resist the pressure of defense priorities and to press for generous civilian allocations, assumed the responsibility for hounding OPM to go to war. To their everlasting credit, Henderson and his shrewd and resourceful deputy, Joseph L. Weiner, urged OPM to end the illusion of guns and butter and to concentrate on providing guns while there was still time. Thanks to this reversal of role between OPM and OPACS, the auto industry's drain on the reservoir of supplies was checked. In May, OPACS prodded OPM to prod the War and Navy Departments to raise their production goal. To find the wherewithal for more guns, the auto manufacturers were told to cut production by 20 percent during the year beginning August 1, 1941.

By this time the debate over guns and butter had reduced itself to a debate over the role the auto in-

dustry was to play in the defense program. The manufacturers were perfectly willing to take on any and
all jobs thrown at them—but as contractors outside
their own plants, not as manufacturers inside them.
Inside their plants they proposed to continue making automobiles. And their expectations, they insisted,
expressed not their self-interest as businessmen so
much as their special knowledge as technicians. It was
as technicians that they informed Knudsen-Hillman
that nothing but automobiles could be made in auto
plants. Knudsen-Hillman had no reply; Hillman because it was Knudsen's end of the business, and Knudsen because it was policy. To the manufacturers'
astonishment and anger, the answer came not from
Washington, but from Detroit. It announced the debut
of Walter Reuther.

In a managerial society whose political, business,
and labor relationships separated the sources of ultimate power from its administrators, where articula-
tion was stereotyped and responsibility stratified,
Reuther was an upstart. Not only did he rush in where
Hillman feared to tread: if Hillman, Murray, Green,
John Lewis, and the Railway Brotherhoods together
had debated with management on such an issue, they
would have been criticized as presumptuous. Yet
here was Reuther, intruding upon the sancta of his
technological betters, but having no passport, no
badge, and certainly no empire.

For Reuther was just another Vice-President of the
rowdy and upstart and not very united United Auto
Workers Union. His puritanical drive had, to be sure,
galvanized the General Motors Department of the

Union into a social phalanx. But, on the other hand, the Union as a whole commanded little respect from the respected leaders of labor, while Reuther himself at that time commanded neither respect nor confidence from the Union's then leaders. The fashionable view of Reuther was that he had little chance of emerging as the symbol and director of a new era in labor relations. He was discounted as an intellectual. All the cumulative clichés of labor politics echoed against him: "Labor is interested in take-home pay for itself not in balance for the economy"; "Labor will never understand the difference between dollar wages and purchasing power"; "Labor does not trust theories and will never follow a theorist." How could a theorist hope to survive, much less to dominate, the rough-and-tumble of labor politics?

The skeptical view of Reuther was half right; his ideas were a tactical liability. But it was only half right, for these unsettling and ambitious ideas were his decisive strategic asset. Admittedly, there was a question about his future career, but the question was not whether this could be made by tactical opportunism. It was whether the force of his ideas could, in 1941, make him a career in spite of his aloofness from the tactical game.

During this chapter in the history of UAW, the tactical game was played at an unusually mercenary level. The objective of the various anti-Reuther leaders was not leadership. It was merely to win and, however precariously, to hang on to recognition from CIO headquarters in Washington. Once duly designated as the Detroit walking delegates of the CIO, the UAW could claim patronage plums from City Hall and State House. Contemptuous of ideas, servile toward Washington, united only by their hatred and fear of Reuther, they were divided among themselves by endless plots and counterplots, feeding on scandal and scurrility. Their traveling poker game, from which Reuther's aloofness removed him, was the meeting ground and market place for the "pork choppers" on the Union payroll (and there was no end of them).

Reuther's strength was lodged in the hard and permanent core of the Union—the Detroit auto workers who had fought to build their organization, who were prepared to fight to keep it, and whose highly developed sense of political independence found security for the rank and file in the factional brawls which divided their leaders. But in sharp contrast to the political maturity and discipline of Detroit's labor vanguard were the shallowness and gullibility of the mass of recruits streaming from the hills and the kitchens into the aircraft plants of the West and the South. This gold rush offered the "pork choppers" a lush opportunity for power and patronage—and slot-machine privileges—inside the Union; and they seized it. Reuther was excluded. Jurisdiction over the new war membership was divided up among the anti-Reutherites. This hurt the war economy administratively, but helped Reuther politically. For by the time the postwar fight for control of the Union came to a head, the opportunists could no longer count on their locals of unskilled war workers while Reuther's permanent organization of skilled Union veterans stood solidly behind him.

Now, in 1941, as Washington was financing the construction of a new war industry alongside our basic industries, Reuther was pressing to win a place on the home front for the auto workers and their tools. The Reuther plan for turning the auto plants into arsenals produced a sensation but no munitions. Reactions ranged from indignation that he should have raised the question to scorn at his answer. Labor spokesmen seemed embarrassed that he should have wandered so far afield from conventional Union responsibility. OPM regarded the problem as one for the industry to decide.

From this attitude, Nelson, who was a responsible executive of OPM and who had the ear of the Administration, did not publicly dissent. He was beginning to be built up by the New Dealers as the coming man in Washington, as the competent liberal businessman whom Roosevelt could trust to coordinate the home front, if, in the end, all the arguments against the delegation of power to an "Assistant President" had to be discarded. But Nelson did not protest OPM's loss of this fight by default. And, because he was a party to the default, his *Arsenal of Democracy* omits all mention of the contribution the Reuther plan made toward turning America into a genuine arsenal of democracy.

Equally ungenerous and distorted is the Budget Bureau history's failure to acknowledge the country's debt to the Reuther plan. Incompetence explains this omission more plausibly than bias. Certainly the New Dealers, crowding behind Henderson into OPACS and bristling across Washington's administrative No

Man's Land at the businessmen in OPM, were fired
with enthusiasm for Reuther's scheme. And, more
important, so was Roosevelt. Not that his enthusiasm
was a commitment of support or, indeed, anything
more than the most general of promises to watch,
with interest and sympathy, while Reuther fought to
convert the automobile plants into arsenals.

As the country was to discover, few men knew how
to fight more doggedly, more resourcefully, or more
imaginatively than this boyish model of the intellectual as a family man. Unfortunately, Reuther's effectiveness in this first crusade was marred by his failure
to take account of certain technical facts which in-
validated his specific proposals, and thus could be
used against him, though they did not touch the principle for which he was contending: for instance, the
tools used for automobile sheet-metal work were too
small to grind out plane fusilages; automobile plant
layouts left too little space between machines to permit the movement of plane parts; automotive engine
equipment could be used to build only the smaller
components of plane engines; automotive production
practice was not disciplined to observe the meticulous
standards of precision required in the manufacture of
planes.

But although the original Reuther plan reckoned
without many of the difficulties involved in converting the automobile plants to plane production, it
ignored the possibilities they offered for quick and
easy conversion to tank production. So did Knudsen:
reacting to the defects rather than to the possibilities
of the original suggestion, he dismissed it with the

comment that conversion would add nothing but floor space to defense production.

History is full of men with a knack of discovering stimulating ideas and ignoring facts; what made Reuther great was that he combined fertility of ideas with a respect for facts and an eagerness to educate himself to use them. One of the world's great engineers now gave him an opportunity to reconcile his general idea with the facts of production. Alex Taub had been an immigrant boy from England and Knudsen's engine man during the great days of mass-production pioneering at Chevrolet. At Vauxhall, General Motors' English subsidiary, Taub had played a distinguished role in the reequipping of the British Army after Dunkirk, designing the engine for the Churchill tank in sixty days. So impressed was Beaverbrook with Taub's talents that, confronted with the confusion of Anglo-American plane production, the British Aircraft Ministry had sent him back to Washington to deal with his old chief, Knudsen.

It was Taub's mission to tell Knudsen that Britain's Sabre engine, which the aircraft lobbyists—and especially the General Motors' aircraft lobbyists—were saying could not be made, was actually in the air; and, further, to persuade him that the British artisanship which had fashioned this complicated engine could be adapted to American mass production. Knudsen was persuaded; OPM was committed to the Sabre project; and, nevertheless, the Sabre was never made in the United States. Fortified with Knudsen's blessing, Taub had gone directly to mass-production headquarters—to the Chevrolet organization in Buffalo, where operating management had been hoping for a challenging war job.

The response to Taub's request was enthusiastic. Buffalo was delighted with this chance to compete with the official General Motors airplane engine. But above operating management was top management; and top management vetoed the project, not merely in Buffalo but in Washington as well. The prospective competitor with General Motors' unfortunate new product—the Allison—was suppressed, and not just within the General Motors organization. OPM, impotent in the face of pressure from both the Army and General Motors, was neutralized. Knudsen, disappointed but loyal to the idea, was able to clear no more impressive source of supply than the small engine subsidiary of Timken Roller Bearing, from which no more than a couple of engines a week could be promised—in a couple of years.

But by this time the British, sensitive to Army hostility and anxious not to wear out their welcome, called off the entire project. Fearful of jeopardizing the American aid in prospect, they decided to sacrifice their immediate hopes of American fighter planes and to concentrate on building fighters themselves. The War Department, they knew, was enthusiastic about developing a major 4-engine bomber program. This suggested an obvious division of labor—British fighters would hold the Nazis at bay in 1941 while American bombers to carry the war back over the Continent in 1943 were a-building—and the British were practical enough to seize it.

The result was a paradox. On the one hand, America

was a neutral, openly friendly to Britain and professing to fear attack. But, on the other hand, America was refusing to accept Britain's best defensive weapon and offering, instead, a long-range bomber program for offensive use. Little wonder that, right down to Pearl Harbor morning, a great many Americans of strong internationalist leanings agreed with a great many others of isolationist leanings that our policy was sheer hypocrisy. On one point, and one point only, Secretary Stimson and Senator Wheeler agreed: that it was neither as a neutral power nor as a people on the verge of being attacked ourselves that we were helping Britain. But whether our purpose was self-defense as stated, or intervention in Britain's behalf as suspected, it was clearly to our interest to accept the offer of Britain's best fighter engine. If we were soon to stand openly as Britain's ally, the common sense of a common effort called for the mass production in America of equipment proven on the front line. But logic wins few arguments and no wars; and, therefore, we prepared our bomber fleet for victory over Europe by preparing our fighter squadrons for defeat over the Pacific at the hands of Japan's Zero pilots.

In the end it was not reason which converted the auto plants, but Pearl Harbor. The manufacturers continued to press OPM (which was supposed to be limiting or, where necessary, curtailing civilian supplies) for priorities in order to maintain auto-production schedules, while they bluntly resisted all pressure from Henderson's OPACS (which was supposed to be protecting civilian supply quotas) to choke production down. But on Monday morning, December 8, 1941, as they sat down to a meeting that had been planned to stop once and for all the pressure for curtailment of their production, Paul Hoffman, of Studebaker, asked for permission to make a statement before the meeting officially opened. "I think the country expects an announcement of a cut in auto production from us this morning," he said.

Once the plants were converted and outfitted as arsenals, they produced as no arsenals in the world produced. Whatever the companies had lacked in imagination or flexibility at the top level of management, they more than made up for at the operating and creative level as soon as the job was laid out for them. Nowhere was their genius for production more apparent than in the lesson they proceeded to teach their teachers in the uses of accuracy. Pre-war automotive standards had accepted tolerances of one-thousandth to two-thousandths of an inch for production pieces of average size. When Detroit went to war, the Army technical officers instructed the automotive engineers to discipline themselves to the standards of aircraft artisanship, which worked to tolerances of only half a thousandth of an inch—to be sure, on a hand scale of production. The agitation against the Reuther plan had prepared business and Government to expect the worst from Detroit. But to everyone's surprise, the automobile arsenals did not limp behind the aircraft industry. Instead of combining the limited scale of aircraft operations with the familiar inaccuracy of automotive operations, they produced faster than they ever had and more accurately than the aircraft artisans ever had. Before Detroit finished winning the war, it was mass-producing pieces at routine tolerances of two-tenths of a thousandth of an inch.

But if, in one sense or another, Reuther's talents were employed to the country's advantage, Knudsen's were not. And this was more than a wanton waste of great talents: it was a cruel misuse of a great person and, incidentally, a thoughtless indignity to a great symbol. In modern American society, the idea of Production corresponds to the Gods of Fecundity which primitive societies held in awe. Knudsen himself was both high priest and devotee. He had grown into this symbol by the power of his devotion. The Horatio Alger story of his success impressed the public, but amazed him. Sincerity too simple to be suspect prompted him to ask, half-incredulously, with each promotion: "How can a man like my boss trust an immigrant boy like me to handle such a job for him?" He asked himself this question when the President of General Motors made him head of Chevrolet, when the heads of GM made him President of the Corporation, and when the President of the United States made him head of OPM.

Of great help to Knudsen was the revitalized Ford organization, which began to supply exactly the kind of creative initiative the defense effort needed. Belatedly, for example, the War Department discovered that it had rushed into tank production with an inadequate transmission. The problem was referred to Ford. Its solution was not merely a new transmission but an altogether new and well-engineered tank.

Another difficult problem solved with equal dispatch, thanks to the Ford reorganization, had grown
out of the expansion of the Pratt and Whitney engine
program. Ford, Chevrolet, Buick, and Pratt and
Whitney all had contracts. The program called for a
prodigious expansion of capacity for making precision
gears. Pratt and Whitney's original supplier had been
a small, specialized Chicago machine-tool company.
In 1940, before the Pratt and Whitney program had
reached so large a scale that only the automobile
companies could be expected to handle it, more than a
million dollars of expansion money had gone into the
Chicago plant. Now, while the entire engine program waited, Pratt and Whitney called on Washington to allocate another $5,000,000 for new construc-
tion and new tooling. Washington complied, being
quite content to commit its scant supply of materials
as demanded by the rigid assumptions of the exclu-
sive guild of defense specialists. At this point, however, Ford intervened, explaining to the authorities
in Washington that 90 percent of the gear-making
equipment specified in the new allocation duplicated
Ford facilities then idle as the result of the curtailment in automobile production. This left 10 percent
of specialized new machinery that would still be
needed, but the Ford engineers insisted that this
could be secured in much less time for only $100,000.
To prove its good faith, the Ford management took
the further responsibility of getting an agreement from
the Chevrolet and Buick production people to accept
the Pratt and Whitney gearing which Ford was con-

verting to produce. Neither Government nor country could have expected more of industry.

Meanwhile, the directors of General Motors, seeking a successor to Knudsen, had found in C. E. Wilson a man whom they could trust never to be invited to Washington by a Democratic President. Knudsen had reacted to Reuther's question as a mechanic, Wilson as a moralist. An honest mechanic is always reluctant to operate on the policy level, and OPM, accordingly, had proven incapable of either adopting or rejecting the Reuther plan. Instead, it put the issue up to a kind of town meeting of top personnel in the war agencies and the interested companies. In the free-for-all that followed, C. E. Wilson (not to be confused with his namesake at General Electric, who was to serve at WPB) stated his credo: everyone admits that Reuther is smart, he argued, but this is none of his business. He is a labor leader, and it is a prerogative of management to deal with this kind of question. If Reuther wants to become part of management, G.M. will be happy to hire him. But so long as he remains Vice-President of the Union, he has no right to talk as if he were Vice-President of a company.

Industrial feudalist that he then was, Wilson diverted the issue from the merits of Reuther's case to the right of a man like Reuther to present it. Many of those present were shocked by Wilson's stand. A number of those with a stake in the management and ownership of companies realized what a costly disservice this regression to the caste psychology of Judge Gary was perpetrating upon American business. But of all those who listened to Reuther and to Wilson, only one man, Ferdinand Eberstadt, had the courage and the simplicity to say: "This young man may have something, and I'm dumb enough to think we ought to give him a chance to find out."

STIMSON ends his account of America's passage through what he calls the "Valley of Doubt" by reporting a talk he had with Harry Hopkins on August 19, 1941, about the unsatisfactory progress of American production. Hopkins, to begin with, was free to criticize the performance of Knudsen-Hillman—he had gone off to London to establish his new position on the inter-Allied policy level when OPM was created and, consequently, he bore no responsibility for its obvious inadequacy. Moreover, his return had established him as *the* authority on what the fighting front needed from the home front. This new position in turn entitled him to operate as a principal factor in the clearly impending reshuffle of the expendables on the operating level in Washington. Since by this time the civilian Secretaries of the War and Navy Departments were also established as principal factors (in contrast to the successive teams of transients staffing the emergency agencies), Stimson was a strategic ally for Hopkins and an authority well worth invoking in criticism of OPM. Armed with Stimson's criticism, Hopkins and Frankfurter could implement their alliance by devising a formula for superseding OPM and arbitrating the growing conflict between the War and Navy Departments and the emergency agencies.

Stimson's views were usable but not quotable. For

he believed and, with characteristic bluntness, said: "that there was no objective like a war to stimulate production." He also paid his respects to what he called the "persuasive" handling of labor. His suggestions on this score Hopkins and Frankfurter knew better than to convey to Roosevelt. But they could and did make capital of his insistence that control over the production program had to be concentrated in one responsible executive. For now Hopkins and Frankfurter had settled on a candidate for the "Pooh-bah-ship." They were in a position to assure Roosevelt that Nelson was *their* businessman and that it would be safe to build him up as the prospective czar.

That a czar was needed, everyone was begining to admit. But if the issue was no longer *whether,* it was not yet *who*: it was *whose*. OPM's bankruptcy invited business and the New Deal to bid more angrily and eagerly than ever for control of the impending receivership. OPM's crisis was Harry Hopkins's opportunity. He and Frankfurter proceeded to build Nelson up as the answer to both pressures. This was shrewd political strategy, and Nelson's record as a competent and progressive purchasing agent made it plausible. Certainly he was entitled to share in the credit for the outstanding job done by businessmen like Robert Stevens in the wool field: late in 1940, shipments of Australian wool were brought in on a scale large enough to supply the armed forces and to prevent a shortage. By the same token, Nelson had leveled unanswerable professional criticism against the Army's naive and costly buying habits. The Army had put out its mass orders for cantonment lumber as casually as if it had been ordering a plank or two, and the War Department had been alternately surprised and unconcerned when the price doubled and lumber virtually disappeared from the regional markets. The Army's shoe buying had been equally irresponsible, and Nelson's criticism equally sound. And so, because Nelson had proved useful to the Administration as a purchasing agent, Hopkins and his cohorts proceeded to make use of him as the New Dealers' new exhibit of a businessman in command of the situation in Washington.

In every sector of the war economy, meanwhile, administrative disintegration was beginning to retard and divert the momentum of production. An urgent problem, for example, was presented by the threat of a power shortage. The utilities, alarmed by the rapid expansion of the power load, reacted as the railroads had—by flooding the press with claims of a comfortable margin of reserve capacity. And, like the railroads, they then had to suffer the embarrassment of being caught short. Stettinius's office, gullible as usual, confirmed the utilities' denial of a power shortage. The statement was reported in the Washington *Star*, Nelson recalls, alongside a dispatch from Birmingham, Alabama, reporting a brown-out to conserve current for the steel mills.

Threats of Government ownership (which railroad management had come to believe) were conjured up by railroad propaganda. But public ownership was more than a propaganda bogey in the utility business. It was a vigorous and expanding movement, no longer justifying itself as mere reform but, on the contrary, claiming to be necessary to the national security. In order to prevent the movement from growing at their expense, the utilities had to grow faster than the demand for power.

Unlike the railroads, the utilities had anticipated this problem realistically as early as 1938, when they worked with Louis Johnson to connect power-company expansion with preparedness. But when their plan was frustrated and the companies were unable to finance expansion programs of their own, they found themselves, when the defense boom came, unwilling to admit the existence of a shortage on the one hand and unable to do anything to overcome it on the other. But the Government's great power projects, which the utilities had fiercely fought to block, had surplus power. The Tennessee Valley Authority quickly emerged as the hub of a significant new industrial area, and even Wendell Willkie admitted its usefulness. Congress appropriated another $75,000,000 to enable it to step up aluminum output. Another concentration of strategic production grew up around Bonneville and Grand Coulee in the Columbia River Valley. Indeed, without Roosevelt's Tennessee and Columbia River developments, the stupendous aluminum and atomic programs, with their enormous power requirements, would not have been possible.

For, already, OPM had begun to review proposals for plant expansion with minute attention to the available power supply. Power priorities became a distinct possibility, as the power companies joined with Government to press General Electric and Westinghouse to speed up deliveries of new equipment. Fairbanks

Morse developed a self-contained Diesel power unit, which it promoted energetically wherever companies were worried about power rationing. Up and down the Atlantic Coast, from Boston Edison to Georgia Power, the utilities serving the great Middle Atlantic production centers shuttled kilowatts back and forth to make up each other's temporary deficiencies; and this, while production was still mainly on a one-shift basis. In Georgia the cotton textile industry, with all the labor, raw material, and customers it needed, still faced the prospect of a cut-back because of the power pinch. Prophetically, Roosevelt considered subordinating to Ickes the power and fuel divisions of OPM and the agencies of Government concerned with power and fuel problems.

To be sure, the period of the czars had not yet begun. Nevertheless, on May 28, 1941, the President designated Secretary Ickes Petroleum Coordinator for National Defense, and the stormy petrel of the Roosevelt Administration responded in characteristic fashion. Just as a cargo of oil was about to leave Philadelphia for Japan, Ickes stopped it. The State Department was furious. The President, thoroughly irritated, instructed Ickes not to interfere in matters of foreign policy. Ickes sent two trunk loads of approving letters to the State Department, and his resignation to the White House. The President made peace by prohibiting further oil shipments to Japan from the East Coast, where war threatened to create an immediate shortage. But, according to Forrest Davis and Ernest Lindley, Secretary Hull complained that public opinion continued to "rawhide" the State Department with demands for an embargo on the stream of war supplies to Japan. At last, on July 25, 1941, the order freezing Japanese assets was issued. This formalized the outbreak of economic warfare. Henceforth, every cargo for Japan had to be specifically approved in Washington, and any and all export licenses were balanced against imports of silk and other shortage items from Japan and the area under her control. By this time, Ickes was appealing to Eastern oil consumers to cut down fuel consumption, and Roosevelt felt obliged to explain publicly what he called the "method" behind the admitted madness of fueling the Japanese war machine.

Fuel tied the power and transportation problems together. Leon Henderson wrote Budd urging him to start a pipeline construction program, a need which became even more intense when the United States turned 50 tankers over to the British. Budd did not answer this letter. Worse still, he did nothing, thus setting the stage for the grisly days of 1942 when tanker after tanker carrying oil up the Atlantic Coast was torpedoed. The railroads were not major petroleum carriers, particularly in the Eastern states, which, consequently, remained dependent upon tanker-borne supplies. The Eastern utilities, in particular, looked to tidewater for their fuel. When at last tanker traffic failed, even though oil supplies were still adequate, the railroads could not begin to take over the load, and gasoline and fuel rationing became inescapable. Ickes, who had predicted that the railroads would be unable to do the normal work of the coastal tanker fleet, and who had anticipated the suspension of tanker traffic, fought loudly and relentlessly for a pipeline. But by the summer of 1941, Washington was no longer free to adopt recommendations as to what should be done: the steel shortage dictated what could be done; and OPM ruled that the steel shortage made a major pipeline project unthinkable. Ickes won a higher priority from Senate investigators than from OPM.

Claude Wickard, recently elevated from Under-Secretary to Secretary of Agriculture, was also pressing Budd for action. Light trucks for farm hauling were what he wanted. But neither Budd nor Knudsen-Hillman was willing to divert auto capacity to truck production, although by this time the War Department was beginning to clamor for trucks of all kinds. Wickard found cases where truck production was at a standstill because parts makers could not get aluminum for magnetos.

By this time the railroads had a car-building program which, they argued, justified their opposition to any diversion of crop traffic to trucking. But by harvest time this program was admittedly going to be 7,500 cars behind schedule—the car shops were half shut down for lack of steel. In desperation, the railroads considered the feasibility of turning the clock back to the day of wooden freight cars. In Schenectady, the American Locomotive Co. and, in Philadelphia, the American Car and Foundry Co., both prominent railroad equipment builders, had grown defeatist about conventional business prospects. They went directly to Washington to enlist for defense work. To their profit and to the country's, their idle facilities were put to work before the available steel supply was rationed out among the country's steel fabrictaing plants.

PATRIOTISM being the last refuge of a prophet, by December, 1940, OPM's Priorities Director Stettinius had adopted a new line in answer to predictions of an aluminum shortage. "Creation of such anxiety which has no basis in fact," he warned Ickes and the others, "serves no patriotic purpose." By February the aluminum shortage was an undeniable fact, and it was interfering with every patriotic purpose. It was also disorganizing OPM. On March 14, 1941, OPM's Priorities Division conceded defeat. It established a critical list of all items to which the Army and Navy could automatically assign priority ratings. Aluminum headed the list. But the rush of aluminum demand was aggravating the shortage much faster than priorities could begin to free supplies. To honor our bomber commitment to the British, and to equip our own air force, a major national effort was needed to make up the deficit.

The Aluminum Company of America (Alcoa) was making an impressive corporate effort. In 1940 it produced more than 400 million pounds, and in 1941 more than 600 million pounds. Granting that concentrated Government demand was underwriting Alcoa's risks, nevertheless its physical achievement in stepping up operation by 50 percent within one year was remarkable if not unique. By conventional standards of corporate performance, as contrasted with public policy, this record justified monopoly. When in March, 1941, the agencies interested in the arithmetic of aluminum concluded that Alcoa's record new 600 million pound capacity had to be doubled, Alcoa insisted that the entire expansion program be entrusted to it.

There now unfolded a drama at once exasperating and inspiring. Democracy, racked by the dilemma of reconciling efficiency and morality, promptly agreed upon what had to be done and just as promptly disagreed about how it was to be done—and by whom. To win the race for control of the air, America had to have aluminum, whether suspect monopoly aluminum or virtuous competitive aluminum. Stimson, whose strength lay in his bluntness but who was the first to concede Roosevelt's superior wisdom in avoiding issues and delaying showdowns, put the problem succinctly when he exclaimed: "I'd rather have some sinful aluminum now than a lot of virtuous aluminum a year from now." And, indeed, on pain of going the way of France by 1942, America was under pressure in 1941 to pursue efficiency as a value in itself. But though common sense dictated putting efficiency first, America started an argument instead of an aluminum program. This cost months and, therefore, lives. It was reckless. But for America it was necessary, and, therefore, it was in the end wise. The months of seeming futility reconciled public policy and national urgency. The momentum of monopoly was conserved, and the spur of initiative was added. Administrative dissension in Washington was inefficient. But it expressed symptomatic doubt and determination from which it generated limitless new energy. And this, in contrast to mere efficiency, was to prove irresistible.

From March through July, 1941, OPM and the War Department argued about sites, about how many sites Alcoa was to have, and about who could be given the others—if any. The disagreements were punctuated by sharp reminders from Secretary Ickes that any arrangements the Army Engineers and the OPM experts might make would be subject to review by him before Columbia River power could be used. To these warnings of a veto, Ickes added the reminder that OPM and the War Department were taking an unconscionably long time to provide the aluminum so desperately needed. The Government officials in charge of TVA, who enjoyed administrative autonomy but who also received correspondence from Secretary Ickes on monopoly and related subjects, found themselves effectively restrained from committing TVA power to the expansion program until Ickes decided what kind of aluminum contract—and contractor—would qualify to buy Columbia River power.

This Washington battle developed into a Sitzkrieg by June, when Hitler invaded Russia. Harry Hopkins went to see Stalin, who gave him a shopping list, headed by anti-aircraft guns, "which the Army had forgotten to buy," and aluminum and high octane gasoline to fly the planes made with it. "Give us anti-aircraft guns and the aluminum," Stalin told Hopkins, "and we can fight for three or four years." Incisiveness was Hopkins's strongest quality, and the impact of his report to Washington forced action upon OPM and the War Department.

By this time the aluminum problem had been thrown at Jesse Jones. His solution was to let Alcoa control the program. But Ickes had already prevailed upon Alcoa to build a plant for Reynolds to operate at Bonneville; and OPM was recommending that, of seven new plants, four should go to prospective competitors of Alcoa. It concluded that Alcoa should design and build plants for two of them, and that the other two—Reynolds and Bohn (which withdrew) — were qualified to build plants of their own.

Weeks later nothing had been done. The teeming Northwest, which looked to power and aluminum to insure the permanence of its wartime growth, was outraged. At least one of the companies on the OPM list knew no more about its participation than it had read in the newspapers. Not one piece of equipment had been inquired for, nor had any arrangements been suggested for power contracts. Jones had decided to negotiate man-to-man with A. V. Davis, Chairman of the Alcoa Board. All other companies, and all other Government officials, were excluded. Meanwhile, the Navy lost priority on its plane production. The "new" heavy bomber program agreed upon with the British —by this time it was the old program—remained in the paper stage for lack of aluminum at Tulsa, Wichita, and the other mushrooming arsenals. America was taking on a new production commitment to the Russians, but it was already in arrears on its less ambitious British commitment.

Nevertheless, Jones haggled on. When the Truman Committee scrutinized the result, it concluded that he would have done better not to have haggled at all. For its investigation found Jones's deal a bad one for the Government, and Truman himself demanded that it be abrogated. What Jones had done was to give Alcoa control over the wartime rate of operations in the plants the Government was financing to compete with it. He exacted no penalties on Alcoa for failure to perform. Operating costs in the Government-financed plants were so high that a price yielding them a modest profit would guarantee Alcoa an exorbitant return. Alcoa retained effective control of alumina, the semi-finished product into which bauxite must be processed before being turned into aluminum.

Nor was this all. After the war, the contract stipulated, the Government would shut down the new low-cost capacity about to be built and turn the market back to Alcoa's older, smaller plants. On this point in particular, Jones was righteous. For he had come to live in fear of the day when the return to "Normalcy" would flood the market with unwanted aluminum. And on this very point Truman was particularly indignant. For he assumed, rightly, that the economy would want the aluminum.

Jones was outraged. The source of his mythical power had been his mythical control of the Senate. But now he refused to answer the Senate's questions. Instead, he referred to Hugh Fulton, the Truman Committee Counsel, as "that whippersnapper." Still more infuriating to him and damaging to his position, the press turned against him. One by one, the New York *Times*, the New York *Herald-Tribune*, the Washington *Post*, *Business Week,* and the *Wall Street Journal* took him to task as the chief bottleneck in Washington.

CHAPTER X

THE ADMINISTRATIVE RECEIVERSHIP

ALL through 1940 Roosevelt had protested that the wherewithal to defend America and save Britain was on order; and, by the time he dissolved the Defense Commission into OPM, the makings of a vast expansion were at last on order. Before its demise, the Defense Commission had cleared contracts involving more than $10,000,000,000, of which the Army and Navy had placed $9,000,000,000 with industry. Ships claimed $3,300,000,000, and the construction of new plant and of defense housing $1,500,000,000. Another $1,500,000,000 had gone into the airplane program. Of the other major ingredients of the effort, ammunition had absorbed $600,000,000, guns $500,000,000, and trucks and tanks $400,000,000.

These contracts, added as they were to the earlier British and other foreign orders, called for the production of: 50,000 airplanes; 130,000 engines; 17,000 heavy guns; 25,000 light guns; 13,000 trench mortars; 33,-000,000 loaded shells; 9,200 tanks; 50,000 trucks; 300,-000 machine guns; 400,000 automatic rifles; 1,300,000 regular rifles; ammunition for all of these; 380 Naval vessels; 200 merchantmen; 40 Government arsenals; 210 camps and cantonments; 80,000 miles of road construction and repairs; and clothing and equipment for 1,200,000 men.

In the last two months of 1940, a million jobs opened up. Prophetic of coming developments was the fact that no less than five and a half million men and women—Negroes as well as whites, migrants as well as those with skills or experience—were registered by the United States Employment Service as available for defense work. Over and above the absorption of men into the armed services, by the end of 1941 the war economy had created some five million new jobs. Hillman brought Isadore Lubin in from the Department of Labor to supervise a broad training program which, fortunately, instead of being limited to the vocational level, was projected at the prospective managerial and personnel management shortages as well. Hillman and Lubin established an "in-training" division at OPM, headed by Channing Dooley, of Socony Vacuum, and Walter Dietz, of Western Electric. These men rendered invaluable assistance to the many companies, large and small, which were struggling to train and absorb droves of unskilled workpeople.

As an administrative automaton, the Defense Commission had served its purpose. But what it left to OPM was the mere makings of a program, not the needed program. OPM's mission, accordingly, was to achieve coordination by balancing requirements. This it failed to accomplish. Instead, it served, like the Defense Commission before it, as a recording device, ringing up each new series of demands upon the war economy and registering them with the armed services and the other agencies of Government, but not calculating the demands and the capacities of the economy as a whole and, consequently, not regulating its workings and not providing for its expansion.

Expansion was now the key to coordination. Materials and facilities normally available for production had been diverted into the construction program, which was continuing to grow without plan and without control. Plant construction quickly became the fashion. Everything constructed, from arsenals to warehouses, increased the demand for raw materials. The very progress of the program, accordingly, plunged it into its first great crisis. This was a crisis of imbalance between the supply of basic industrial materials and the demand for them. The problem was to expand the flow of materials as fast as capacities were installed to process them. OPM began by failing to anticipate the problem and ended by failing to recognize it. While it temporized with the aluminum shortage, the steel shortage overwhelmed it.

STEEL followed the pattern of aluminum, but on a larger scale. Beginning in February, 1941, steel capacity was subjected to tremendous new pressure by the Maritime Commission program. This program for 200-odd Liberty ships was rapidly increased to 1,200, intended to add 13,000,000 dead-weight tons to our merchant fleet. By the spring of 1941 nine new shipyards and 131 new shipways—notably the dynamic Kaiser "ship assembly lines"—were springing into action.

In February, 1941, Roosevelt instructed the Maritime Commission and OPM to cooperate in scheduling

shipbuilding priorities. But one of OPM's major failures was its failure to prevent—or even to referee—the
steel race between the Maritime Commission and the
armed services. Not until the spring did the Commission win representation on the Priorities Committee of
the Army-Navy Munitions Board. Not until August
did it win mandatory priorities. As the Budget Bureau
history admits, the 136 merchantmen delivered between July 1, 1940, and December 31, 1941, were "less
than had been scheduled and . . . far short of war
needs." All through 1942, the shipbuilding program
was admittedly hampered by the delay in recognizing
and rectifying the steel shortage of 1941.

As late as February, 1941, OPM, through Stettinius
and his advisor Gano Dunn, was still claiming the
existence of a surplus of steel. Roosevelt, carrying his
trust in Stettinius past the point of absurdity, went so
far as to repeat Stettinius's charge that talk of shortage was unpatriotic. To the horror of his advisors, he
branded the claim of a steel shortage "a deliberate
lie." By the spring Gano Dunn was calling for a 13,-
000,000-ton expansion program; Forrestal thought
15,000,000 tons of new capacity would be safer. August
1 brought a full priority system to pig iron. But the
expansion program was not adopted until September,
1941. And then, in spite of Pearl Harbor, Nelson says,

For some reason not clear to me, no action was taken until
both OPM and SPAB had been laid to rest. The report
was not placed before the War Production Board until
March, 1942, and it was only in May that the report was
approved. . . . And then on June 30, 1942, the program

was cut back to 10,000,000 tons, not because we couldn't use more steel, but because this tonnage seemed about the limit of our facilities.*

During this nine-month period of gestation which Nelson complains was shrouded in darkness for him, he served successively as Executive Director of SPAB and WPB and was the ranking executive empowered to deal with production, priorities, requirements, and capacities. During these months America's capacity to produce, to fight, and to aid its fighting Allies was hampered and held back for want of the new steel that had been "on order" since the spring of 1941.

Dislocation in steel caused dislocation in agriculture. When aid to Britain began, the British were grossly underestimating their needs. Milo Perkins, for example, in a striking display of initiative, took the responsibility for multiplying the initial British order for cheese. This solved Britain's problem. But the American cheese-makers soon faced a problem of their own. Thanks to the butter shortage, to Army buying, and to prosperity demand for food of all kinds, they moved to increase their capacity. But they could not get steel for vats. Neither could the chemical and alcohol manufacturers. Nor, more controversially, the brewers and distillers.

The difficulty was not, as farmers thought, that OPM was discriminating against agriculture, but simply that it did not know what it was doing. As late as July, OPM, while issuing priorities hand over fist, did not have statistical data as to the flow of steel

* Donald M. Nelson, *Arsenal of Democracy* (New York, Harcourt, Brace and Company, Inc., 1946), p. 143.

into industrial channels or as to inventories. It relied on the trade papers for its facts and figures. The steel companies felt free to book orders and to protect customers' inventories without regard to priorities. Some large steel producers found that 70 percent of their new business carried A priority ratings. But Gresham's Law—that bad money drives out good—had already affected the priorities system, which was war economy scrip, this inflation made OPM priorities worthless, and provoked the Army and Navy to promulgate their own "priorities critical list," which quickly grew to embrace some 300 steel items. Nevertheless, a National Association of Manufacturers' survey of over 500 defense manufacturers, all of them presumably big, revealed that material shortages were a major obstacle to 82 percent of them. OPM admitted its inability to determine to what extent steel producers were favoring valued customers and discriminating against customers having priorities but regarded by steel companies as undesirable.

Henry Kaiser was the most conspicuous of these. He had been on the prowl in Washington ever since defense spending began, but his energy did him little good until his New Deal contacts sent him to see Tommy Corcoran, who by early 1941 was practicing Washington law. Todd Shipyards was a veteran bulwark in shipping emergencies, and Corcoran was close to its management—hence Todd-Kaiser, which dissolved when Kaiser developed what the Todd people regarded as delusions of grandeur in fields unrelated to shipbuilding. Corcoran brought Kaiser to Jesse Jones and got him his first RFC loan. Kaiser and Corcoran

broke off relations when Corcoran sent Kaiser his bill.
"I thought Tommy was an idealist," protested Kaiser.

Meanwhile, however, Kaiser had created a major
sensation, and an inspiring one, in his new West Coast
shipyards. Instinctively grasping Roosevelt's rule that
energy was more efficient than efficiency, he reveled
in his new role; it was a sand-and-gravel contractor's
dream come true—at cost-plus. At a time when experienced managements in all industries were holding
back against committing themselves to spend Government money and to assume public responsibility
for unfamiliar tasks, Kaiser reached out for every
derrick, crane, and bull-dozer he could lay his hands
on. He hired every floater willing to take the highest
pay to be had, without regard to qualifications, on the
assumption that everyone who could be had could be
used. He persisted even when newspaper reporters
produced affidavits that Kaiser workers spent their
shifts playing cards, and when neighboring plane
manufacturers complained that Kaiser was stealing
skilled labor for unskilled work at higher pay. It was
unbelievably extravagant—at cost-plus—but it paid
for itself in time saved and security won.

For it built ships—that is, as fast as steel to build
them with could be found. Kaiser bought steel exactly
as he hired manpower, by spending money faster than
the average businessman could count it. The average
businessman hesitated to hire people when he had no
material for them to work with, and he hesitated
to bid up to the sky for material for which the Government expected him to pay no more than approved
prices. Kaiser hired the people, bought the material,

and sent the Government the bill. Everyone who read the newspapers knew what his results were, and only a few Government comptrollers knew what his costs were. They philosophized that the men who got results are invariably men who break rules, and they hoped that, come "I-Day"—Investigation Day—Congress would agree that the results *at the time* were worth the price.

By normal standards of value, the product itself was not worth the price. Even Kaiser granted that his ships were not built for immortality. Along the waterfront the word spread that his ships could not be trusted to get back to port. They certainly fell far short of traditional shipbuilding standards. But, on the other hand, traditional shipbuilding standards were much too high to meet the need for time and for tonnage. Admittedly, Kaiser bought time at the expense of durability. But this was realistic. All through 1942 and 1943 the chances were that every Kaiser ship launched would be sunk before it could be repaired.

In that desperate situation, Kaiser's drive and the scale on which he had the audacity to spend public money improvised a new technique. Pre-Kaiser merchant shipbuilding had been a job of construction. Kaiser transformed at least part of it into a reasonable facsimile of line production. As much cutting, shaping, and fabricating as possible was done behind the ways, while the steel moved up to the keel. This reduced to a minimum the time each ship delayed its successor in the ways. In 1941 the average time taken to deliver a Liberty ship was 355 days, and total deliveries barely

exceeded a million tons. Within a month after Pearl
Harbor, the demand for our shipping was double the
supply. To fulfill our contract with the Russians, to
defend ourselves in the Pacific, to support the combined Anglo-American operation, top priority had to
go to create new cargo space. In January, 1942, Roosevelt set our 1942 shipbuilding objective at eight times
the 1941 figure. We achieved it. The time necessary to
deliver a Liberty ship was slashed to 56 days. One of
Kaiser's yards completed a Liberty in 14 days.

This was very upsetting to United States Steel and
Bethlehem Steel, the dominant factors in West Coast
shipbuilding and steel marketing. They had been
building ships for many more years than this upstart
contractor, and they had fixed ideas about how much
inventory was needed to support even his rate of construction. They resented his shipbuilding leadership,
and they refused to accept his demands for steel to
support it.

Kaiser was quick to retaliate. He turned on his ac-
cusers with charges that they ignored his priorities
and deliberately lost "steel" earmarked for him. To the
echo of steel industry blasts against black-marketing
and hoarding, and Kaiser's counterblasts against steel
industry conspiracy, Corcoran—still his friend—took
him back to the RFC with a bold new program. If
Kaiser's priorities could not buy him steel, he was
going to make it in the West himself. On this occasion,
Jesse Jones moved swiftly. Kaiser was given the authority and the wherewithal to create an integrated
steel operation in the West. He was many months and
still more obstacles away from having enough steel to

feed his shipyards. But the mere threat sufficed overnight to get his priorities honored. Suddenly steel
showered upon him (in spite of which he allowed the
Government to put him into the steel business).

In this war of nerves OPM was a bystander, and
not a well-informed one at that. OPM's statisticians
despaired of their ability to trace the movement of
steel, industry by industry and product by product,
until the auto industry and its parts suppliers got onto
a defense basis!

THE auto industry was getting ready to go to war. By
January, 1941, Packard, Studebaker, Ford, and General Motors were working on plane engine projects. In
addition, Ford was collaborating with Consolidated
Aircraft. Chrysler, over and above its tank contract,
was working with Goodyear and Glenn Martin. General Motors was helping North American. The result
of this auto-aircraft collaboration was a steady acceleration in the flow of subassemblies for bombers. The
industry was also producing a great variety of ordnance, armored cars, and trucks. Willys-Overland
went to work on the jeep.

Companies associated with the industry, like Timken Roller Bearing and Houdaille Hershey, pioneered
new ordnance techniques, Timken in armor plate and
Houdaille Hershey, a parts supplier specializing in
shock absorbers, in machine-gun manufacturing. It
found that it could eliminate costly and elaborate tooling which Army engineers had assumed to be necessary. The troops using this gun had been improvising
sticks to replace the shiny aluminum handle, which

broke easily. Houdaille Hershey developed a substitute which functioned more efficiently and saved aluminum. The application of mass-production methods to defense production problems also began to earn dividends in the form of manpower saved.

But in spite of the volume and variety of defense activity, automobile production continued to consume materials and man-hours and machine time at a capacity rate. The Army and Navy were up in arms because work on their contracts waited while auto-parts makers completed orders for Detroit: the Army-Navy Munitions Board accumulated a dossier of a few hundred such cases. Moreover, because the auto rush continued through the normal summer shutdown period, manufacturers of farm implements, cans, and other products needed by the war economy could not get steel.

By July, 1941, auto production was being forced to an austerity basis. But far from relieving the shortages, Detroit's improvisations threatened to aggravate old ones and create new ones. Wherever possible, all the companies substituted plastics for metal: the result was a plastic shortage. They cut down on chrome, but tried to substitute stainless steel. They eliminated brass, which was going into shot and shell, but tried to substitute copper, which was in hopeless short supply.

By mid-July, OPM reluctantly conceded that the original 20 percent cut-back in auto production had not been enough. It prepared to force a further cut of 50 percent and, at the same time, to force truck production up by some 60 percent. Output for 1941 was running at the rate of over 5,000,000 cars and trucks a year. OPM felt obliged to reduce this to 2,500,000 vehicles, and, at the insistence of the Armed Services, to allocate 1,500,000 units of this quota to trucks which, beginning August 1, became subject to priorities. This schedule would have left the auto companies free to work at the rate of only a million cars a year.

The companies protested, and with good reason. For the industry could not begin to break even at the rate of one or even two million cars a year—even if the Government could prevent inflation of costs. OPM, they complained, was being mealy mouthed; it did not want the responsibility for stopping auto production altogether, and yet it well knew that the effect of rationing the industry to a one-million car-production rate was to make further commercial operation impossible. But for this OPM wanted the public to blame Detroit, not Washington.

The squeeze was too tight for Detroit to worry about blame. The problem was now employment. By making too much of a good thing for too long, while insisting that conversion to defense operations was impossible, Detroit had missed its opportunity to organize a gradual, and profitable, transition from production for the market to production for the Government. The question was no longer whether conversion was possible, but whether it could be made profitable. The auto companies were not finding it so because the defense program had not yet accumulated mass-production momentum. Chrysler, for example, reported 12-month earnings of only $13,295 on defense deliveries of $31,666,171. With $4,000,000,000 of new defense business about to be placed in Detroit, the auto companies wanted to know whether they were about to pass from prosperity-as-usual to priorities unemployment and thence to profitless capacity production. While they wondered, Ford received a new $140,000,000 order for nearly 5,000 Pratt and Whitney engines. Chevrolet, also a major factor in the Pratt and Whitney program, moved to convert its great Buffalo and Tonawanda operation to plane engines. Chrysler took a $42,000,000 subcontract for Glenn Martin parts, and Hudson $12,000,000.

For labor these new orders came in the nick of time. Priorities unemployment had sharpened into a bitter reality for the working people of Detroit, Toledo, and the other auto centers. In midsummer General Motors' labor negotiators stated that only 5 percent of its man-hours had been absorbed into defense work. Between this figure and the obvious fact of General Motors' big defense orders there was a discrepancy, accounted for by the fact that most auto company contracts called for new construction instead of for the conversion of existing facilities. During the summer these projects were still in the construction phase: they were not beginning to absorb production labor. But by the time priorities unemployment made the absorption of production labor imperative, Washington had run out of appropriations.

"This defense program," said C. E. Wilson of General Motors, "is big business. We might just as well make up our minds to that. It is big business and it isn't going to be handled by thousands of small businesses alone. Small plants can't make tanks, airplanes or other large complex armaments." This announcement, Wilson's manner assumed, made it official. That it represented a complete about-face did not embarrass him. But it infuriated OPM and the War Department. Both organizations had accepted at face value the industry's original polemic against the Reuther plan; and, understandably, both resented the industry's belated discovery of the uses to which a defense program could put auto plants. Even more did they resent Wilson's bland assertion that General Motors "could have handled a larger volume of war business if the Army and Navy had placed it with us." More bitterly ironical still, while most of the companies which converted to defense work had been unable to get materials, the auto companies which had refused to convert had continued to get materials.

Moreover, thanks to the incompetence of the Priorities Division of OPM, a good deal of the material still flowing into civilian channels was spoiled. Yellow Truck, for example, had 900 buses in production. It obtained priorities sufficient to justify cutting up materials for 900 chassis. But then it was able to get priorities for only 500 sets of wheels. Not only did this waste freight cars and other services in short supply: it forced the lay-off of 3,000 men. And it spread distrust of the priorities system. Admiral Land, of the Maritime Commission, expressed the attitude of every businessman in the country when he said he "never lays a keel until he has enough steel to start the ship after the one at hand." No system based on paper can function when everyone hoards. Material hoarding turned OPM's priorities orders into so many rubber checks.

FOR the auto companies the problem was a passing one: the war economy was going to need their facilities, and sooner rather than later. But upon the Union it inflicted a cruel blow. The UAW was the most defense-minded labor organization in the country; and it was also the strategic battleground on which a labor leadership intent on making American Democracy work was leading the fight against a labor leadership which exploited the assumption that American Democracy could not meet the crisis. Between John L. Lewis and the Communists and the vested interests in unionism-as-usual, the Reuther organization was on the defensive. Stimson and other zealous patriots were impatient with Roosevelt's "persuasive" handling of labor, but Roosevelt was growing as impatient with them as he was with the zealots on the other extreme who were pressing him to turn the crisis to labor's advantage. For while Reuther was fighting against great odds to persuade the vanguard of mass production labor to take the initiative—if necessary, to sacrifice —to speed up OPM's program, OPM had rewarded it with unemployment: not deliberately, to be sure. Little wonder that, when John L. Lewis shut down the coal mines in the spring of 1941 and jeered that Reuther's men were paying dearly for supporting Roosevelt while his men were profiting from his opposition to the war program, Roosevelt did not dare to move from persuasion to coercion. At that point, not merely auto labor but the entire labor movement would have regarded a crackdown on the miners as evidence that labor was about to suffer politically as well as economically. All sections of labor feared that Hillman was becoming a prisoner and that big business had taken over the defense program. What labor wanted to know was whether big business had taken over Roosevelt too.

Agitation over big business control of the defense program was not limited to the labor movement. The fact was that 56 corporations held some 80 percent of the contracts. Not only did the great majority of the country's 45,000 metal-working establishments find themselves threatened with exclusion from the national effort: their communities were suffering from the failure of conversion to take up the slack resulting from the interruption of normal civilian work. Some 27,000 plants employed four workers or less, and OPM conceded that only about 4,000 of them had been given contracts involving sums in the neighborhood of $50,-000 apiece; 6,000 additional firms had managed to find subcontracts. By the summer of 1941, priorities unemployment had thrown the country into turmoil. What came to be called the "priorities mail" poured in upon the pleasant but bewildered Stettinius by tens of thousands, and spilled over, unread and unrecorded, into the space afforded by a Washington police court. Congress too was putting constructive pressure upon OPM and, for once, the press was supporting the efforts of Congressmen in behalf of their constituents. As Nelson admits, during the six months before Pearl Harbor, thousands of communities were threatened with depression in the midst of the boom. To broaden the base of the program, Harry Hopkins brought Floyd B. Odlum of Atlas Corporation to OPM as head of a new Division of Contract Distribution; and Morris L. Cooke, a well-known engineer in Hillman's Division, made a special study of pools in which groups of manufacturers in distress areas joined together to handle defense orders as a unit.

York, Pennsylvania, was the most famous of these, but at one point over 100 communities were operating such pools. The York Ice Machinery Corporation, for example, owned a large boring machine which normally worked no more than 350 hours a year. The York Pool put it into full production making powder presses for du Pont and doing similar jobs which would otherwise have been delayed for months, while duplicate machines were being built for part-time work. Odlum sent traveling exhibits around the country to show people connected with unconverted businesses what kind of work was wanted, while Cooke broke down into geographical subdivisions a list of 650 firms having prime contracts of $100,000 or more. Soon after Odlum came to Washington, OPM's Labor Division, with which he cooperated closely, certified that 10 typical medium-sized industrial communities had been crippled by shortages. Priorities unemployment had cost 120,000 men their jobs in these areas.

Pools were also formed on an industry-wide basis. In October, the 30-odd units in the washing machine business formed an industry-wide pool, with three of them becoming prime contractors on a $12,000,000 machine gun job and the rest taking subcontracts. Indicative of the chaos in OPM, the Iron Fireman

Company immediately protested that the War Department had promised another Division of OPM that it would get this order; and, on the strength of this order, Iron Fireman had invested $500,000 of its own money in equipment needed to convert its plant to handle the job. One by one, makers of jewelry and every other kind of consumer item organized pools of their own. The stove manufacturers, who had been outdoing the automobile and refrigerator companies in their efforts to get materials, finally organized a pool and converted. The small tool shops in Michigan worked with Odlum to pool the production of equipment wanted to blast open bottlenecks. Plants unable to get priorities tried to qualify their machine shops for participation in these pools.

Nelson tells the story of a manufacturer with an artillery contract who decided that he needed $5,250,-000 worth of plant expansion. By this time the pressure upon the War Department and OPM to share the work was forcing more practical investigation of such demands. Inquiry revealed that commercial facilities in the area not yet absorbed into defense work could make 118 of the 121 parts involved in the cannon in question. Accordingly, the manufacturer with the prime contract was tooled up to supply the three missing parts, and everything else was subcontracted. In spite of constructive cases such as this, however, something like half of the country's installed equipment was idle. Moreover, in spite of all the money pouring into expansion projects, OPM failed to put the machine tool industry on even a two-shift day.

All this time, OPM Research Director Stacey May

had been pressing for permission to poll the bigger defense contractors about their materials' consumption and requirements. OPM's Production Division refused this permission, although maldistribution of inventories was hampering production as severely as shortages. OPM's Priorities Division had allowed some companies having tremendous backlogs of contracts to fortify themselves with inventories sufficient to see them through most of the war, while it was allowing other related companies feeding production to or from them to shut down intermittently for lack of supplies. Moreover, the auto companies and others still in civilian work remained free to load up on fresh inventories and to instruct parts makers to process virgin materials for new cars while their own divisions engaging in defense work were slowed down for lack of materials. Thanks to the race for materials, the auto companies, having pioneered the technique of subcontracting, now felt every incentive to ignore its normal advantages and to keep as much work as possible under their own roofs.

On top of all this, OPM was called upon to schedule Russia's new requirements. At the top of the list was aviation gasoline. Ickes, having humiliated OPM and trounced the War Department as Power Coordinator, doubled in brass as Oil Coordinator. While the President stormed at Sumner Welles and, for once, even at Stimson, for the delay in arranging for shipments to Russia, Ickes coyly announced that, following Hitler's invasion, he had undertaken to start the flow himself. This relieved the pressure from Russia; but meanwhile, the British discovered that they had been understating their own needs by half to two-thirds. And, as our own airmen began to accumulate flying time and airfields, our requirements, too, began to rise. For the first time the oil companies were given tentative estimates of what was wanted from them; and the manufacturers of oil refining equipment were spurred into the race for priorities. For the Government alone they eventually installed $203,000,000 of new 100-octane refinery capacity. But in mid-1941 the problem was not yet how much could be built. It was still how to find steel to begin building.

STETTINIUS's new role as Hopkins's nominal successor and political equerry in the Lend-Lease program was "formalized," as the Budget Bureau history puts it, on September 16, soon after he was relieved as Director of Priorities at OPM. Simultaneous with his appointment as a Presidential Assistant, he received a letter instructing him to report to Hopkins. Sherwood's account of this episode in Hopkins's career has him "calmly relinquishing an imposing title and a job of vast importance (Lend-Lease Administrator)—and this in the City of Washington where men in top positions not only fought and bled to hold on to their own jobs but sat up nights figuring ways to take powers and functions away from others of equal eminence." * How Hopkins in his single-minded dedication to winning the war could have justified the promotion of such a universally ridiculed and discredited failure as Stettinius into a job of such vast importance—and,

* Robert E. Sherwood, *Roosevelt and Hopkins* (New York, Harper & Brothers, 1948), p. 376.

later, into the Secretaryship of State—Sherwood does not attempt to explain. He does say that "Stettinius was his friend," which is what Boss Murphy or any other political boss would have said about any hench-man, and what in fact Hopkins did say.

Hopkins soon discovered that his laying down the law to the War Department over the White House telephone was not enough to move the cargoes that had been promised. His characteristically incisive orders had to be followed up. For this Hopkins himself was too busy, too sick, and too impatient. And Stettinius, his front man, was no more capable of doing the job for him than he had been of doing it for himself at the Defense Commission or at OPM. To process Lend-Lease orders for bidding took an average of 120 days, and remained subject to Army control of procurement. We had fallen far behind in our original commitment to Russia, which was being steadily increased. Russia, for her part, was jeering that two-thirds of our Lend-Lease program consisted of food-stuffs, and that our Army, which was not fighting, was sitting on large inventories of fire power needed at the front.

"FEUDING and squabbling in Washington" had become an irritating daily headline in newspapers throughout the country. Roosevelt's reaction was characteristic. He addressed himself not to the merits of the case, but to its public relations. Just as his answer to the charge that he could not work with business had been to bring Knudsen and Stettinius to Washington, so, now that bickering among his appointees had become an issue, he met it by seating a select group of them around a table. This he called SPAB—Supplies Priorities and Allocations Board. He created it August 28, 1941.

Baruch promptly brought his long-smouldering differences with Roosevelt out into the open. He dismissed the new agency as "a faltering step forward." Baruch's reaction was a good deal like Stimson's on another occasion. At a Cabinet meeting, Roosevelt justified one of his compromises with the words, "Well, it's a step forward." Stimson admonished him to "keep on walking," and the entire Cabinet burst into laughter.

The SPAB maneuver was a complicated one—even for Roosevelt. It suspended OPM, but left intact the OPM Council of Stimson, Knox, Knudsen, and Hillman and their entire apparatus. These four became *ex officio* members of SPAB. Appointed to sit with them were Vice-President Wallace, in his new capacity as Chairman of the Economic Defense Board, a Cabinet Committee with a staff created on July 30, Price Administrator Henderson, and Harry Hopkins in his improvised capacity as Special Assistant to the President supervising Stettinius's supervision of the Lend-Lease program. Labor was given recognition in the person of Hillman, but the unforgivable blunder of Stettinius's original War Resources Board in ignoring organized agriculture was repeated: Wallace counted as Roosevelt's man, not as the Farm Bureau's. Whereas only Hillman had represented the New Deal on OPM's four-man Council, the addition of Wallace, Henderson, and Hopkins gave the New Deal a majority among

SPAB's seven. For publicity purposes the force of this New Deal victory was blunted by the emergence of Nelson, a corporation executive, as the key man in the new setup. He became Executive Director of SPAB.

But this was only one of two new jobs simultaneously given to Nelson, and it conflicted with the other. For he was also transferred from the directorship of OPM's Division of Purchases to the directorship of its Division of Priorities, supplanting Stettinius. And this was more confusng than ever. "As Executive Director of the new Board," Nelson complained, "I gave orders to OPM; as Director of Priorities I received orders from OPM."

The double standard governing Nelson's status applied to Henderson too. For his Office of Price Administration and Civilian Supply (OPACS) was split into the Office of Price Administration and a Division of Civilian Supply. OPA remained an independent agency, autonomous *vis-à-vis* the new High Command, while the Division of Civilian Supply became another unit of OPM, subject to SPAB. Thus, Henderson also found himself in the schizoid position of sitting at the SPAB Council table and voting directives to OPM, whose directives in turn he was obliged to follow in his other capacity as one of its divisional directors.

From a purely administrative point of view [the Budget Bureau apologia concedes], the organization erected by the order of August 28 left much to be desired. Critics [it acknowledged] pointed out that Mr. Nelson, as Executive Director of SPAB, was a subordinate of Mr. Knudsen when Mr. Knudsen was acting as a member of the Board and perhaps was an administrative superior of Mr. Knudsen when Mr. Knudsen was acting as Director General of the Office of Production Management. As Director of the Division of Civilian Supply of OPM, Mr. Henderson was a subordinate of Mr. Knudsen, but when he attended sessions of SPAB, he met Mr. Knudsen as an equal.

This cannot be dismissed as administrative trivia which did not interfere with the winnng of the war and, indeed, the Budget Bureau history makes only a half-hearted attempt to do so. It admits that the transfer of the civilian supply function from OPACS to OPM separated price control from production control, thereby jeopardizing and complicating both, as Baruch had predicted it would. "This basic decision was made," the history admits, "without a great deal of consideration of its basic consequences." One consequence was the failure of production control under Nelson. Another was the pillorying of the price administrators, whose role should have been a popular one. For the time being, however, Henderson was anything but a martyr. He was regarded as the protégé of Hopkins and as the brains behind Nelson, which made him the key operating man of the moment in Washington. Knudsen's reaction to this partial demotion was characteristic. "All I want to do is make pieces and parts," he said. "I don't care about the glamour and I don't want the policy responsibility anyway. *That* job requires working with lots of figures, and I can't do that."

Nevertheless, conceptually if not administratively, SPAB, with all its shortcomings and all its overtones of musical comedy, represented a bold step forward and an historic one. For the first time a central agency was empowered to determine the requirements of our armed forces, our civilian economy, and our Allies-to-be. On this occasion, no doubt, Roosevelt would not have been justified in boasting that he had "planned it that way." Nevertheless, this reorganization, which established Leon Henderson as the administrator of prices on the one hand and civilian supply on the other, achieved a coordination more practical than many planned in more businesslike fashion. When, for example, the Cubans began to inflate the sugar market, the civilian supply administrator eliminated this source of deadly pressure upon the price administrator by asking the Cubans what they needed. By releasing from civilian supply enough of the goods requested, he made it possible for Cuba to get what it required. Then, as price administrator, he was able effectively to freeze the price of sugar.

Conceptually, the period of administrative isolationism was over. It was over in fact, too. The President suddenly found himself in urgent need of an administrative device for underwriting international if not domestic priorities. The Moscow Protocol, approved early in October, guaranteed to Russia priorities on aluminum, machine tools, and other necessities of war up to a billion dollars. But the priorities system was still in chaos. Everyone had priorities and no one could get them honored. To make good the overdrafts which OPM was issuing daily on our strained capacities, SPAB began to allocate calls on capacity without regard to priority scrip. Thus, the Navy commanded priorities on aluminum and on new tooling. So did Russia. But the Navy was closer. It used its position inside OPM to get its priorities honored at Russia's expense. By specific instructions from the President, however, the Secretary of the Navy was restrained from favoring his colleagues at the SPAB Council table with his views on the Russian situation; and SPAB's allocations established Russia's prior claim to the priorities OPM had issued.

In spite of the fact that the President found himself forced to use SPAB to veto OPM, in spite of the fact that he was intervening in the squabbles between the military and the civilians in his capacity as Commander-in-Chief and at the level at which Heads of Government were pooling inter-Allied resources, the Army and the Navy fought a stubborn rear-guard action, forcing SPAB repeatedly to reaffirm its directives from the White House. A month before Pearl Harbor, the Secretaries of War and the Navy went further. They demanded the subordination of SPAB to a new super-priorities committee to be controlled by the military; and, presumably to be empowered to countermand SPAB's exercise of the Presidential veto over OPM.

This demand for open military control of the home front was, of course, rejected. The realities of war on the Russian front dictated its rejection—for the Army and Navy were insisting that America's armed forces be supplied before Russia's and Britain's were helped. Administratively speaking, it was the responsibility of the War and Navy Departments to do this, and, consequently, even the outspoken internationalists at the head of both services admitted that the military proposed to use the power demanded to slow down shipments to Russia and to Britain. But rejection of this demand did not solve the problem. Until the war economy could produce enough to go round among our own armed forces and the anti-Axis forces, the problem could not be solved. Pressure of new appropriations for the Army, the Navy, and the Maritime Commission continued to compete with pressure from the fighting fronts. Between August and October the armed forces were given $12,000,000,000. But money was not munitions. They could buy matériel only if matériel was there to be bought. The legacy of NDAC and OPM, however, was shortages. Their failure to launch in time the necessary expansion program was the root of the bitter, fruitless struggle for supplies between the military and the advocates of allocations abroad. In recognition of the realities aggravating the agitation in Washington, the RFC was authorized to issue an additional $1,500,000,000 of notes to finance new expansion projects supervised by Jesse Jones's various lending agencies, and Jones himself was coopted onto SPAB, which by this time was pushing the idea of expansion. But again, it was a case of too little and too late.

SPAB had been an admitted compromise. To begin with, it was a compromise with the public, which was demanding a reorganization of the defense general staff. But it was also a compromise with the defense general staff, which wanted the controls left inside OPM. Roosevelt's compromise appeased both the public and the defense general staff. To SPAB he gave public responsibility for the defense program. But the real power to operate the program remained with OPM.

SPAB was not put on top of OPM, as advertised, but in front of it. For SPAB was not an organization. It was nothing but a policy board attached to the OPM organization, which continued to direct production, short of explicit Presidential vetoes provoked by the pressure of the Russian crisis. Nelson himself had been so elated to become Executive Director of SPAB that he had failed to protect his position as its boss. The Executive Order creating SPAB did not name Nelson Executive Director. It merely provided for a seven-man Board and an Executive Director who, it specified, would act *ex officio* by virtue of being priorities director of OPM. Thus it was as one of Knudsen's divisional superintendents, and not as his boss, that Nelson controlled any part of the apparatus of production. SPAB itself had no apparatus other than OPM. To implement its policy decisions it had to depend in emergencies upon Presidential intervention or, as a matter of routine, upon the OPM Council. Individually and collectively, Stimson, Knox, Knudsen, and Hillman remained in control of the administrative machinery.

Roosevelt had invented SPAB to mediate the fight between the forces symbolized by Knudsen on the one hand and Henderson on the other. To a certain extent it did this, but at the price of provoking a much fiercer and more explosive fight between Nelson, whom the public regarded as having taken over, and the

OPM Council, whose members were still entrenched in control. The weird administrative contraption looked like a Rube Goldberg cartoon and, as Nelson quickly discovered, the joke was on him. Understandably, he resolved to revenge himself on OPM and on the military politicians behind it.

The military politicians were vulnerable. On the one hand, they felt obliged to press for supplies and equipment that had to be allocated to Russia and to Britain. But, on the other, for all their demands, their own budgeting still fell amateurishly short of the requirements of war.

Thus, the OPM research staff contrasted the Army-Navy Munitions Board estimate of aluminum requirements with the facts. The Industrial Mobilization Plan had calculated that the maximum effort of a 4-million-man Army would absorb less than 500 million pounds of aluminum in two years. OPM was positive that military requirements alone would exceed a billion pounds. The discrepancy in the case of copper was 4 to 1. "Obviously," the staff concluded, "the Industrial Mobilization Plan estimates for the 4-million-man effort bear no relationship to the realistic demands under the present program."

Knudsen, whom the War Department regarded as its ally and advocate, was provoked to rebuke the Army for its failure to heed his technical and even his statistical warnings to improve the quality and multiply the quantity of antitank guns and other ordnance. As to the Navy, "unbelievable revision upward or downward" was OPM's disrespectful comment on the admirals' estimates of requirements. Yet OPM was virtually the civilian auxiliary of the War and Navy Departments.

To be sure, OPM itself had underestimated steel demand. But even OPM knew enough to question Navy steel estimates for ammunition which, in September, 1941, provided for nothing more than target practice. For large shells the Navy's estimate of its wants was doubled. For anti-aircraft shells, it was trebled. But before the civilians multiplied the military's estimates of military requirements, shortages prevented production up to even the initial schedules. Early in October, the British considered sending artillery to the American Army, which did not have enough to practice with.

WAR was now weeks away. Hitler, confident that Russia was crushed and that his war was won, threw the controls of the German war economy into reverse: he ordered matériel production slashed, and materials diverted for civilian use. Roosevelt, on the other hand, was never more serious, never more dedicated. How could he have maneuvered such confusion into such chaos? As he said on another occasion, he "planned it that way." For, while Washington seethed, the momentum piled up as the dollars poured out. In SPAB's first month of existence, production rose 15 percent, and in its second month 26 percent. Even the Budget Bureau history is frank to admit, however, that "No causal relation can be inferred between the order [creating SPAB] and the upward production trend." As a matter of fact, there was a causal connection, but the other way. It was because the production trend was upward that Roosevelt dared to play his game with SPAB. It was because momentum outside of Washington had begun to mold policy inside Washington that he let SPAB debate the arithmetic of expansion with OPM and the military politicians. He trusted the momentum outside of Washington to make the arithmetic come out right inside Washington.

Inside Washington he trusted two mavericks to prod his appointees on SPAB to keep pace with the momentum. The first was Ickes, the other was Thurman Arnold. Ickes was not a member of SPAB, while Arnold was barely tolerated as a member of the Administration. Unflustered and articulate about "Harry Hopkins' sell-out of the New Deal to the Cartels," Arnold jeered at the pressure groups entrenched in OPM and SPAB and retaliated like the competent politician he was—by forming an alliance with the most potent lobby in Washington, the American Farm Bureau Federation, which was the one pressure group ignored by SPAB's complicated balancing of forces. Organized agriculture was always rowing with the transportation and processing interests, and now, in particular, it was bitter against "Big Business control of priorities." Farm strength was concentrated in Congress, which was becoming increasingly hostile towards OPM and SPAB. It was to the farm bloc that Arnold now turned for support in his feud with the war agencies. He timed a major speech in Kansas City on "Restraints in Transportation" with the seasonal peak of traffic pressure on the railroads. He threatened to bring an anti-trust action against the entire structure of freight rates. He managed to prevent a major truck merger. He hinted that the can companies should be dissolved. He warned municipalities, which by this time were up in arms not merely because of priorities unemployment but because of priorities as well, that collusive priorities were victimizing them as purchasers of transportation, utility, and hospital equipment. He opened a Small Business Bureau to serve as an unofficial court of appeals for independents denied contracts, subcontracts, or a fair hearing for new processes for defense production. And, finally, he attacked the Teamsters' Union—whose cheering and devoted leaders had spearheaded Roosevelt's campaigns—as a monopolistic conspiracy. Altogether, his incantations, although dire, were needed.

Needed also was the constant threat that Ickes would open a second front of his own against the war agencies in Washington. On the one hand, he had accumulated more strategic power than most of their members combined. But, on the other, he was excluded from their councils; this fact satisfied him that there really was a conspiracy against him and spurred him to new outbursts of righteousness. He had a good deal to be righteous about. Standing up to John L. Lewis was man's work, and Roosevelt had entrusted it to him. Coal was his barony and, therefore, Budd as well as Lewis was his quarry.

Budd himself was not expecting the autumn freight peak to reach the danger line of 1,000,000 carloadings a week, which, he admitted, the roads could not handle. But for over a year the warnings which he was now echoing had been coupled with the practical suggestion that the autumn coal traffic be moved forward into the slow pre-harvest summer months. This he had ignored and, consequently, the coal and crop movements were straining the railroads simultaneously —in spite of which they were reaching for the oil traffic no longer traveling by tanker.

Oil was another of Ickes's baronies and an East Coast pipeline was his crusading objective. To thwart him, the railroad spokesmen turned to "astronomical statistics" themselves. They claimed that the railroads had a surplus of tank cars sufficient to take over the oil business. As Ickes had no difficulty in establishing, this was a thoroughly irresponsible claim. East Coast terminal capacities were already being taxed to capacity; tank cars owned and operated by industrial shippers and needed to move chemicals, foods, and so on, were included in their calculations; hundreds of locomotives nowhere to be had would have had to be diverted to tank car service.

Now the pipeline issue had preceded SPAB into the headlines, and Henderson had gone on record as favoring it. But SPAB tried to avoid voting on OPM's refusal to release steel for the project. Instead, it hoped to put through a compromise plan for the use of concrete barges carrying oil in drums and barrels (prolonging the drain on steel supplies). When Connecticut's powerful Senator Maloney, who was investigating the oil situation, heard this, he exclaimed: "You can't sink a pipeline."

Meanwhile, perversely, steel was released for a pipeline from Portland, Maine, to Montreal: this threatened to siphon oil out of New England, where the shortage was acute, and to tie up tankers delivering fuel at Portland for Canada. Altogether, the transportation crisis dramatized SPAB's inadequacy and Ickes's effectiveness. Of this situation Ickes made the most, securing general agreement that a pipeline must be built after all, but commiserating with Baruch that both the Curmudgeon and the Sage were being ignored and neglected.

BARUCH was indeed being neglected, and he was making the most of it. The administration of the home front, Baruch had been saying since the end of World War I, had to begin with the gauging of requirements. Belatedly, SPAB had been commissioned to follow this advice of Baruch's, but without the benefit of his counsel. And it had failed. Moreover, Baruch had indicated at the time that it would. As SPAB, having begun as a receivership, began itself to need a receiver, this slight to Baruch was converted into an asset.

Less than sixty days after SPAB's launching, Baruch's "availability" to administer the Victory Program in the making was being described as "logical." As he himself was frank to admit, he was at least as spry as Stimson and Hull. So far as any personal feeling of Roosevelt's might be concerned, the President found it expedient to keep Knox as Secretary of the Navy and to deal with him through Forrestal and Ickes (Knox's comrade of the Bull Moose days). Baruch, certainly, was more of an asset than Knox. On the one hand, he symbolized business sagacity. On the other, his criticisms of the businessmen in the defense agencies had been more devastating and more outspoken than any ventured by the New Dealers.

The press catered to him and he made a great point of catering to no one.

All too often, the merits of a claim are at variance with the ballyhoo of public relations. Baruch's claim to take over from SPAB, however, was as sound as it was plausible. In terms of policy, his advocacy of coordinating requirements was about to be given recognition. In terms of men, his becoming the Chairman of the next Board would keep Nelson working as a purchasing-agent and enable Knudsen to go to work as a production engineer. Knudsen and Nelson were competent journeymen at the operating level, miscast and expended at the policy level. But Baruch was a seasoned journeyman at the coordinating level. Nothing is more abhorrent to a journeyman than to go unemployed—nothing, that is, than to go unemployed while masters of other trades make failures of his. At this point, however, Baruch was available, as ever, politically, but unsuitable: he was disappointed but certainly not discredited. Nelson was promoted from the protection of the purchasing agent's procedures to conspicuous responsibility and eventual oblivion.

STATISTICS furnished the arguments in the pre-Pearl Harbor debate over the Victory Program. But the question at issue was one of time, not of figures. It was not *how much* of *what* America could produce under one or another set or combination of circumstances, but rather for *how long* the precarious security and the precious opportunity offered by the months of War-in-Peace could be trusted to continue.

The debate upset the rules of occupational advocacy. The civilian calculators of the statistics of victory clamored for immediate conversion to a war economy whose controls, they, ardently hoped, they would be allowed to regulate. But the military insisted that, short of war, preparedness had to remain a subordinate and relatively specialized function of the civilian economy over whose workings, however, they demanded veto and supervisory power. In this situation, which was neither war nor peace—which was war-in-peace—the civilians and the military were trying to do each other's jobs.

The fact was that, as only Stimson was blunt enough to say in so many words, only war could force the job that had to be done. A great many people realized this, but their minds had room only for the question, How can America enter the war in Europe? Roosevelt shrank not only from the answer, he shrank from the question. Between the time the defense program began to improve business conditions and the last quarter of 1941, Roosevelt's evasions were supported by a new and most welcome prosperity. Consumer income rose from the rate of $75 billion early in 1940 to the rate of $100 billion late in 1941, and consumer expenditures rose with it. But, on the eve of Pearl Harbor, priorities unemployment and, worse still, priorities reemployment forced a leveling off in the consumer boom. To be sure, consumer income was due to double in four years, reaching a prodigious rate of $150 billion by the beginning of 1944, and prices were about to be effectively controlled. Nevertheless, the scarcity of goods and services, of manpower and necessities, was forecasting an abrupt and imminent decline in the standard of living or, at any rate, in the standard of convenience; and this warning of dislocation in store for the economy was in turn forecasting a new round of protest from the voters.

At this time of dislocation and insecurity, Roosevelt received his most valuable advice from that widely publicized symbol of Bad Government, Boss Kelly of Chicago. Kelly told the President that too much subtlety was self-defeating in politics—that paradoxes and fine shadings only confuse the people and never evoke a mass response. He recognized without hesitation that Roosevelt was right in assuming that most of the country was against war, and he even declared that most of the people who supported Roosevelt did so because they believed he would keep them out of it. The lower income groups, he asserted, were not concerned about world problems, and supported F.D.R. because they remembered what he had done for them in dollars and cents, and they were either grateful or they expected more. Up to then, Kelly believed, the voters had accepted the emergency because of the boom. "But your problem," he told Roosevelt, in so many words, "is to keep your supporters bought. They're not in any mood to pay a price to go along with you."

Kelly's conclusion, however, was far less cynical than his reasoning. Since the people are going to discover simultaneously that war is inevitable and sacrifice inescapable he counseled, tell them so, and

assure the working people and the little fellows that they won't do all the sacrificing. You've got to give everybody the feeling that the fellow making $1,000 a year more than himself will be making more sacrifices. Right now, most people suspect that everyone with more money will have to sacrifice less. The voters want to be told the truth —and, if it's as grim as they suspect, they will want you to put the Emergency program into the hands of a man who commands your respect and who can win theirs.

From Stimson these words had sounded like mere principle and, when Roosevelt discounted them, Stimson himself agreed that he was no politician. From Ickes the same words had sounded like mere opposition, useful in a negative way but requiring no action.

Hopkins was present when Kelly in his own inimitable patois echoed Stimson's prose and Ickes's invective, and he resented it as Roosevelt did not. Hopkins did not speak up to Roosevelt himself, and he eyed anyone who did as an intruder. He has been glorified as the New Dealer who put principle above faction. Yet in this crisis, when Stimson and Ickes, who were not machine politicians, and Kelly, who was, pressed for plain-speaking, Hopkins opposed them for the usual political reason—war was unpopular and prosperity was not.

Roosevelt, however, was anything but resentful of Kelly. He took the shrewd old boss's testimony as evidence that he faced another crisis—reminiscent on a larger scale of his election campaign crisis in 1940—which he could hope to control only by ignoring politics-as-usual and invoking the politics of principle. Then he had defied all known taboos by launching the draft. Now he embraced the Victory Program, which frankly anticipated war production and not war boom.

PEARL HARBOR soon supplied the war. Roosevelt immediately stipulated what the economy would have to supply: 60,000 planes, 45,000 tanks, 20,000 anti-aircraft guns, and 8,000,000 tons of shipping by the end of 1942. More significant than the figures was their impact. By the end of 1941, munitions accounted for only 15 percent of our production. In 1942 production rose substantially and more than half of it went into munitions. Appropriations exceeded $100,000,000,000 and war production (at controlled prices) exceeded $30,000,000,000. Civilian output, on the other hand, fell by more than a quarter.

Kelly had urged Roosevelt to talk war and to act through a man—through one man—whom the people would trust to administer equality of sacrifice. This clearly eliminated everyone who had been in control of OPM. It also eliminated Henry Wallace, who, as Chairman of SPAB, should have been in control of OPM but who was not even in control of himself. Those having to press him for operating decisions took to referring to him as "the Prisoner of Zenda"—Mme. Zenda was a fashionable Washington astrologer. Members of SPAB complained that his self-conscious giggling and his self-deluding mysticism had turned its meetings into travesties. And SPAB itself, instead of leading the economy or, for that matter, of following it, had further complicated the OPM procedures it was created to simplify, and was plainly disintegrating.

Roosevelt had recognized for some time that the home front had grown too big, too complicated, too controversial to be administered personally by him. He lacked the time, the energy, and the firsthand experience that would be needed to arrive at solutions of the problems involved. This exposed him to the daily hazards of a disturbing dilemma: either he had to proclaim, for instance, on the authority of lieutenants like Stettinius, that the country enjoyed a surplus of steel, or he had to disavow his own experts. The first alternative had already compromised him, and the second threatened to demoralize his Administration.

The problem was a standard one in the business world, and it called for a standard solution—the principal must recognize that the time has come to promote himself to the Chairmanship of the Board, and to find a successor qualified to represent him as deputy without and executive within. This reality Roosevelt accepted, criticism to the contrary notwithstanding, and he improvised a brilliant, and simple, political analogy for it: if the Constitution called for a Vice-President, the situation called for an Assistant President.

Roosevelt was right, and his instinct for timing was right. In deciding that he needed an Assistant President, and in resolving to look outside the emergency agencies for the right man, he was trying to put behind him the period of his dependence upon businessmen as public relations exhibits. Because his businessmen had failed, an administrative receivership was at hand; and this, in turn, forecast the coming of a political receivership in 1944. For Wallace had wasted the opportunity presented by the Chairmanship of SPAB to convert the Vice-Presidency into the Assistant Presidency; and, although he happened at the

moment to be growing into a formidable political symbol of the latter-day New Deal, his administrative
fecklessness had already sentenced him to certain political death in 1944.

Wallace's default might have been expected to open
the way for Baruch to take over the administrative
receivership. Instead, it eliminated the wily Sage. For
the fact that the war Presidency was now headed inescapably towards a political receivership outweighed
every other claim Baruch had upon the administrative
receivership. Roosevelt wanted the man to whom he
entrusted the administrative receivership in 1942 to
grow into the political receivership in 1944, and he
said so. His choice was Supreme Court Justice Douglas, for whom he had shown special affection and regard. Douglas had already demonstrated his capacity
for administrative leadership, and Roosevelt believed
him capable of developing the attributes of political
leadership as well.

"Whoever takes this job and does it as you can do
it," Roosevelt told Douglas, in offering him the Chairmanship of what was soon to be the War Production
Board, "will have the first call on the Democratic
nomination for President in 1944." "You will run
again," Douglas replied, accepting the offer.

CHAPTER XI

THE POLITICAL RECEIVERSHIP

HARRY HOPKINS had, by this time, attained a position which transcended the realm of conventional politics. As Assistant to the President and plenipotentiary to heads of associated governments, he had put the New Deal and all ordinary Party transactions behind and beneath him. Hence Sherwood and his other admirers, and even those who hated him for deserting the New Deal, conceived the illusion that he had become a selfless, dedicated soldier and nothing more. But in fact, to protect his new position, he could still maneuver, and had maneuvered, as ruthlessly, cynically, and masterfully as ever.

One of the most dangerous aspects of Hopkins's manipulations was his penchant for staffing the centers of political and administrative power with weak and amateurish men as a means of preventing able men from gaining position from which they could threaten his ascendancy. One such protégé was Stettinius, whom he installed in Lend-Lease and in the diplomatic succession. A second was Wallace, whom, in 1940, he put into the Presidential succession. Robert Sherwood has depicted Hopkins's role in the 1940 convention as that of a man who unselfishly undertook a disagreeable duty in a convention which was "vulgar" and "unruly." But the convention was no more

vulgar, no more unruly than those other Democratic
assemblages which nominated Roosevelt in 1932,
1936, and, later, 1944. Nor was it, in fact, more reluctant to nominate Roosevelt. What it was reluctant
to do was to award the Vice-Presidency to Henry
Wallace. History has already given a striking perspective on the judgment of those elements which were
"unruly" in their resistance to having Wallace thrust
upon them. But Hopkins had made Wallace his candidate, and persuaded Roosevelt to endorse this
choice, had isolated Roosevelt from Farley, and had
then brought about a situation in which neither
Byrnes, nor McNutt, nor Justice Douglas could be
nominated in opposition to his protégé.

Now Roosevelt's arrangement with Douglas to appoint him to the chairmanship of the WPB sent Hopkins searching frantically for a third protégé—Nelson.
Douglas was a strong man, and no amateur. Moreover, the Executive Order creating SPAB had recognized that the production authority needed jurisdiction over requirements and allocations for the entire
home front, including the area of off-shore aid. SPAB,
to be sure, had been a paper body; but for that very
reason, the Assistant Presidency awaiting the new
production czar was bound to carry real power to
supervise and limit Hopkins's Assistantship to the
President. Consequently, Hopkins opposed Roosevelt,
and resorted to political manipulation to defeat Roosevelt's purpose. He succeeded.

Like any other politician at work on a job of
eliminating a candidate he could not hope to control,
Hopkins proceeded on the time-honored rule that

"You can't beat somebody with nobody." He therefore provided himself with Nelson as his "somebody,"
and set out to beat off the threat he saw in Douglas.
He used three lines of attack. First, and most effectively, he exploited his influence with Churchill and
Beaverbrook to conjure up a picture of Douglas as a
callow, shallow, "bleeding-heart liberal," greedy for
personal power but unawakened to the urgencies of
the situation, uninformed as to the administrative
problems involved, unsympathetic to the businessmen
who alone could be trusted to solve them, unap-
preciative of the need for underwriting the British
Empire, and, more sinister still in Hopkins's thumb-
nail sketch, anxious to see America's productive power
brought to bear across the Pacific in time to save
China. Hopkins was appealing to Beaverbrook in his
ex officio capacity as the British Hearst, at a time
when Beaverbrook, as Minister of Supply, was quite
properly agitating for more Lend-Lease. Duly aroused
by Hopkins, Beaverbrook exercised against Douglas a
veto power which Roosevelt was bound to respect—
after all, it was Beaverbrook with whom the new production czar would have to work. Churchill, who was
visiting in Washington, and with whom Roosevelt was
feeling his way—and disagreeing—had also been
alerted and was also quoted. Hopkins thereupon used
the high-frequency channels of the Frankfurter broad-
casting system to spread the word that the British
were dismayed with Douglas and hoped that the President would realize how impossible a choice he was.
Meanwhile, Nelson was exposed to Churchill and, more
particularly, to Beaverbrook under Hopkins's benevo-

lent auspices, and word was duly passed around Washington that the British found him sound.

Hopkins's second stratagem was equally unworthy of a single-minded patriot-soldier dedicated to victory. He cautioned Roosevelt that to plan on running with Douglas in 1944 might not be good politics—this would merely substitute one New Dealer for another as Vice-President. A businessman, he suggested, might make a more effective running-mate. That Nelson was the most plausible businessman available for a political build-up was evident.

These two operations were conspiratorial. But Hopkins's third tactic was printable and therefore he disclosed it to Sherwood. In a memo dated January 14, 1942, and reproduced by Sherwood, Hopkins admits that "the President . . . played seriously with the idea of getting Bill Douglas off the Supreme Court and, in fact, talked to Douglas about it." The memo continues as if Hopkins had been in Douglas's confidence, and as if Douglas had not given his whole-hearted assent to the proposal: "but Douglas never had much enthusiasm for it."

At Hyde Park the week-end of January 10–11, after Douglas had accepted Roosevelt's offer, the memo goes on, in a tone of suppressed exasperation,

> The President talked of getting a three-man committee made up of Willkie, Douglas and Nelson. . . . I urged very strongly that this not be done, primarily because neither Willkie nor Douglas knew anything about production and because Willkie was apt to use it as a political football.
>
> He came back to the idea again later and I told him for

the second time that I thought he was making a great mistake. I told him that if he were going to move in this manner, my suggestion was to appoint Don Nelson, who was the best of the lot.

He was sympathetic with the President, had had a good record under severe conditions; that furthermore he belonged to the school that wanted to increase production and believed that it could be done; that he was easy to get on with and that the President liked him. I told the President that the most important asset, apart from the man's ability, was that he had the President's confidence.

Upon our return to Washington, the President told me that he thought Nelson was the man. I then urged him to make the appointment at once because it would surely spread all over town and all the people who wanted the job would be bombarding him with reasons why Nelson should not be appointed.*

This statement was clearly dictated by an uneasy conscience and in shrewd anticipation of violent repercussions. It was a record in Hopkins's own defense, and yet it reveals the flagrantly selfish and political nature of his motives. To begin with, it was shallowly prejudicial to Willkie, who had impaired his candidacy by the extent of his cooperation with Roosevelt, and whom Roosevelt was to trust enough to offer the Secretaryship of War later on. At the same time, it was hostile to Douglas, by innuendo, and from Hopkins's personal standpoint. Nelson was easy to get on with, the memo says, implying that Douglas was not (as if Hopkins himself was). A genuinely unselfish soldier would have recognized that Douglas had no trouble getting on with Roosevelt, and that camaraderie was hardly a

* Robert E. Sherwood, *Roosevelt and Hopkins* (New York, Harper & Brothers, 1948), p. 475.

qualification for the Assistant Presidency one month after Pearl Harbor.

Camaraderie was the outstanding characteristic Nelson brought to the responsibility of command; and Hopkins, by his own testimony, was the palace politician who manipulated him into the office.

But it was not only to Douglas as Assistant President, it was to the very idea of an Assistant President, that Hopkins was opposed. This was a fundamental point. But Roosevelt had resolved to create an Assistant Presidency—and rightly so. For, with the coming of war, mobilization ceased to be merely a problem of production. Instead, the problem had to be solved at the level at which the two components of national energy, production and manpower, gear in with one another. The merging of the familiar, and profitable, flow of war production with the new, and controversial, demands for manpower meant that the problems of production had to be dealt with at the White House level and not at the agency level, by a Presidential deputy and not by an agency head.

It was because war production had to be administered at the White House level that Roosevelt had fastened on Douglas. And it was because he wanted to eliminate Douglas that Hopkins had argued that the new production czar had to qualify at the agency level as a technician. In persuading Roosevelt to pass over Douglas and pick Nelson, Hopkins had accomplished half his purpose—he contrived to have Douglas bypassed. But he did not prevent the creation of the Assistant Presidency: he merely postponed it by ten months; James F. Byrnes left the Supreme Court for the White House in October. By then, Nelson had been chopped down below the level of the agency and Department heads whom he had been appointed to direct; and his production czardom had been deflated into one of many rival baronies. Moreover, thanks to Nelson's failure to qualify for the Assistant Presidency, Hopkins ended by being as far from controlling the succession as he had been when Wallace failed to seize the opportunity of the Vice-Presidency.

In any case, Nelson's failure as production czar confirmed Roosevelt's judgment, and refuted Hopkins's advocacy—what was needed after Pearl Harbor was not another businessman to follow Stettinius, Knudsen, and Nelson as production czar, but an Assistant President authorized to mediate the running conflict between the requirements of the war production program and the capacities of the war economy.

Ten months of war convinced Roosevelt that he needed an Assistant President, but to do a job altogether different from the one projected in January. Pearl Harbor had shaken his faith in the adequacy of momentum: this faith had rested on his original assumption that America had enough time to trust momentum and, momentarily, Pearl Harbor challenged this assumption. Roosevelt had made his mind up to appoint Douglas because he felt the need to hedge his standing bet on momentum with a new bet on leadership. Instead, he appointed Nelson and stayed with his bet on momentum without leadership. He won it. The momentum was not long in swamping Nelson. But, meanwhile, it took the pressure off Roosevelt to find the ablest and most vigorous and

imaginative deputy with whom he could make war
against the country's enemies. Momentum, accelerated
after Pearl Harbor, was soon to make possible the
planning of the invasion of Africa, and his need was
for a deputy who would be content to make peace
among the country's leaders.

The *ex officio* mediator in the Presidential circle
was Byrnes and, accordingly, it was he whom Roosevelt finally made Assistant President. As director of
the administrative receivership, Byrnes became heir
apparent pro tem to the political receivership. He
made a perfect foil for Roosevelt to use against Wallace and, in the process, became fair game himself.
Hopkins had dismissed Douglas with the sneer that
to replace one New Dealer with another was pointless.
But Byrnes's bid for the succession put the burden on
Hopkins, and on Roosevelt, of answering a new question: Could Wallace be replaced by anyone not a 100
percent New Dealer?

THE maneuvers which finally installed Nelson as production czar deflated Knudsen-Hillman into a pair of
pathetic victims of political persecution. Every headline proclaimed their failure. Hourly rumors foretold
the time and the details of their being purged. In vain
their friends pointed to the progress of production
outside Washington. This merely intensified the criticism. Credit for the country's achievements went to
Roosevelt; blame for Washington's administration of
those achievements fell upon his appointees. Well
might he have reminded his political enemies that
their familiar taunt—he planned it that way—had

become a boast again. Within a month after Pearl Harbor, he was ready to elevate a new expendable. The idealistic young king-makers in OPM who looked up to Nelson as *their* businessman declared open war against Knudsen.

Nelson's own story of his appointment, told long after the event in *Arsenal of Democracy*, is definitely misleading. He declares that he had no idea why he was asked to come to the White House; that he did not understand what the "new and mysterious" War Production Board (about which all Washington was talking) could be; and that news that he was to head it was "the shock of my life." But we have Hopkins's accurate version of what happened in the White House on that fateful day. Nelson apparently forgot all about Hopkins's part in his promotion and, incidentally, about Hopkins's presence at the meeting. Sherwood quotes from Hopkins's carefully filed memorandum of January 13:

At 5:30 that afternoon he [Roosevelt] asked Wallace and Nelson to come to his office and wanted me present. . . . He . . . told Wallace that in order to give Nelson the kind of authority he must have, Nelson would have to be Chairman of the Board and the Chairman would have to have all the power. I had a few hours earlier seen Nelson to prepare him for the meeting.*

What Hopkins reveals shows not only how far from mystified and surprised Nelson was, but how mystified and surprised he had to pretend to be lest Wallace discover that he had dissolved without notice the

* Robert E. Sherwood, *Roosevelt and Hopkins* (New York, Harper & Brothers, 1948), p. 20.

Wallace-Nelson partnership, solemnized by their joint venture in control of SPAB. For Wallace, it was necessary to succeed as Assistant President in order to survive as Vice-President, and his success as Assistant President assumed a combination of his political dynamism and Nelson's technical competence. But Nelson had discovered that, in the political atmosphere of war (especially of defensive war), technical competence quickly generates a political dynamism of its own. Throughout, Nelson was sensitive to his obligation to Wallace as his senior partner and sponsor in SPAB, and, therefore, he was careful to include the genuinely mystified heir-apparent in his "faint suspicion" of what the President was leading up to. Actually, as all the participants in the Washington game except Wallace and his intimates were quick to see, Wallace's silent partner had now emerged as his open rival.

Hopkins's disclosure of Nelson's duplicity makes Nelson's subsequent narrative coherent and rational. On his own showing as a bewildered bystander, it is not. For how does he recall reacting to the shock of discovering at long last that he is to be head of WPB? Like any other successful conspirator. He returns to his office to be "greeted by a rather jubilant group of my associates," whom he does not name but who were named at the time in publications throughout the country as his campaign managers. The most energetic and influential members of the cabal were Robert Nathan, to whom great credit was in fact due as the imaginative economist principally responsible for formulating the Victory Program objectives; and the

precocious personnel manager and scout for Justice
Frankfurter's Washington organization, Edward F.
Pritchard. Nathan was an idealist interested only in
ideas, and Pritchard was interested only in their ex-
ploitation.

Nathan was a principal author of the Victory Pro-
gram, and Nelson was the chief whom he trusted to
make it a reality. But Nelson, sitting in the White
House with Churchill, Beaverbrook, Hopkins, and
Knudsen, admits that he was "startled" and "alarmed"
to hear the President say that we would need—and
could build—45,000 tanks and 60,000 planes in 1942.
Roosevelt did not conjure these figures out of thin air.
He settled on them after studying data supplied by
Nathan and like-minded economists in OPM, of which
Nelson was Priorities Director. These economists were
exasperated with Knudsen because he lacked the
imagination to believe that the objectives they visualized could be achieved. They believed in Nelson because he assured them that these same objectives were
practical. It was this program which inspired Nathan
and the rest to campaign for Nelson as the realistic
idealist behind whom they could hope to carry it out.
Yet at the climax of their campaign, weeks after the
program itself had been reduced to a slogan and accepted by the President, Nelson was "startled" and
"alarmed" to hear Roosevelt say what the program
was and that he meant to get it accomplished.

NELSON's predecessors were foredoomed to failure by
the circumstances of their appointment to office. The
Presidential directives creating SPAB, OPM, NDAC,

and the WRB were, one and all, administratively unworkable and politically vulnerable. The WPB order,
on the other hand, was as nearly perfect as any single
Presidential instrument can be. Nelson's predecessors
were denied power commensurate with the responsibilities thrust upon them. The power given Nelson, on
the other hand, was greater than he ever dared use.
Indeed, he lived in mortal fear of having to use it.
Inevitably, his failure gutted the concept of WPB
and scrapped the Executive Order creating it. Thus
he was the one plausible candidate for the Rooseveltian succession who failed in spite of the administrative instrument Roosevelt gave him to work with.

Nelson's failure followed swiftly and inexorably from
his decision—if decision it was—not to use the administrative apparatus which had been put at his
disposal. That his understanding of the WPB order
was limited to fear of the power it conferred upon him
seems clear. Certainly, he was content to take office
under the order handed him without tracing its origins
back to the suppressed Baruch Report for the discredited War Resources Board. Bruce Catton, who
worked for Nelson and believed in him, quotes Nelson
in his own book—*The War Lords of Washington*—as
admitting that he never studied the War Resources
Board Report.

Actually no more than a handful of people, all bound
to confidence, knew what the Baruch-Hancock report
had recommended. (Months after the war, Secretary
of War Patterson told John Hancock that he had
never seen the report, and, when informed that it had
constituted the basis for the order creating the War

Production Board in 1942, confessed that no copy of it was to be found in even the top secret files of the War Department.) Consequently, the political high jinks that had bounced the Stettinius Board into the national spotlight and out again in the autumn of 1939 threatened Roosevelt with no embarrassment when at last, in the winter of 1942, he adopted the forgotten plan that had been prepared for the Board. For, weighed politically rather than in terms of efficiency, the practical effect of dissolving the Board and suppressing its report without publicity in 1939 had been to free Roosevelt to follow its recommendations at any time thereafter without mentioning Stettinius or Baruch—and without confiding in Nelson. And this is exactly what he did.

The powers Roosevelt gave to WPB were the simple and inescapable ones outlined in the Baruch-Hancock report to the Stettinius Board. They were sweeping, and they carried jurisdiction over the entire war economy. After peace had come and Roosevelt had gone, Baruch complained to a Senate Committee that Roosevelt's refusal to act on his report at the time had wasted untold lives and resources. The "adviser of Presidents" had a real grievance. In the summer of 1939, he had described the function that had to be performed. And, in the winter of 1942, Roosevelt had authorized Nelson to have WPB perform them. Baruch's suppressed report of 1939 had indeed served as the blueprint for Roosevelt's "discovery" of 1942, and it was this which, with appropriate fanfare, Roosevelt christened the War Production Board. To prove that this "discovery" was his own and worthy of him,

Roosevelt let it be known that his War Production Board bore no resemblance to anything that had been recommended to him by anyone connected with the discredited War Resources Board. And, although the War Resources Board had been Roosevelt's promotion, by this time all memory of it had come to be associated with Baruch. In 1939 the only assignment Roosevelt had given the hapless and bewildered Stettinius had been to work with Baruch. And in 1942 the only assurance Roosevelt had had to give the hapless and bewildered Nelson, as head of WPB, was that Baruch had been repudiated. Nelson took this to mean that the cliché called militarism had been repudiated.

Nelson believed the gossip of the moment about Baruch and, for the moment, it was true. But nothing is more treacherous than a truth which swings with a political pendulum. This was such a truth. For implicit in Roosevelt's assurance to Nelson was a threat to him; and, by the same token, implicit in Roosevelt's repudiation of Baruch was a commitment to him. Indeed, early in 1943 the truth of 1942 did turn into its opposite—Roosevelt repudiated Nelson and pressed Baruch to take his place. But Nelson could see neither the threat of the future nor the pattern of the past.

Nor could he see the simple, single problem of problems—the problem of gauging requirements and allocating capacities to meet them. Because he proved incapable of moving vigorously to anticipate requirements before they turned into pressures, he was found incapable of rationing out priorities among the people with a plausible, or powerful, claim to them.

The immediate reason why Nelson—that is, one man, one civilian—had been given unprecedented and far-reaching power over the war economy was that SPAB, an unwieldy committee, divided and paralyzed, had failed to fulfill its mission, which was to set requirements. Nelson's default had given the military control over the production of all lines of matériel. But who was to say which schedule of priorities would produce too much, and which too little? Which would produce planes without fuel to fly them and which shells without guns to shoot them, and which combat troops without landing craft to carry them? All that could be said was that the military, when working in the dark, must as a matter not merely of power but of duty, control any and all home front operations. When the military did, the civilians protested. The military acknowledged the force of this protest. The War and Navy Departments agreed that the home front was *the* civilian theater; and readily consented to the grant of every last iota of power the civilians demanded in the WPB order. Not only did the military cooperate with this effort of the civilians to reassert their proper claim to control over the home front: they stood aside—irresponsibly, as they soon discovered—and let the civilians settle on who the new czar was to be.

Roosevelt, moreover, protected Nelson against any new invasion of his sphere of command by the military. For it was at the Presidential level, and not at the agency level, that the over-all munitions objectives for 1942 were set. This was a directive of the Commander-in-Chief, accepted by him at the suggestion of the civilians and binding on the military. All that remained for Nelson to do was to schedule the production requirements—by industries, by products, by components, by materials, by man-hours, and by months—needed to meet the President's estimate of matériel requirements. The President had settled the controversial question of How Much. What he delegated to Nelson was the technical question of How.

THE War and Navy Departments immediately reorganized themselves to attack the problem of How. Under the broad and simple division of labor contemplated in the WPB Order, contract procurement remained the administrative responsibility of the military. To meet its obligations to the home front commander, the War Department created a home front command of its own. In February, 1942, the Army Engineers, the Signal Corps, the Medical Corps and, of course, the Quartermaster and the Ordnance Departments were lumped together into the Services of Supply, under the command of General Brehon Somervell, a man loud and strong, stubborn and shrewd, destined for controversy and not frustrated. The Services of Supply, presently streamlined into the Army Service Forces, centralized into an aggressive and disciplined military formation the entire procurement function—and purchasing power—of the War Department (with the exception of the aircraft specialists who remained under the combat control of the Army Air Forces).

Forrestal had previously agreed with Patterson that the War Department was to buy certain of the equip-

ment and supplies needed in common by both services, notably small arms ammunition and food. This
left the Navy Department responsible, in turn, for
other items, such as fuel oil and for its specialized
needs: for construction, for transportation equipment,
for ordnance. Its parallel reorganization to gear these
specialized home front operations into WPB's machinery of command is perhaps best described by the
then Secretary of the Navy in a letter to the author,
dated July 4, 1944:

What I regard (maybe other people wouldn't agree) as
my principal contribution to the acceleration of the Naval
building program was the creation of the Office of Procurement and Material, headed up by Vice Admiral S. M.
Robinson. Without this I believe the Navy Department
would have been unable to function. These are the reasons:

1.   There are five main procurement bureaus in the Department—Supplies & Accounts, Ships, Aeronautics, Ordnance, Yards & Docks. In peace time the Bureaus operated
on a competitive bidding basis with the technical contracting work and the legal work being done by Supplies &
Accounts and the Judge Advocate General's Office, respectively. Each Bureau operated on a highly individualistic basis although a certain amount of control was exercised by Supplies & Accounts, on a detail level. There
was, of course, no such thing as negotiated buying in the
normal commercial sense, because everything had to be
done by competitive bidding.

2.   As I have said, all these Bureaus were fairly individualistic. There were cross lines between Bureaus. For
example, Aeronautics decided what planes it wanted to
buy, held consultations with the individual companies,
agreed on specifications, terms, etc., but then all of this
had to be shoveled over to Supplies & Accounts for what

Frank Folsom used to call "flyspecking." The papers then came back and were again shoveled up to the Judge Advocate General's Office for legal clearance.

3. It was obvious that these procedures could not obtain when we were swelling from around a half a billion a year in expenditures up to twenty-eight billions and when practically everything had to be bought on a negotiated basis. Furthermore, with various controls put into effect by OPA, WPB, ODT, etc., the Navy had to deal with these agencies as a whole rather than through individual divisions.

4. In order to bring together all of these loose ends and threads and to give solidarity for the Navy in the presentation of its material requirements, its priority demands, etc., I set up, in March of 1942, the Office of Procurement and Material. Admiral Robinson, who was the Chief of the Bureau of Ships, was made Vice Admiral and head of the new office. He set up an organization which did three things:

(.01) *Statistics*: I got Don Belcher from American Telephone & Telegraph as head of the Planning & Statistics Division. His task was to set up a bill of materials for Navy procurement—that is to say what its lump requirements were in terms of steel, copper, aluminum, etc., and to keep track of progress of our various building programs, this being accomplished in the form of a monthly Status Report and a semi-monthly Progress Report.

(.02) *Procurement*: You may remember that Nelson was given powers by the President for over-all supervision of Army and Navy Procurement. I immediately got Frank Folsom from his staff at WPB to become the head of Procurement. To him Nelson delegated his powers and I mine (this knit together the WPB and the Navy, and in due course the Army, which followed suit by taking Al Browning as Folsom's opposite number).

(.03) *Production*: Joe Powell, and subsequently Admiral Jones, became head of Production, and by that I mean merely the follow-up of production where it was spotty, getting managements for concerns that had poor ones, etc.

I don't believe anybody else except Robinson could have performed this job for me. He had been Chief of the Bureau of Ships, is a brilliant engineer, and has a most extraordinary personality which commands the respect of the whole Navy. Incidentally, he had a son in the Navy who is now a prisoner of war, taken at Wake. The other two main things that loom in my mind are Logistics, about which I became a fanatic after a visit to the Pacific in the summer of '42—just after Guadalcanal. It was obvious that the old concept of Naval logistics— the ship coming to port and the supply officer being left to fill his requisitions at the base—was no longer valid. It was clear that the Pacific war meant a dynamic and continuous flow of supplies. The Navy's logistic organization now is good, although there is still need for indoctrination—competent officers would rather be at sea than behind a desk, but even the most ardent seagoers are now aware of the fact that no matter how hard your fist may be it is only as good as your reach. My view of logistics is not unique with me; as a matter of fact I don't want to give the impression that the Navy wouldn't have become alive itself to its needs in this respect. It would have, I am sure, and I also know that my ideas could not have been put into effect without the equally zealous support of Vice Admiral Horne and his crowd, who include Rear Admirals Farber, Purnell, Good, McCormick, Poco Smith, and Captain Chapline. (Another good man was Rear Admiral Oscar Badger, now in the South Pacific.) Logistics is of course a very broad term and includes munitions, equipment, personnel, interlocked and precise planning on railroad transportation, ships, depots, shipping points, etc. Walter Franklin of the Pennsylvania Railroad was a great help to us on shipping. I hope to see a course in logistics included in the curriculum at Annapolis.

As far as other jobs are concerned, the ones that I took the greatest satisfaction in were Destroyer Escorts and

Landing Craft, particularly because in both cases the statisticians said that they couldn't be done. I think you are fairly familiar with the Destroyer Escort story. We were scheduled for 260 in the year 1943 and we got 306. Here again, however, it would be dangerous to attribute this to any individual effort. It was the contributions of Admiral Cochrane of the Bureau of Ships, Admiral Irish who was in charge of the Material Coordinating agency in New York; Francis Gibbs of Gibbs & Cox; Captain Morgan Watt of the Bureau of Ships; and Charlie Wilson and Cap Krug of WPB. Incidentally, these programs, in my opinion, could not have been accomplished—neither could have a good many others—without Eberstadt's Controlled Materials Plan.

If there is any meat in the above you are welcome to it. I hope you will keep in mind my constant cry that it is the team and not the individual. I am not being modest when I say that none of these things that occur to me as I write could have been done unless I had the strong and competent people who are available in the Navy. By and large they are as good a crowd of men as is found anywhere, and for practical as well as generous reasons I would rather give them credit than myself.

Sincerely yours,
James Forrestal

P.S. A man to whom I would also like to give some credit is H. Struve Hensel, who became head of what I designated the Procurement Legal Division. Under him we put young and competent legal talent in the Bureaus where they could do work on contracts at their inception rather than at the end—(contracts used to come to me for reading after they had been processed by the Judge Advocate General's Office). It was obvious that such a reading was of no constructive value. By having the work done down at the roots we were able to get procedures much more nearly like ordinary commercial practice. To get this done without upsetting the Judge Advocate General and the usual procedure of the Navy was a delicate task, because the civilian procedures had to be meshed in with the military organization. It is due to Hensel's ability and personal tact that this was accomplished. He and Admiral Gatch, the Navy Judge Advocate General, now work in the closest harmony and cooperation.

ELEMENTARY efficiency dictated these moves by the military. But, once made, they served a political purpose too. The WPB order had established absolute civilian control over the home front, and it taxed the military with reducing the directives of the civilians to contractual form and to military reality. Paper work is a notorious hazard for the military mind, and Somervell was charged with coping with it. Boasting that no subordinate of his "ever made the same mistake twice," he deputized General Lucius D. Clay to administer the process of continuous and automatic translation, back and forth, between fighting front requirements and home front commitments, between fighting front commitments and home front requirements.

No appointment was more strategic or more fortunate. An officer of unlimited courage and crystalline resolution, Clay happened also to be a virtuoso at the art of General Staff planning of matériel flow and logistical support. His was the responsibility for budgeting enough of everything in the right place and at the right time for each fighting unit; and his was the responsibility for transforming paper budgets into fire power.

Politically, in terms of the running duel between the civilians and the military, the military needed such a home front command, and such a commander, to meet their obligations to their civilian superiors. Granted competence and firmness on Nelson's part, the reorganization of the War and Navy Departments was dictated by considerations of political self-defense—they had to brace themselves to hold their own against the civilians. In fact, far from having to resist civilian encroachment on their proper preserves, the military soon found themselves charging into the vacuum created by Nelson's default.

The clearest account of this default is provided by the Budget Bureau history, which is avowedly pro-Nelson, and by Nelson himself. WPB's Requirements Committee, says the former,

like SPAB, was plagued by the inadequacy of data on which to base decisions and by the inadequacy of arrangements to assure that its broad decisions were executed in detail. . . . [It] was made up of representatives of the leading claimants, each fighting to keep the other fellow's piece of the material pie small and his own big. Though the decision always rested with Mr. Nelson's representative in this struggle, the lion's share went to meet immediate military demands, to the undue sacrifice at times of equally good claims of the railroads, of housing for workers, mining machinery and agricultural tools, or of aid to the Allies.

Lost in this expression of pseudo-liberal resentment against the military is all recognition of the reality that wartime shortages disrupt General Staff planning into a succession of over-the-field risks, rather less than more calculated, and involve the assignment of priorities under conflicting pressures to one theater of war over another—or, worse still, the assignment of priorities of one type of fire power to one theater and of other types to other theaters, diluting the effectiveness of all. Civilian control of a war economy rests, after all, on the ability of civilian commanders to avoid shortages, genuine or imaginary. Shortages spread confusion; and confusion invites the substitution of military pressure for civilian control. The fact was, as the Budget Bureau apologia does not admit, that the civilians failed to use their pre-war opportunity to prepare the civilian economy for mobilization. After Pearl Harbor, the hope of imposing orderly civilian controls upon the war economy hinged upon Nelson's ability and determination to eliminate the administrative confusion responsible for shortages; and, therefore, it was foredoomed to disappointment.

"In order not to disturb a going system and cause delay," the Budget Bureau history explains, "Mr. Nelson continued the priority system which had been built up under the Office of Production Management, and immediately authorized the Army-Navy Munitions Board to assign priorities to all Army, Navy, Maritime, and Coast Guard procurement." This defense of Nelson gives him the benefit of an inaccuracy in the facts, in spite of which it is still a scathing indictment. In fact, Nelson did not merely inherit the priorities system. It had been his system before OPM was created, and it had set the pattern for OPM's failure. The indictment appears in the admission that his first act upon being assigned and empowered in 1942 to restore civil control over priorities was to renew his ruinous default at the outset of this "synchronizing" power to the military. Contrary to Hopkins's pressuring at the time, and to the Budget Bureau's later apologia, the fact that Nelson was certain to continue his ineffectual priorities policy was reason enough not to give him control over production in 1942.

The consequence of this default by Nelson, as the Budget Bureau history itself admits, was endless waste and dislocation:

Locomotive plants went into tank production when locomotives were more necessary than tanks. . . . Truck plants began to produce airplanes, a change that caused shortages of trucks later on. . . . Merchant ships took steel from the Navy, and the landing craft cut into both. The Navy took aluminum from aircraft. Rubber took valves from escort vessels, from petroleum, from the Navy. The pipe-lines took steel from ships, new tools, and the railroads. And at every turn there were foreign demands to be met as well as requirements for new plants. . . .

We built many new factories, and expanded many others [continues this official defense of Nelson's regime which documents his downfall as few exposés could], which we could not use and did not need. Many of these new factories we could not supply with labor or with raw materials, or if we had, we would not have been able to fly the planes or shoot the ammunition that would come out of them. But in the process we used up critical material which might better have gone into something else.

It was not merely to the military that Nelson surrendered his power over priorities. The very corporations which held contracts and needed regulation were invited to regulate themselves. Again, the most devastating testimony against Nelson is that volunteered by his defenders, the Budget Bureau historians: "Any contractor who had an 'A' priority order could place that priority on any material which he in his own judgment decided that he needed to do the work." Their priorities were, as it says in a masterpiece of understatement, "extensible."

The solemn priorities sign had replaced "the silly-fool dollar sign" as the scrip to be honored in the war economy; and it had been debased before it could be put to work. The result was a gigantic and uncontrollable inflation of the war economy scrip system which threatened to unbalance the war economy.

The Budget Bureau history details the facts and figures of this entirely unnecessary dislocation:

The Services were equipped with high priorities, which gave the contractors confidence that they would be able to get the materials and components they required, price arrangements were generous and elastic, and the manufacturers were not unwilling, under pressure, to sign additional contracts even when their plants were already full, hoping to expand, or to find some other method of discharging their inflated obligations. With this combination of circumstances, over $100 billion of contracts were placed in the first six months of 1942. In other words, industry signed up to deliver for war more than the total production of the American economy in the Nation's most prosperous and productive prior year. At the time, there were also some $20 billions of orders outstanding, mostly for munitions. The new orders included $68 billions for munitions, $12.6 billions for industrial expansion, and $6.9 billions for military construction.

Because the larger corporations to which the War and Navy Departments looked for quick and reliable production held most of the "extensible" priorities, and were receiving most of the new construction and expansion contracts, the Budget Bureau apologists for WPB go on to admit: "the result was . . . an over concentration of contracts in the larger corporations and a failure to fully [sic] utilize the facilities of many small manufacturers whose plants could have produced 'bits and pieces.' It did not escape the attention of Congress that better utilization of small plants could have reduced the necessary expansion of facilities." Indeed, the Truman Committee forced this scandal upon the attention of Congress and the country, and thereby gave the chief investigator of the war economy an added opportunity to compete with its administrators for the political receivership.

As early as March, 1942, WPB's Planning Committee warned that uncontrolled expansion was threatening production. But not until the second half of the year did the tide of wasteful construction ebb. And then, it was not regulation but the combination of criticism and shortages which stopped the abuse. Indeed, shortages became so acute in the early summer of 1942 that, in addition to curtailing reckless and aimless expansion, they interfered with production. By July 4, 1942, the ship program, than which nothing was more basic, had to be cut back for lack of steel plate, as well as of glass, turbines, engines, and valves. The consequence was that other programs suffered when, in the fall of 1942, the Navy and Maritime Commissions in self-defense tied up all of the country's valve-making capacity. No more ironical commentary upon the self-defeating irresponsibility of the expansion authorized during the Nelson regime could be imagined. WPB had authorized the expansion of everything except what was most urgently needed.

The galloping inflation of contracts and priorities

was piling up surpluses, on the one hand, and running headlong into shortages on the other. This process of inflation, to be sure, was spurring over-all production to new highs. But production would have broken all records in any case: the output of economic energy reflected the volume of Government spending, not the skill of Government regulators. Semi-supreme powers had been given to Nelson in recognition of the reality that the objective of a war economy is not mere production, measured as an end in itself, but balance in developing units of fighting power. This was the objective Roosevelt had set. But Nelson's toleration of "priorities inflation" sent some divisions of War Production racing far ahead of the Victory Program goals and forced others to lag behind.

Again, the official defense of the Nelson regime summarizes the extent of its failure. "All semblance of balance in the production program disappeared because of the different rates of contracting and of production that resulted from the scramble to place orders. If there ever had been a planned balance between men, ships, tanks, planes, supplies, weapons, ammunition and new facilities, and there is no evidence that there was, that balance disappeared."

"Resignation of power by WPB" to the military is the Budget Bureau's rueful evaluation of the reality behind the ballyhoo of Nelson's crusade against "militarism." And the more abjectly Nelson resigned power to the military, the more shrilly he accused it of "militarism." Indeed, as Nelson and his adversaries in the War Department had now taken to shouting back and forth at each other, there was a war on; and the purpose of war production was to fight it. Everyone claiming a place in the war effort and, above all, the military was daily pressing Nelson for payment of the endless drafts of priorities he had issued against the economy.

THE most formidable representative of those with claims against WPB was, inevitably, the spokesman for the armed forces, Ferdinand Eberstadt, who had become Chairman of the Army-Navy Munitions Board at roughly the same time Nelson had taken over WPB. A most formidable creditors' representative he was. He brought unusually versatile equipment to the task. A financier intimately acquainted with the workings of industry, a magnate frankly sympathetic with the claims and contributions of labor, a remarkably blunt and forceful character of scholarly attainments and penetrating intellect, an administrator able to master endless detail and yet to formulate comprehensive and workable over-all policy—such was the relentless antagonist whom Nelson had to look in the eye each morning and tell which of WPB's promissory notes he would make good.

In desperation, in the summer of 1942, Nelson put forward a plan which had been tried piecemeal by OPM for months on end and without success. It was called PRP (Production Requirements Plan), and it was foredoomed to failure. For instead of simply resigning the priorities power to the military, PRP turned it back to every manufacturer with a contract: it defaulted not to an imaginary threat of militarism, but to a very real threat of chaos.

PRP instructed each contractor and subcontractor to file his priority needs—that is, in effect to issue to himself the priorities he would "need" as fast as he accepted orders. Admittedly, this was wrong and reckless. Nevertheless, PRP's sponsors felt that it was a necessary expedient. For, as late as July, 1942, indeed as late as November, Nelson had neglected to use the powers delegated to him by the Commander-in-Chief to establish a procedure for gauging, much less controlling, the accumulation of inventories. While, on the one hand, the advocates of PRP granted that the plan would tempt manufacturers and, in many situations, force them to call for materials in excess of their strict needs, on the other hand, they argued that PRP would at last give Government some rudimentary machinery for polling manufacturers on their inventories. PRP provided that manufacturers failing to file their priority needs would be cut off from supplies, which meant that PRP gave WPB the power to punish those who did not respond to its order to take over—and abuse—its powers.

Inevitably, PRP detoured production out of the straight line it should have followed from raw material to the finished product. With each subcontract along the way from fully armed and fueled tank to raw ore, there went an irresistible invitation to add an automatically legitimized bonus of priorities—on materials, on manpower, on machinery, and on plant—necessary or useful for completing past orders or getting future ones, or serving corporate purposes at the expense of the war effort. So long as neither WPB nor the military nor companies letting contracts for parts, for components, and for equipment and construction, could guarantee actual deliveries on priorities, every company fighting to keep and to get orders and, for that matter, fighting to protect or to raise profit margins, had to rustle for itself. Little wonder that companies of all sizes felt justified in building their own banks of items in short supply for their own purposes. At last the doctrine of momentum was on trial. Could it make up for all the lost motion WPB was forcing on it?

Within WPB, fortunately, momentum was not trusted to answer the question. By August, Roosevelt and the War and Navy Departments, sensitive to the scrutiny of the Truman Committee and to criticism by both our Allies and our troops, became thoroughly alarmed by the rate at which tank treads were accumulating without armor plate, at which carburetors were accumulating without sets of instruments. North Africa was about to be invaded. Our offensive had to be broadened and supported. The time had come to impose not merely a director upon Nelson but direction as well.

It was on October 3, 1942, that Roosevelt, exasperated and genuinely disturbed, took James Byrnes off the Supreme Court and put him into the White House as Director of Economic Stabilization. Nelson, seeing the handwriting on the wall in September, had invited Eberstadt to become Vice-President of WPB in charge of priorities. But the situation was too far gone for this concession to save Nelson. On October 6, Nelson's devoted brain-truster, Robert Nathan, calculated the total of the various unbalanced programs underway at

$115 billions, which, as all agreed, was the measure not of what to hope for but of what to fear. "What we urgently need," Nathan concluded, "is an authoritative body that would represent fully and competently the strategic, economic, and political (in the sense of broadly social) factors that must jointly determine a well-formulated production program." But what else had Nelson been appointed to do in January?

Now, after Roosevelt had been forced to discard Hopkins's self-serving theory that the home front had to be run by a production man, after Nelson's staunchest supporter—Nathan—had called for new leadership at the political level, and after Roosevelt had called upon Byrnes to supply it, Nelson concluded that WPB would have to take over and exercise a greater degree of control over the balancing and timing of programs. But it had of course been created in the first place to exercise precisely such control in a definitive way.

But Roosevelt had long since learned to discount Nelson pronunciamentos. Instead, in mid-October, Roosevelt, Byrnes, and the War and Navy Department chiefs decided to impose Eberstadt's Controlled Materials Plan, which was formally adopted on November 2. It saved the situation by asserting Government's right to regulate the war economy, and equipping the Government to do so. It was as simple as any workable system of regulation has to be. Where Nelson and his predecessors had attacked the administrative problem at all points and solved it at none, Eberstadt concentrated on the strategic problem of controlling the flow of three essential materials —steel, aluminum, and copper; and, by solving it, solved the others. Proceeding from the fundamental premise of Eberstadt's collaborator and intimate, Baruch, that production objectives must equate with capacities, CMP resulted in the placing of orders for finished products in full and precisely calculated balance of all the parts, components, and materials involved in producing the finished product in question. Thus, because the production flow followed steel, aluminum, and copper, each order for 1,000 tanks became an effective order for every item, no more and no less, needed to work off the prime contract; and each manufacturer working off a prime contract found himself sending his supplies and parts-makers and subcontractors in a straight line to the source of the precise items, no more and no less and no other, specified in the original order.

CMP, in short, ordered finished products on the businesslike assumption that WPB meant to supply the fighting fronts with units of fighting power and not merely to cut up raw materails and build plants and employ manpower. It quickly balanced the input of economy energy and the output of fire power. In 1942 the war economy produced something over $30 billions of finished munitions. In 1943, at virtually the same price level, munitions production fell just short of $60 billions; and, in 1944, the achievement of 1943, continuing to function automatically, carried production well over $60 billions.

CMP flooded the fighting fronts with fire power. In a miraculously short period of time after Pearl Harbor, the question: How soon will our troops have enough to fight with? was transformed into an immeasurably less anxious question: How soon will our troops begin to fight with what they have? The miracle of production never was in question. The fundamental question was one of time. The miracle of administration, consummated by CMP, organized the miracle of production into usable form in time.

That CMP truly engineered a miracle of organization is proven, if proof were needed, by the fact that it doubled the economy's finished, usable production in 1943 without increasing the civilian labor force, without curtailing consumer expenditures, and while slashing plant expansion from its inflated 1942 peak to a normal and necessary rate. But proof is not needed. For the Budget Bureau history, defending Nelson as it does, nevertheless appreciates and acknowledges "the significance of Mr. Eberstadt's epochal reforms." And Nelson himself, by way of explaining that "in the end it proved impossible to integrate his policies with those of WPB," admits that Eberstadt "rendered very effective service to the war effort by devising and putting into operation the Controlled Materials Plan, which proved so useful during the rest of the war period." *

FOR 20 years Baruch had warned that priorities are the problem of problems for a war economy. For three years Nelson and his predecessors had failed to face this problem. During the last of these three years, mo-

* Donald M. Nelson, *Arsenal of Democracy* (New York, Harcourt, Brace and Company, Inc., 1946), p. 364.

mentum had produced a vast amount of various parts
of the program, but Nelson's failure to dispose of the
priorities problem had admittedly unbalanced the war
economy and threatened it with chaos. In three
months Eberstadt solved the problem of balance by
eliminating the problem of "priorities inflation." It
was a lasting solution. Because it was, victory came
much more rapidly than any had dared hope in 1942.
For it was the winning of the war on the home front
late in 1943 that made possible the winning of the war
in Europe by early 1945.

Eberstadt himself was rewarded with dismissal. He
fell victim to the most masterful achievement of Nelson's career as Chairman of WPB. It was characteristically an achievement of intrigue. But while it
purged Eberstadt, it did not undo his work and it did
not save Nelson for very long.

When the priorities system Nelson built had collapsed, he found himself obliged, in September, 1942,
to invite Eberstadt to become Vice-Chairman of
WPB, and to allow him to take over its priorities
operation. What Nelson won with this move was control over raw materials—for WPB. What he lost was
his fictitious personal issue, "militarism." To salvage
it, he pitted Eberstadt against another Vice-Chairman of WPB—Charles E. Wilson, of General Electric,
a well-meaning and forward-looking man of high resolve, who later headed President Truman's Committee on Civil Rights, and who returned to Washington in 1950 to run the Office of Defense Mobilization.
Nelson put Wilson in charge of production, and demanded that the military allow Wilson to schedule and

control its production programs as fully as it was allowing Eberstadt to direct the materials operation.
This was a shrewd tactic, and a bold one. It blurred
over the Army's obvious and emphatic desire to have
WPB control the scheduling of critical components,
such as valves and bearings, and provoked the Army
to fight to control the scheduling of weapons, ammunition, and other items directly geared to military operations. Nelson recalls the success of his maneuver with
understandable satisfaction:

> The Army's unceasing insistence that we restrict our
> controls to materials only led it to support the job Eber-
> stadt was doing and to oppose Wilson's work. The situa-
> tion became more and more strained, and developed into a
> conflict between Wilson and Eberstadt themselves, with
> Eberstadt having strong Army backing. I did my best,
> but without success [sic!] to resolve this conflict, and it
> became evident that the two men could not continue to
> work together in WPB. In the circumstances, of course,
> there could be no question as to whom I would retain. . . .
> Early in 1943 I realized that our task was becoming
> more and more a production scheduling job. It seemed
> logical, therefore, to transfer additional authority over
> the control of WPB's operations from the Program Vice-
> Chairman, Mr. Eberstadt, to the Production Vice-Chair-
> man, Mr. Wilson. This was done, but the Army people
> bitterly resented the action.*

Indeed they did. For they saw through this transaction and attacked it as the shabby device to "divide
and rule," which it was. Patterson and Forrestal, supported by Stimson and Knox and, more impressive
still at that particular point, by Byrnes and Baruch,

* Donald M. Nelson, *Arsenal of Democracy* (New York, Harcourt, Brace and Company, Inc., 1946), pp. 387, 388.

went to Roosevelt and documented their charge that
WPB was being torn apart by the senseless and un-
principled row Nelson was stirring up between Eberstadt and Wilson. Roosevelt agreed that Nelson had
been a mistake, and that WPB, created the year
before to serve the armed forces, was now rendering
them a disservice. He agreed, moreover, to appoint
Baruch Chairman of WPB, going so far as to make
Baruch a formal offer by letter—a rare admission of
past error. Recognizing that the apparent friction between Wilson and Eberstadt was merely an outgrowth
of Nelson's campaign against Eberstadt, he authorized Baruch to make Eberstadt his Deputy.

This counterattack inspired Nelson to a still bolder
and shrewder tactic. Late in the night of February 16–
17, Nelson was awakened by a call from Nathan,
whom he identifies merely as "one of my most trusted
assistants." They breakfasted at 7:00 A.M., February
17, when Nathan informed him in detail of the Order
which Byrnes had prepared for the President to sign
at 2:00 P.M. that day. How had Nathan come by
this valuable bit of White House intelligence? His
friend Pritchard was in the White House, and had
given it to him.

When Byrnes became "Assistant President," one of
the decisions he had to make was how to deal with
the Frankfurter organization. Non-recognition would
have meant war. But his mission was peace. So, with
some misgivings, as he took leave of his brother Justice, he agreed to hire Pritchard although he admonished this voluble prodigy to "quit going to cock-
tail parties and gabbing to columnists." This most

damaging of all Pritchard's leaks actually obeyed
Byrnes's instruction to the letter. It was a confidential violation of confidence.

Pritchard coupled it with the most flagrant act of
surreptitious insubordination in the history of the
Roosevelt Administration. Nelson's crisis called for
direct action, and this precocious manipulator of power
was ruthless enough to counsel it. That Frankfurter's
most valued friends among the senior members of the
War Administration—Stimson and Patterson—were
pressing for Nelson's removal, did not complicate
Pritchard's view of what had to be done. On the contrary, he dismissed any question of consideration or
deference for them on the grounds that both had come
under the domination of Forrestal, who thought ill of
Frankfurter and said so; and that both were about to
put themselves into the hands of Eberstadt, who was
notoriously unsusceptible to manipulation. Pritchard's
advice to Nelson, transmitted through the literal-
minded and naive Nathan, was simply to fire Eberstadt in the morning—before the 2 o'clock meeting
at which Roosevelt was scheduled to act.

Nelson followed the advice; and, as Pritchard had
so cynically calculated, Roosevelt shrank from the
scandal threatened by any attempt to undo the
fait accompli with which Nelson confronted him. In
the middle of the war which America had to win for
the world on her own home front, when the high command of the home front had broken down and Roosevelt himself had put aside pride and admitted it, this
Machiavellian genius dared to bluff the War President
out of a firm commitment to the country's first private

citizen, to humiliate that statesman and deprive the country of his badly needed skill, and to betray his own chief, the Assistant President, who was at once the trusted friend of the Elder Statesman and the trusted broker of the President.

Eberstadt went, and Baruch's health suffered a convenient relapse. Pritchard was punished by being drafted. As for Nelson, he got off, for the time being, with this homily, delivered by Roosevelt at the end of the day which was to have been Nelson's last:

> I wish the job could be accomplished without these head-on collisions. I believe that there are ways of maneuvering so that head-on collisions can be avoided. It is my experience with businessmen in Government that they always get into these battles, not merely with one another but with the heads of other Government agencies. They don't know how to administer the things they must administer as well as the politicians know how. Now, I probably could have appointed, let's say, a man experienced as a Governor or a Senator to head the War ProductionBoard, and he could probably get a production at least 90 or 95% as large as businessmen are getting.
>
> But I am satisfied with the way the job is going; and I should like to see it continue. See if you can't keep the head-on collisions down some.

It was to be 18 months before Roosevelt exiled Nelson by sending him on a mission to China. For Nelson these were months wasted in anxious waiting for the end of the reprieve he had bought with the purge of Eberstadt. As Stimson says:

> Having tinkered for nearly two years with boards and commissions . . . [the President] finally gave power to the wrong man. Then when that man got into trouble,

the President coasted along; he neither fully backed Mr. Nelson nor fired him. Stimson believed that it was Mr. Roosevelt's irritated but indecisive tolerance of men lacking strength of character that lay behind many wartime administrative difficulties. Disagreements with men like Hull and Morgenthau were painful, but in these cases Stimson always knew where he stood; disagreements with men who backed and filled were extremely irritating.*

Of the two qualities Hopkins had listed as qualifying Nelson for the Chairmanship of WPB—technical skill and the President's confidence—the former had been exposed as irrelevant and the latter had been dissipated. Now Nelson admits that he checked with Stimson the information "leaked out" by Pritchard. Nevertheless, his account, characteristically, creates a false impression by speaking of the proposal to replace him with the Baruch-Eberstadt team as a mere proposal by his critics (including his Chief, Byrnes), and not as the Presidential decision it was. And in this intrigue which upset the Presidential decision, when insubordination saved Nelson in the place incompetence had imperiled, how was Hopkins serving Roosevelt?

"I have heard and read many different versions of this episode," Sherwood confesses, with an air of embarrassment over this lapse of Hopkins from the character he had established for him. "I do not know just what part Hopkins played in it, but it seems evident that he backed Nelson and persuaded the President to give him another chance. He also persuaded Nelson to delegate a very large amount of authority for the

* Henry L. Stimson, *On Active Service* (New York, Harper & Brothers, 1948), p. 494.

direction of WPB to Wilson." * Hopkins's role in protecting his vested interest in Nelson against the President's decision was necessarily an undercover one. For the responsibility for the relationship between WPB and the military had been given to Byrnes; and Byrnes's first words to Hopkins as Assistant President had been: "There's just one suggestion I want to make to you, Harry, and that is to keep the Hell out of my business." Sherwood reports Hopkins saying that Byrnes "smiled very pleasantly when he said it, but by God he meant it and I'm going to keep the Hell out." Sherwood's indulgent comment—"It is improbable that Hopkins was entirely faithful in living up to this resolve" †—implies that Hopkins was not one to let a commitment to a politician stand in the way of seizing every opportunity to serve Roosevelt and the war effort. Actually, Hopkins understood full well that Byrnes was threatening him as one politician to another; and, by playing the role Sherwood admits he played in Nelson's coup to save his WPB post, Hopkins served neither Roosevelt nor the war effort but himself.

Wilson remained, ostensibly as Nelson's Deputy. But the elimination of Eberstadt changed Nelson's need for Wilson. He had brought Wilson in to serve as a foil against the "militarists." Now, to keep his issue agitated, he found himself obliged to attack Wilson as a "militarist" too. This abrupt and cynical transformation of Wilson from instrument to ex-

---

* Robert E. Sherwood, *Roosevelt and Hopkins* (New York, Harper & Brothers, 1948), p. 700.

† *Ibid.*, p. 634.

pendable, from ally to enemy, he effected in exactly 23 pages of his book. On page 388—the page of the Eberstadt purge—he characterizes Wilson as the very personification of his fight for the principle of civilian control. On page 411, the scorn heretofore reserved for Eberstadt is rifled at "Charlie Wilson, in particular, who tended to agree with the Army's point of view."

CMP ended all worries about how fast the home front could deliver how much to the fighting fronts. Instead the question became, With how few men could the home front keep the war fronts supplied? Soon after the creation of WPB, in April, 1942, Nelson had re-linquished control over the manpower component of production to Paul V. McNutt, who, as Chairman of the War Manpower Commission, became the most har-assed of the Washington czars. Nelson's motive was no doubt to simplify his job; but, as so often happens in such cases, this ill-considered move added further complications. For it committed the flow of materials to one set of controls and priorities, and the flow of manpower to another and generally conflicting set. Thus, in the Seattle area, when the shipyards com-manded top priorities, wages in the airplane industry were frozen at a higher level than in the shipyards. Inevitably, this cross-purposing multiplied manpower turnover and defeated the efforts of priorities control.

This was to be one of the most troublesome of the problems Nelson bequeathed to Byrnes; and it in-tensified the clash of claims over manpower allocation. Each of the pressure groups—agriculture, labor, in-dustry, mothers, wives, educators, clergymen, and all the rest—engaged in an endless economic, ideological, and sentimental free-for-all, the objective of each participant being to tell the Army whom it could not draft.

More than 80 per cent of all draftees up to February, 1943, were single men under 30, and most of the remainder were single men under 38. With the Second Front still a year away, and with draft calls running at the rate of 400,000 a month, the Administration had to choose between occupational status and family status as a basis for deferment. Its freedom of choice, moreover, had been limited in November, 1942, the month after the invasion of North Africa, by an act of Congress granting a priority on deferments to agriculture. Throughout 1943, the hunt for trainable draftees among husbands, fathers and, finally, "pre-Pearl Harbor fathers" conflicted with the resistance of the various occupational groups and with the rich economic incentives offered by shifting opportunities on the home front. By September 1, 1943, farm deferments exceeded 2,000,000 and industrial deferments exceeded 1,500,000. At the end of 1943, Congress recognized that, as the Budget Bureau history says, "the selection of men for military service was never part of a long-range and comprehensive manpower program." It legalized the anarchy by removing Selective Service from the jurisdiction of the War Manpower Commission.

Then, early in 1944, when no one could estimate at what rate casualties would begin to require replacements, the Army announced that young men would have to be taken first. Moreover, the President, al-

though he was a believer in momentum and in the
free play of incentives among the pressure groups—
especially labor—decided at last to include in his State
of the Union Message a call for "national service
legislation," making "available for war production or
any other essential services every able-bodied adult
in this Nation." He did this under pressure from the
military, and without clearing with McNutt.

It was a gesture, but a meaningful one. Short of
total war which, fortunately, was no longer a threat,
Congress was determined to resist the War Department's pressure for manpower mobilization. But by
and large its members were practical enough to recognize that an attack on manpower anarchy was essential and could best be made via inflation control:
Government had to stabilize the cost of living before
it could call upon working people to stop seeking
better jobs. In January, 1942, Congress passed the
Emergency Price Control Act, giving OPA general
authority to fix price ceilings subject to the stipula-
tion that any ceilings on farm prices would have to
be higher than prevailing prices. In May, 1942, OPA
issued the General Maximum Price Regulation, putting a ceiling on most non-farm prices but leaving
wages and farm prices free. Rent ceilings—in 20 cities
to begin with—were imposed in the same month.
Rising food prices provoked demands for higher wages,
and, by July, a labor policy had to be formulated.
This the War Labor Board supplied in the "Little
Steel" case, holding wages to 15 percent above the
January, 1941, level (except in cases involving sub-
standard conditions). Finally, in October, Roosevelt

was forced to reassert control over the manpower and price functions which WPB had vacated. He appointed Byrnes to accomplish by negotiation what Baruch had insisted could be done only by regulation. Byrnes promptly insisted on Congressional authorization, which he received in the Stabilization Act of 1942. This empowered him to control wages even when both parties to collective bargaining agreed upon increases.

By May, 1943, the wage-price negotiating process in Washington had turned every occupation into a pressure group. OPA was caught in a cross-fire. On the one hand, industry and agriculture accused it of being too stern while, on the other, labor and consumers accused it of being too pliant. The pressure process had forced living costs up 27 per cent, and the beneficiaries were as dissatisfied as the victims, while the draftees felt cheated. Democratic losses in the 1942 election made an expendable of Henderson. Ex-Senator Prentiss Brown replaced him. "Hoosiers" and hillbillies in the boom centers rebelled against rationing. The entire Northwest buzzed with the story of the lady welder who snorted, "I'm going back to Missouri, where they don't have ration books."

By early 1943 the Farm Bloc was demanding inflationary prices *and* draft exemptions, but expecting to settle for either or to compromise on both; and the labor and industry blocs were taking a similar bargaining position. In April, 1943, the President moved on all fronts to stem the tide. He vetoed an inflationary farm bill; he issued his "Hold-the-Line" wage order; and when 400,000 miners refused his appeal not to strike, he took over the mines. To rectify the damage that had been done, he launched a $400,000,000 program to subsidize price "roll-backs" to consumers. This was effective: after May, 1943, wartime living costs rose only 1 per cent. But without such subsidies to cover the margin between the prices agriculture had won and those consumers could pay, neither OPA nor the "Little Steel" formula could hold the line.

To complicate matters, the "roll-back" program was submitted to Congress without consultation with Chester Davis, the Food Administrator. Although Roosevelt had assured him that he would have "authority commensurate with his responsibilities," and, the President might have added, with his influence on Capitol Hill, Davis heard about the new stabilization program over the radio. He thereupon resigned without being given an opportunity to talk with the President. The Farm Bloc mustered enough votes to defeat the subsidy program and began to clamor for a food czar. Roosevelt dealt with this in much the same way as he dealt with the demand for a rubber czar— by refusing the grant of statutory power and instead appointing a czar whom Congress trusted to represent its point of view in the Executive arm of Government. His choice was Marvin Jones, who, in the New Deal days, had been a farm bloc spokesman in the house and whom he had kicked upstairs to the Federal Bench.

Roosevelt's call for "National Service" legislation in his 1944 State of the Union Message was at once an offer of a trade and a warning. It offered a *quid pro quo* to the warring farm and non-farm factions—the restoration of subsidies benefiting labor in return for the regulation of labor. It also portended the Selective Service Order canceling occupational deferments to young men in the controversial 18 to 21-year age bracket. As late as February, 998,400 men under 26 enjoyed occupational deferments. Fully 910,000 of them were not fathers and 562,400 were farm deferments. The military had at last persuaded Roosevelt to draft the young men it had wanted from the beginning. This decision focused all the pressures on the Administration's lack of a manpower policy. And this lack, in turn, went back to WPB's failure to exercise the authority given it over the manpower component of production. "Under the general theory of WPB," the Budget Bureau history notes, "it would have been able to indicate to WMC the order of priorities which should be followed in referral of available manpower to civilian employment and, likewise, to indicate to Selective Service considerations of labor supply for its guidance in the withdrawal of manpower from the labor market for the Armed Forces." Instead, WPB allowed its foundation to be pulled out from under it by the czars and its roof to be removed by Byrnes; then Byrnes was called upon to improvise a roof, after Roosevelt's refusal to integrate production, price, and manpower controls (as Baruch had advised) had precipitated an emergency.

Eberstadt's CMP regulated production and won the war on the home front in 1943. Roosevelt and Byrnes, by measures heroic and practical, prevented the inflationary pressures from disturbing the regulated momentum of production; in this they were ably assisted by Fred M. Vinson, later Secretary of the Treasury

and Chief Justice of the United States, who resigned
from the Circuit Court of Appeals to direct price and
wage stabilization. A past master of the delicate arts
practiced in the House Ways and Means Committee,
Vinson was the very model of the experienced poli-
tician-administrator; and, relying on Vinson's judgment of when to be firm and when tactful, Roosevelt
freed himself of further fear of the costly "head-on-
collisions" in which his businessmen appointees were
constantly involving him.

But, if production and prices were finally brought
under control, the movement of manpower never was;
and, consequently, manpower crystallized into the
crucial problem during the year which intervened between the winning of the production war and the winning of the shooting war.

IF the movement of manpower posed a many-sided
administrative problem, it also reflected a many-sided
social revolution. This the war effected. The temper
and outlook of the country changed. Whereas the depression had left a residue of feeling that America was
finished, that expansion was at an end, the war re-
vived the restless and adventurous spirit of frontier
days. New productive energies were unleashed. Evan-
gelism and experimentation pioneered new industrial
techniques.

The most powerful force transforming the social
fabric was the endless demand for labor. At the peak
of the war effort, no less than 9,800,000 separate enter-
prises were in operation: about 6,000,000 in agriculture, about 3,800,000 in industry and commerce.

Nearly all of them were humming with energy. Everybody seemed busy, everybody was making money, everybody was sure not merely of winning the war but of enjoying security afterwards.

With immigration practically stopped (relatively small groups of Mexicans, Porto Ricans, and West Indians were absorbed into the economy), a demand existed for every hand. This meant that women were much more widely employed than in the First World War. In fact, by August, 1945, the proportion of women in the civilian labor force rose to 36 percent. Shipyards and plane plants and assembly shops of all kinds recruited women eagerly, and even machine shops and explosives factories welcomed them. Particularly conspicuous were the women war-workers between the ages of 25 and 35—most of them wives of service-men and girls waiting to be married. And these women workers came to stay; after demobilization, industry employed some 600,000 women more than before the war. Relaxation of child-labor regulations was another natural by-product of the emergency. When the labor pinch was sharpest, no less than three and a half million teen-agers from fourteen through seventeen were being employed. This, happily, proved a transient phenomenon. Peace brought a more vigorous enforcement of the Fair Labor Standards Act, with new child-labor laws adopted in some states like Georgia, and a stricter application of all laws in others.

While women were breaking down traditional barriers, so were colored folk. The country's thirteen million Negroes supplied more than a million men to the armed forces. The Navy, traditional stronghold of the

South, led the way to the discarding of segregation. But the Army, despite some progress resulting from the widely discussed "Gillem Report," segregated all too many Negroes into labor battalions and special Negro service units. In combat, Negro troops, including an air-fighter group, made good fighting records. On the home front, the President's Executive Order No. 8802, creating the Fair Employment Practices Committee, had a most far-reaching effect. It established the principle that the nation should create equality in employment opportunity for all, without respect to race, ancestry, or creed; and, though the Committee had but limited power with which to enforce its decrees, and was defied by powerful corporations and unions alike, it did give a fair chance at jobs to Negroes, Mexicans, and other long ill-treated groups. Although it was but a temporary agency, it paved the way for permanent committees for fair employment in a number of states—New York, New Jersey, Massachusetts, Indiana, and Connecticut leading the procession. Great numbers of Negroes who found new horizons opened by army life, and who met little social discrimination in Britain, France, and Italy, ultimately returned home with a conviction that the doctrines of the "Atlantic Charter" and "Four Freedoms" should be made good; and while the war still raged American democracy began to adjust itself to the realities awaiting it after V-Day.

Nowhere was the process of interracial adjustment more dramatic than in the home front's factories. The CIO anticipated public policy by banning Jim Crow practices; and many progressive managements cooperated energetically and imaginatively. But policy, like legislation, could lead only as fast as human relations followed. And, at the human level, progress tempered prejudice with experience. Thus, the novelist John Dos Passos heard one Southerner exclaim: "As if we didn't have enough trouble organizing this pile of mule-skinners into decent union men and citizens without having these longhaired wiseacres come down from Washington to stir up the race question!" On the other hand, he heard another talk more reasonably: "We have found that to get fair play for the poor whites we've got to fight for equal rights for poor Negroes." The upshot of this process of fermentation was to change the question of equality of opportunity in America from whether to when.

No wartime change was more remarkable than that in the status of the farmer. When the war began, vestiges of his traditional poverty and insecurity still clung to him; but the conflict brought him responsibility, dignity—and wealth. Crop production rose steadily throughout the war years. It would be roughly accurate to say that it increased by about one-third between 1939 and 1946—this in the face of an almost stationary crop acreage, and a reduction of 5 to 10 per cent in labor force. In other words, the tremendous expansion in food output was accomplished by a larger use of fertilizers, increased mechanization, fuller control of insect pests and plant diseases, scientific soil conservation, and distribution of better seeds and livestock varieties. Some of these factors responsible for the farmers' changed status were bound to be permanent. The prosperity of the six million farm families, with better land, better houses and barns, little debt, and money in the bank and in securities, contributed significantly to the post-war boom. The electrification of farms, chiefly through the Rural Electrification Administration, was in itself a striking advance. American food habits continued to improve, and despite the discontents of rationing, the people were better fed than ever before.

The total picture had both dark and bright aspects. If the appearance of new industries, like electronics, was encouraging, the heavy depletion of vital natural resources—iron ore, copper, lead, Canadian nickel— was alarming. If the strong population movement to California and the Pacific Northwest improved the sectional balance, the renewed flow from country to city (including a large transfer of rural Southern Negroes to slum-congested Northern industrial centers) presented new problems of housing and welfare. What was certain was that America had regained all its historic dynamism and more: it was on the march. Roosevelt's theory was vindicated by the facts. America's energies were serving it better than any plan could.

CHAPTER XII

THE MOMENTUM OF VICTORY

ONE word—cut-backs—tells the story of the time lag between the winning of the war on the home front and the winning of the war overseas. Not until the spring of 1944 did the shooting war reach its climax. Cut-backs on the home front began in 1943; and, exactly like the beginnings of war production, they suffered from being too poorly planned. This was as excusable, however, as it was unexpected and unprecedented. The very thought of cutting war production back half a year before the enemy had been engaged on the vital front—and at the very time when the enemy's war production was rising to a new peak —was as bizarre as the achievement was epic.

The calendar speaks for itself. The production curve reached its peak in October, 1943, the time of Tarawa and the recapture of Kiev. Prophetically, the pressure of surpluses struck at the same strategic point where the pressure of shortages was first felt—in aluminum. In December, four aluminum pot lines were closed down. The previous month, the Senate had created a Special Committee on Post-War Economic Policy and Planning under Senator Walter F. George. It promptly began hearings on war contract cancellations, surplus property disposal, and over-all demobilization and reconversion. Byrnes, meanwhile, asked Baruch and John Hancock to survey the problem; and, in January, 1944, the President, in his annual Budget Message, stressed the importance of reconversion for the period of offensive war at hand. "Demobilization begins long before hostilities end," he said. A few weeks later, Baruch and Hancock made specific recommendations to create machinery for throwing the entire program into reverse, and the President issued appropriate Executive Orders immediately.

By February 3, 1944, Stimson announced that military procurement programs had been slashed no less than $12,800,000,000. Early in 1945, Byrnes reviewed an ambitious new Naval program, projected for completion in 1947–48, and denied allocations for 70 ships. At the same time, the merchant shipbuilding program was cut in half. Proof positive that the production war had been won came in Byrnes's directive to cancel orders for 40 tankers. Moreover, Byrnes was able to report on January 1, 1945, fully four months before V-E Day, that renegotiations for the fiscal years 1942 and 1943 had already returned $4,355,268,000 to the Government; and that other price reductions had reduced its commitments by another $3,887,597,000. Thanks also to the wise provision of the Excess Profits Tax, which allowed companies to claim refunds on their wartime excess profits tax payments to cover post-war losses, the Government was free to cut war production back without fear of precipitating a crisis of working capital or a wave of bankruptcies. It was also free to concentrate on the financial and economic aspects of demobilization without fear of exposing the reconverted economy to a failure of mass purchasing power.

Full employment had boomed individual incomes between 1941 and 1944. At the same time the combination of rationing, price control, debt reduction, and moderate wartime taxes had accumulated a prodigious pool of savings. At the time of Pearl Harbor, the liquid assets of individuals (including unincorporated businesses) totaled $50 billions. By the end of 1944, cash plus war bond holdings by individuals came to $140 billions, a record reserve available for purchasing power. In 1944 alone individuals earned $138 billions of spendable income, of which they saved no less than $20 billions. Virtually everyone held war bonds; and, since their yields rose rapidly as they neared maturity, everyone had a strong incentive to hold them past the expected period of post-war adjustments. This, added to the new sources of purchasing power which demobilization of the armed forces promised to provide, guaranteed the economy against a reconversion depression. Moreover, because so large a share of these new assets was held by groups of previously marginal consumers (Negroes, farm workers, newlyweds, students, and, above all, women); because, also, so much of this pool of purchasing power was concentrated in areas which had benefited from wartime population shifts, the momentum of the economy's wartime expansion was precipitating a new and still more impressive move of post-war expansion.

WHEN Roosevelt had gone to Casablanca in January, 1943, automobile pleasure driving was being banned.

When the Russians triumphed at Stalingrad, we
rationed shoes. By the time the Battle of the Atlantic
had been won, and the invasion of North Africa had
spilled over into Sicily, however, Washington was able
to authorize the resumption of production on no less
than 10 household items. This first relaxation of austerity was achieved a month before the Japanese were
driven from the Aleutians—such was the time lag between victory on the home front and Victory. At
Teheran, in December, 1943, the principal issue resolved was the timing of the all-out air offensive
against Germany and the Second Front. Our economy
was already in a position to support commitments for
the relief and rehabilitation of countries which had
been invaded. And the production problem had been
narrowed to a series of critical items.

Some of these critical items remained problems in
1944 because of administrative blunders and omissions
in 1942. Thus, although the objective of the entire program from the beginning had been the invasion of
Europe, and although no invasion could be contemplated without landing craft, the success of the program uncovered a staggering and scandalous shortage
of landing craft.

Eisenhower reports Army concern with the problem
as early as February, 1942. But, he explains,

it was difficult to develop a widespread interest in them
when everyone was desperately concerned with defense.
Although the Navy would have to take charge of building
landing craft, it informed us that it could not even provide
crews for them. General Somervell promptly retorted
that he would do so. With characteristic energy he set

about the task and performed it successfully. Months later, when he tried to transfer [these landing-craft crews] . . . to the Navy, we ran up against the curious proposition that the Navy could not take drafted men.*

Sherwood reproduces a memo pad sketch of a naval landing craft drawn by Roosevelt at about this time. He reports that landing craft stood tenth on the Navy's Shipbuilding Preference list in March, 1942. The pressure of the North African invasion forced them up to second place momentarily, but, as soon as the immediate urgency passed, they dropped back to twelfth place. A year later, at Teheran, the problem was rediscovered. In fact, General Marshall reported that it was the most critical shortage impeding the progress of the Conference. In January, 1944, accordingly, a drive was launched to build no less than 65,000 landing craft in time to support the Second Front.

Other critical shortages were, notably, those of rubber and high-octane gasoline. "The armed forces," the Truman Committee found in its scathing Report of May 3, 1943, "failed by a wide margin to anticipate wartime needs for aviation gasoline. A year after Pearl Harbor, the armed forces were still raising their sights. Their estimates made last September will apparently be met by production this summer. But during last fall and winter—after almost a year of war—these estimates were tremendously increased. This, of course, intensified the priorities jam."

From the beginning, the rubber and petroleum dislocations had been interchangeable. The public, irri-

* Dwight D. Eisenhower, *Crusade in Europe* (New York, Doubleday & Company, Inc., 1948), p. 38.

tated with gasoline rationing and aware of the over-all adequacy of oil supplies, never understood that the purpose of gasoline stamps was to conserve rubber. During the summer of 1942, OPA, WPB and the Petroleum Coordinator were squabbling about whether to ration gasoline. But the issue had to be resolved in terms of rubber, and this seemed too explosive for WPB and the Army to agree about. But not for Congress. In July, 1942, seven months after WPB had been created to provide over-all direction for the War Economy, Congress moved to abrogate the Order by passing a Bill to create a rubber czar independent of WPB, and to make an automatic statutory grant of overriding priorities as fast as the rubber czar demanded them.

Because Jesse Jones had been dollar-wise and rubber-foolish while there was still time to stock-pile natural rubber, he has also been held responsible for the War Administration's failure to anticipate the need for an American synthetic rubber industry. This is unfair to Jones. At the outset of the fight over synthetic rubber, he was a neutral bystander awaiting instructions from the policy-making level which did not come. At the end of the fight, when a scapegoat was needed, his administrative reputation drafted him for the role, which his political insecurity led him to accept.

The real culprit was Wallace. He had used his immeasurable authority as Vice-President, as presiding officer of SPAB, as head of economic warfare and as symbol of the succession, to block the frantic demands of Forrestal, Somervell, and Eberstadt for a major

synthetic rubber program. Wallace's dogmas led him
to insist that all the rubber the war effort would need
could be grown—and in time!—in Latin America
where, he argued, it would serve the additional purpose
of financing emergent democracy. What fate would
overcome this emergent democracy if America failed
to protect it for lack of rubber, did not seem to concern
him. Equally prominent in Wallace's irresponsible distortion of the realities of war was the consideration
that a commitment to produce synthetic rubber would
threaten the pre-war pattern of world trade, that it
would give respectability to a product of Germany's
cartelized industry, and that it would establish Standard Oil in post-war control of a protected industry. To
hindsight, Wallace's use of his wartime position to
wage post-war politics seems fantastic. To the men
responsible for waging war, it was a nightmare. Jones
certainly cannot be blamed, as he has been, for not
financing new installations when the men empowered
to authorize them could not agree whether they were
necessary. Nelson had been armed with sweeping
powers to make precisely such decisions in behalf of
the President. This he lacked the force of will and the
clarity of mind to do. On the one hand, Nelson hesitated to oppose his patron Wallace on an issue so
meaningful in Wallace's pseudo-liberal patter. On the
other hand, Nelson was feuding with Forrestal, Somervell and Eberstadt in public; and he had no appetite
for giving them such a major public victory over
Wallace.

For months Nelson walked the tight-rope while the
issue raged. Then Forrestal, as plenipotentiary for the

desperate military, took the issue to Hopkins. This was precisely the kind of issue on which Hopkins's incisiveness seized again and again—far from involving a threat to his position, it enabled him to fortify himself in the White House by dissociating himself from his now suspect protégés—Wallace and Nelson. To his everlasting credit, Hopkins took the fight to Roosevelt, who quickly resolved it in favor of synthetic rubber. As soon as Jones was given his orders, he acted on them; and production soared to 800,000 tons by 1944. Infinitely more significant for the post-war world, the synthetic rubber commitment coincided with the decision to gamble on the Manhattan Project.

The synthetic rubber scandal annoyed Roosevelt with Wallace, and disillusioned him with Nelson. At the level of public relations, he had to reconcile himself to gradual liquidation of both liabilities. The abuse Wallace and Nelson so richly deserved was heaped upon Jones. But, inside the circle of White House reality, Roosevelt never forgave Nelson for the embarrassment which Congress' rubber offensive caused him.

The embarrassment lay not only in the exposure of Administration errors, but in the price that had to be paid to cover them. For Roosevelt could not veto Congress' bill without making concessions: the situation would be investigated by Baruch, to whom he was therefore placed under obligation, and a rubber czar would be appointed. Baruch, assisted by James B. Conant and Karl T. Compton, surveyed the situation for the President and recommended nothing less than "complete reorganization and consolidation of the governmental agencies concerned with the rubber program." Baruch, Conant, and Compton threw their combined prestige behind the proposal to ration gasoline "as the only way of saving rubber." In addition, they urged a 35-mile an hour speed limit for the entire country. Baruch and his associates warned that 1942 had produced a minimum rubber deficit of 211,000 tons, and that the synthetic capacities under construction left a margin of safety of only 100,000 tons. But the aviation gasoline and synthetic rubber programs depended at certain points on the same facilities, over which Jesse Jones's Rubber Reserve Company and the Petroleum Coordinator were in conflict. The bottleneck was butadiene. "Under an agreement with four large rubber companies," the Budget Bureau history explains, "only Rubber Reserve could give out information about synthetic rubber processes to others; but the WPB Rubber Branch had to work six weeks to get such data released."

The Baruch Committee called for an additional 300,-000 tons capacity, and for the appointment of a Rubber Administrator. Baruch, however, in spite of his criticisms of WPB's rubber record, allowed the White House to prevail upon him to advise that the Rubber Director "should be located within the general framework of WPB." Where Congress had written an automatic claim on priorities into its Rubber Bill, Roosevelt's compromise obliged the Rubber Director to join Ickes and the rest in the free-for-all fight for deliveries. But the Rubber Director he appointed in September, 1942, William M. Jeffers, President of the Union Pacific Railroad, was more than competent to take care of himself. He proved to be a vigorous model of how effective and fearless a businessman can be in Government. If Roosevelt had picked him instead of Budd to do the transportation job in the beginning, the entire story of the home front might have been different. In any case, Jeffers created rubber capacities, and his partitioning of Nelson's empire constituted yet another reason why Roosevelt needed an Assistant President in charge of keeping the peace among the czars. Rubber remained in short supply until the end, and Rubber Czar Jeffers was obliged to fight the battle for rubber to the end.

Still other dislocations arose unavoidably from the conditions and lessons of combat. In the air the B-24 Liberator was supplanted by the more formidable B-29 Superfortress, and the A-20 attack bomber by the A-26 Invader. On the ground the tank program was finally reengineered. By 1942, the more obvious weaknesses of the tanks originally rushed into production had become apparent; and, preparatory to the invasion of North Africa, engineering improvements had been made to fit them for combat. Nevertheless, in 1944, the engineers had to be put to work again, and the General Sherman model was supplanted by the vastly superior General Pershing.

Eisenhower describes a masterpiece of practical engineering in the middle of No Man's Land by a sergeant named Culin. The Germans had constructed a system of obstacles which forced our tanks to "climb almost vertically, thus exposing the unprotected belly of the tank and rendering it easy prey to any type of armor-piercing bullet." Culin averted a new crisis along the Washington-Detroit axis by the simple expedient of "fastening to the front of the tank two sturdy blades of steel which, acting somewhat as scythes, cut through the bank of earth and hedges," * and freed our tanks to move forward horizontally and shooting. Just as considerate of Washington, General Bradley reclaimed the needed steel from the German fortifications on the Normandy beachhead.

Still other dislocations and urgencies centered about a dozen other programs. The production of ordnance, ammunition, and field supplies of all kinds—from Navy rockets to field and assault wire—had to make up for time lost and material requirements miscalculated. Between September, 1944, and February, 1945, calls for military dry cell batteries forced transfers of priorities sufficient to expand output by nearly 75 percent. The sudden acceleration of the draft in the last winter before D-Day pushed up the production of cotton duck even further. As supply lines lengthened and thickened, more light-heavy trucks had to be rolled off what remained of the old assembly lines. Above all, heavy tires had to be manufactured; and this, in turn, called for emergency increases in carbon black capacities. Altogether, during these five months of production cut-backs, the twelve programs classified as critical achieved a gain of well over 50 percent.

Nor was this all. Over and above the requirements of combat that had been predictable since before Pearl Harbor, the historic technological revolution precipitated by the war now imposed an altogether unpredict-

* Dwight D. Eisenhower, *Crusade in Europe* (New York, Doubleday & Company, Inc., 1948), p. 268.

able set of requirements upon the war economy—unpredictable in its total scope and unpredictable in its specific demands for allocations. Pearl Harbor found our fighter planes at a disadvantage against the Zeroes. The answer—in 1942—was to improve and adjust the conventional models. But by 1944 no improvements in conventional models sufficed. Even the claims of the British for their Sabre engine had become irrelevant. For just as we began to win the long and expensive race for high-octane gasoline, the jet engine began to supersede gasoline engines as the standard combat power unit. The change-over to jets forced changes in production requirements, and, since jets burn a kerosene fuel, it reduced the pressure for endless streams of high-octane gasoline. The result was still further pressure upon the administrators of the war economy for flexibility and precision of control. They met it.

At the same time they met calls for radar and rockets and research into the strange and effective new weapons the enemy had started to throw into the fight. Above all, they met the requirements of the epochal and nerve-wracking atomic speculation.

But the most urgent call of all was the simplest. It was for manpower. Manpower had to be drafted to win the shooting war, and manpower had to be kept on the job to supply equipment to the manpower that was drafted. Byrnes was supposed to be the broker between the rival schedule-makers. But only his military client was functioning—on the civilian side of the bargaining-table, neither Nelson nor McNutt was a principal able to use the good offices of a broker. Because the production and manpower authorities were disintegrating, and because the military relied on Byrnes to solve their civilian problems, he found himself not merely coordinating but policing the turbulent manpower front.

More than any other single factor, Byrnes's involvement with the unpleasantness of manpower administration provoked the opposition which persuaded Roosevelt to make his famous last-minute decision not to run with his Assistant President in 1944. For two years the politics of manpower had been complicated by the psychological problems and the political plans of Sidney Hillman. The scars left by the brutal purge of Knudsen-Hillman had never healed. That purge had put Knudsen into a General's uniform and sent Hillman to a hospital bed. His bitterness deepened when Roosevelt passed over him and appointed McNutt manpower czar. Haunted by the realization that the power of labor leaders was coming to be measured by their influence in Washington, from his exile Hillman vowed not vengeance but its bargaining equivalent—political power that Roosevelt would have to recognize and deal with. Hence PAC. Hence the foundation in political reality for the famous Republican taunt—"Clear it with Sidney."

This was Hillman's vindication, and if Democratic Chairman Robert Hannegan resented and denied it and Roosevelt found it embarrassing, Hillman had every reason to be proud of it. But Hillman had no illusions about Wallace in 1944. He backed Wallace exactly as Roosevelt did, for trading purposes, and with full knowledge of Roosevelt's intentions. Hillman's problem was to convert a defeat for Wallace into a political victory for PAC and a personal victory for himself. To do this, he had to defeat the other candidate Roosevelt was backing—Byrnes.

Byrnes was vulnerable to attack by Hillman, and not merely as a Southerner. He was the obvious scapegoat on whom labor could vent its pent-up grievances. These, as its critics never managed to understand, were many and deep—profits were high, the Farm Bloc dominated Congress, wages were frozen, labor's representation in Washington had vanished with Hillman, labor-management committees were a public relations fiction, and Roosevelt had finally joined his War Cabinet members in calling for the hated "Work-or-Fight" labor draft. No labor leader except John Lewis dared use these grievances as justification for turning against Roosevelt, and PAC regarded Lewis's position as reason enough to give Roosevelt credit for all of labor's wartime gains. By the same token, PAC ignored Roosevelt's control over Byrnes's work, as well as Byrnes's many decisions helpful to labor, and made the Assistant President the villain behind everything the President found necessary to do displeasing to labor and pleasing to other pressure groups.

Byrnes returned to the White House from his defeat at the Chicago Convention humiliated and embittered. He felt cheated by Roosevelt and by Truman. Eliminated from the Presidential succession, his position as Assistant President was for the first time dubious. Nevertheless, for all his ill-disguised resentment, which led him to resign just before Roosevelt's death, his effectiveness as war mobilizer was never greater than during these months of greatest challenge late in 1944 and early in 1945.

Byrnes described this challenge in his First Report as Director of War Mobilization, dated January 1, 1945, a model of lucidity:

The development of industrial knowhow on the part of management and labor has made it possible to increase output per worker. As a consequence, we have been able to maintain production on a plateau, even though the number of workers in munitions industries has declined. . . . Increases in productivity will probably continue but at a slower rate bringing with them further reductions in employment in certain types of munitions plants.

That is a natural economic phenomenon. We can use it to our purposes; but we can also misuse it. That is a danger that I must lay before the Congress. Whenever workers are laid off because they are not needed in this shipyard or that aircraft plant, demands immediately spring up to provide them with civilian employment, to permit manufacture of civilian goods. These demands are hard to resist. Yet until we get the critical programs under control, until we can assure General Eisenhower, General MacArthur and Admiral Nimitz, of the critical supplies they need, I feel we must resist these demands, reasonable as they appear on the surface.

We must direct our efforts to channeling this released manpower into critical war programs and to industries and services needed to support them. It is not as if the civilian economy has been starved. Some items are short. But on the whole the volume of consumption has risen. . . . Our level of living is higher than in 1929 or 1940.

Byrnes went on to state quite frankly that the Administration had erred, in the spring and summer of 1944, in assuming that victory was at hand; and large-scale civilian production could be resumed. Nelson had announced a four-point reconversion program June 18. At Byrnes's request, he had agreed to stagger the timing of each order. Thus, on July 15, aluminum and magnesium restrictions were relaxed; on July 22, permission was given to manufacturers to build experimental post-war models; on July 29, unrated orders for machine tools were sanctioned; and on August 15, ten days before the liberation of Paris, the "spot-authorization" order was issued permitting WPB's regional directors to authorize individual plants to resume the production of civilian goods. But, in December, the fury of the German counterattack along the Ardennes front dictated the cancellation of the "spot-authorization" plan and the reestablishment of ceilings on any further expansion of civilian production.

The Congress to which Byrnes presented his stern new policy had been elected when victory seemed imminent. It convened when battle proved inescapable. The reconversion of 1944, Byrnes insisted, had been premature and overenthusiastic. It had

. . . demonstrated that we could not do two divergent things at once, that we could not pursue an all-out war production effort while simultaneously releasing materials, facilities and manpower for civilian production. In the first place, the mere resumption of civilian output convinced some workers and some industrialists that victory was just around the corner; that therefore they had better prepare for peacetime security.

In the second place, it affected even those who continued to feel that the war was our first and main job. They felt that if their friends or competitors were converting to civilian production, they could safely do so.

As Director of War Mobilization and Reconversion, I am convinced that we must give our undivided attention to war production until we can be absolutely confident that victory is within grasp, until our military leaders tell us that they have enough supplies and that we can afford to reduce production.

Byrnes was, of course, a professional politician, and a resourceful and ambitious one. He stands, accordingly, as fair game for political attack; and in 1950 he invited the fiercest attacks of his career when his long-smouldering feud with Truman exploded into open war. But no purely political disputes should be allowed to detract from recognition of his firm and fearless administration of the war program during these months of alternating relaxation and tension, when Roosevelt's flagging energies were increasingly diverted to inter-Allied matters and when inter-Allied negotiations were chiefly concerned with what could be expected from America's home front.

Ambitious politicians tend to be refugees from principle. Frustrated politicians tend, on the contrary, to seek refuge there. Byrnes did. He followed up his "War First" policy with the announcement that the 40 percent cut-back in war production, projected for the year after V-E Day, was being reconsidered with a view to downward modification, and that rationing would continue. Meanwhile, he had closed down the race tracks, traditionally sacred to politicians. He served notice that allocations among civilians, the military, and our Allies would ignore the principle that "the wheel that squeaks the loudest gets the grease." Finally, he warned that V-E Day, far from relieving the strain on the war economy, threatened to intensify it. Necessarily calculating without Hiroshima, he posed the problem of redeploying the entire war machine against Japan. Inside America, the railroads, short not only of equipment but of manpower, had managed to carry double the 1939 freight load with only 20 percent more freight cars and 10 percent more locomotives. Redeployment promised little relief from old pressures and much trouble from new ones.

THIS was "militarism" with a vengeance. To administer it and, incidentally, to remind the military that the Presidential powers vested in him made him *their* Commander-in-Chief on the home front, Byrnes deputized General Lucius D. Clay as Assistant Chief of Staff of the Army Service Forces. Clay had produced, late in 1943 and early in 1944, a remarkable series of analyses forecasting the 1944 production crisis that saddled the war economy with surpluses while leaving it short of critical items. He predicted that it would come to a head before the Second Front opened. Moreover, he showed that the pressure for new production peaks, combined with the steady expansion of overseas shipments, demanded further "intensification" of America's use of her resources. Specifically, he warned that the demand for manpower was about to exhaust the pool available under "present controls."

Clay's call for stricter manpower controls exposed the fatal weakness in Nelson's setup—the weakness that stemmed directly from his waiver of power to integrate manpower with the other productive resources under his authority. Any effort to regulate

production without regulating its human component
was bound to fail. Clay noted that it had failed. Nelson's answer was an attack intended to prove that
coordination between production and manpower control was no longer necessary: Victory was at hand, war
production was being cut back and all that remained
of the problem of regulating manpower was the removal of Governmental restrictions against their re-
absorption into civilian work as fast as reconversion
permitted. This a full year before the Battle of the
Bulge.

Now Nelson's military antagonists were vulnerable,
and on grounds on which Nelson was strong. They had
been cutting war production back indiscriminately and
irresponsibly without regard for the people and the
communities thus abruptly disemployed—or, for that
matter, for future military requirements. And while
surpluses of items ranging from cotton goods to ther-
mometers piled up, they had run short of ammunition
—with the climax of the shooting war at hand. Senator
Kilgore of West Virginia complained to Byrnes that
"Two different departments shut down a plant in my
state at one time, and they not only wrecked a town,
they wrecked every citizen in it." On the other hand,
Eisenhower complained to Marshall, and Marshall
complained to Somervell about the ordnance situation.

On both counts, Nelson could have reasserted the
authority of WPB over the Army. Instead, he continued to clamor for reconversion. On the first count,
he compromised his authority within WPB. Wilson,
his one-time protégé, refused to echo Nelson's criti-

cisms of the "militarists." Instead, because he fought for the integrity of the war program, he was himself stigmatized as a "militarist." On the second count, Nelson's ignorance of the Army's underestimation of its ordnance requirements, Clay established himself in Nelson's place as the arbiter of matériel production.

The demoralizing effects of Nelson's propaganda drive for wholesale cut-backs and decontrols justified a new demand on the part of the military in mid-August, 1944, that the President remove him. This time he did. Nelson left as he came—in an atmosphere of devious and explosive personal intrigue. He says, "The President asked me what I thought about his appointing Charley Wilson as Acting Chairman in my absence. I readily assented, feeling that Charley was not only the best man but the only man immediately available for the job." *

But, on page 413, he goes on, "Stories began to break all over the newspapers. I had received, it was said, 'a kick in the teeth' [in being suspended by Wilson]. I had been 'exiled to Siberia.' . . . Charley thought again that the newspaper stories had been 'leaked' with my consent by members of my staff and the WPB Information Division. Now he was not only annoyed; he was mad."

Nelson insists that neither he nor his "personal staff" had anything to do with this seemingly spontaneous campaign against Wilson. But Bruce Catton, who gave heavy assistance in the writing of Nelson's *Arsenal of Democracy*, says flatly in his own book,

* Donald M. Nelson, *Arsenal of Democracy* (New York, Harcourt, Brace and Company, Inc., 1946), p. 412.

The War Lords of Washington, that it was "a Nelson man" who touched off the spark.

In any case, Nelson and Wilson indulged in a highly personal and well-publicized set-to before the executive personnel of WPB. The next morning the President, furious, sent for Nelson and, by Nelson's own admission, treated him "like a College Senior who had been called before a rather severe dean to explain an escapade." Finally, on page 414, as if page 412 had not recorded his endorsement of Wilson as his successor, Nelson admits telling the President point-blank not to "try to persuade Charley Wilson to stay on the job." At first, Nelson had called Wilson "the only man immediately available for the job." A day later, Nelson "recommended . . . another very capable executive . . . Julius Krug" * (later Secretary of the Interior under Truman). Roosevelt, weary and disgusted, agreed, overruling Hopkins. Nelson had the satisfaction of seeing Wilson go, too. Thomas E. Dewey continued to call Roosevelt a dictator, and Eisenhower continued to call for ordnance and for men to shoot it.

WPB's disintegration transferred its executive responsibilities to Byrnes's Office of War Mobilization and Reconversion. In November, Clay, who had now emerged as the dominant authority on matériel production, became Deputy Director. He took with him his civilian aide, J. Anthony Panuch, a legendary prototype of the anonymous administrative virtuoso. Later as Deputy Assistant Secretary of State under

* Donald M. Nelson, *Arsenal of Democracy* (New York, Harcourt, Brace and Company, Inc., 1946), p 414.

Byrnes, prior to his rejoining Clay during the Battle of the Airlift, Panuch set in motion the machinery that first ousted and then convicted Alger Hiss. Panuch and his former senior associate of SEC days, Benjamin V. Cohen, who was Byrnes's counsel, provided Byrnes and Clay with indispensable support.

Clay's most remarkable single achievement before becoming Byrnes's Deputy had been the breaking of the strategic Cherbourg bottleneck through which the troops and their supplies had to pass on their way to the front. In October, Somervell had released him to Eisenhower for four months. But the mission was accomplished—with a combination of ruthlessness and finesse characteristic of Clay—in exactly three weeks. On his return, he found that Marshall was still worried lest the chronic ammunition shortage delay the final assault planned for early 1945. Clay increased the supply by speeding its passage through the pipe-line.

As Deputy Director of the War Program, his most perplexing problem was how to accomplish an equivalent result for the labor supply. Nelson had taunted the Army endlessly with the claim that unemployment among die-setters in Cleveland would not relieve a shortage of welders in Phoenix. But the fact is that most war workers did not wait for unemployment to send them moving about. Labor shortages were relieved by job-jumping, by mass migration, and by overtime, housing, and other incentives.

All through 1943 and 1944, workers quit jobs in manufacturing plants at the record rate of 5 per 100. In the first quarter of 1945, the Byrnes-Clay regime revoked the draft deferments of 40,000 job-jumpers.

Whereas in 1943 only 30 percent of the population lived in localities classified as critical labor areas, during the last months of the war 44 percent did so.

The accumulation of 77,000 casualties during the Battle of the Bulge, by creating uncertainty over the prospective drain on our troops, forced Byrnes and Clay to estimate the 1945 war manpower shortage at 250,000 to 300,000 workers. In January and February, 1945, new controls and new threats of penalties drew a record high of 2,000,000 workers into war and war-supporting jobs, 400,000 of them in "must" jobs. Neutralizing this progress, no less than 300,000 "must" workers went prospecting for peacetime opportunities. Veterans demobilized, workers released from programs continuing to decline, and new additions to the labor force constituted the reservoir from which manpower was channeled into critical programs. Reflecting the even division of programs between the surplus and shortage categories and, incidentally, measuring the magnitude of the task facing the Office of War Mobilization and Reconversion, the "must" list was altered each month by the addition of some 400 plants and the removal of a like number. Complicating the task still further, labor, its unfriendliness towards Byrnes turned to hostility by his reliance on Clay the "arch-militarist," clamored for abandonment of the "Little Steel" formula.

This was the uneasy stability victory upset. Until victory came, the controls had to remain. War could not make them total, but the pressures generated by the War Economy leavened them into workability. Indeed, the continuous controversy over manpower, over "militarism," and over foreign aid, which intensified as we won the war of production, points the moral of the achievement of World War II and poses the problem of future mobilization. Given the kind of war we were lucky enough to be able to fight—or, more precisely, to join with others in fighting—production was the strategic sector of the home front. No miracle of administration in any or all of the three subsidiary sectors of civilian supply, foreign aid, and manpower would have offset the continuation of chaos in the production sector. But the imposition of order upon the production sector sufficed to free the home front to function one-quarter coordinated and three-quarters uncoordinated. At more or less the same time, CMP brought the flow of materials under effective control and the Russian achievement demonstrated that our flow of materials could win the war. It was because we began to win the war as a war of production that we did not have to fight it as a war of fully coordinated mobilization. Therefore, we did not.

We cannot expect to be so lucky again. On the contrary, by 1950 the Soviets were well on their way to turning the tables upon us—this time they shielded themselves behind masses of allies, in whose hands Russian production is formidable, and it is our manpower which stands to be expended. Their strategy, accordingly, has put us on grim notice to prepare for total mobilization. World War II's experience of "quarter-coordinated" mobilization shows how to achieve it: by duplicating CMP's performance in the production sector, and by applying the CMP technique of allocations control to the three subsidiary sectors of civilian supply, foreign aid, and manpower.

Before this technique resulted in complete victory.

Roosevelt died. Since his death, the conditions that enabled him to fight his "quarter-coordinated" war have disappeared, certainly not to return again. But though his measures cannot be repeated, his War Presidency left, in more ways than one, a lasting heritage. It oriented the American mind to the reality that Isolationism belonged to the past, and that in the present, emergency is "Normalcy." At the time when Roosevelt died, the author wrote in *Life* (April 30, 1945),

With Franklin Roosevelt's death there descended upon America a mood almost epic in its simplicity. To America, standing in the raw daylight of 1945, with a war to finish, with a peace to organize, with the San Francisco Conference to hurdle, the days of mourning became days of soul-searching and stock-taking. The nation which made the last journey to Hyde Park with Roosevelt was deeply conscious of history. For it knew that it had to proceed to make history. Instinctively, it recognized that the question—how great a man was Roosevelt? was one for the future to decide. More urgent for the people who had to win that future was the question: *how* was Roosevelt a great man?

THIS book has attempted to explain the how of Roosevelt's greatness by telling the story of Roosevelt at his greatest—as War President and presiding genius over America's home front. The how of his greatness defies comparison as it will ever defy duplication. Great men following in his wake, and their advisors, will never tire of speculating upon his motives, his stratagems, his assumptions, his luck, and his faith. The better their understanding of the course he followed, the deeper their admiration for his achievement, the more will be their avoidance of any duplication. Great men will not try to use the Rooseveltian How. Little men will not succeed.

The militaristic totalitarianism of Roosevelt's period seemed at the time to be an omnipotent masterpiece of organization. To organize its defeat, he put his faith in the unorganized momentum of American democracy. The momentum of victory left behind it an unprecedented problem of Governmental organization—the Department of Defense. In the structure of big government, it is the Department of Defense which sets the limits of foreign policy and determines the course of the economy, not least by setting the tax rate. To minimize the problems of Defense, to expect genius or opportunism to dispose of them, is frivolous: to await a recurrence of the Rooseveltian miracle is dangerous. The totalitarian militarism of Soviet imperialism is, if not better organized, more doggedly inspired and held together by a more cohesive glue than the Nazi system. To keep it at bay, organization, as efficient as organization can be, is indispensable. But organization alone will neither defeat it nor avert the dangers of Russian totalitarianism. For that we shall need to be more total than any totalitarianism. We shall need to invoke those drives of the human spirit which totalitarianism strait-jackets. Our achievements of organization will have to be driven by the anonymous energies of the millions behind whose momentum Roosevelt followed. The simplicity of the faith which dominated the passing complexities of the crisis and conjured up this miracle is the enduring heritage of Roosevelt's War Presidency.

BIBLIOGRAPHICAL NOTE

INDISPENSABLE to an understanding of American social
and economic history, in general, during these years,
and of American wartime organization in particular,
is systematic use of the files of *Time, Fortune, News-
week, Business Week* and *Harper's*. As a running
commentary admittedly critical of the Administration's dealings with business, and of the role of business and businessmen in the war effort, the *Nation*,
the *New Republic* and, in particular, the defunct daily
PM are illuminating, even if more tendentious than
accurate. So for the sophisticated reader is *Business As
Usual* (New York, 1941) by I. F. Stone, Washington
correspondent of *PM* and the *Nation*.

It is essential to use the best newspapers, and in
particular the New York *Times*, not least for its provocative, learned and shrewd dispatches by Arthur
Krock: also the Washington *Post* and *Star*, the St.
Louis *Post-Dispatch*, the Baltimore *Sun* and the *Christian Science Monitor*. For colorfully biased criticisms
of the Administration, the Chicago *Tribune* and its
associated newspapers must be referred to for their
provocative bearing upon the bitter controversies of
the period. Reports of the various Government departments, and especially the annual reports of the Secretaries of the Treasury, War, the Navy, Labor, Commerce, and Agriculture, must be consulted. Many of
the emergency agencies of the government published

reports, and many issued regular news releases. A full list of the war agencies of the executive branch is given as an appendix of *The United States at War,* prepared by the War Records Section of the Bureau of the Budget (Washington, 1946). This large volume recounts the development and administration of the federal war program in a history which is indispensable for its narrative, and as a key to the main activities of the various war agencies, although it is biased and, at the analytical level, self-contradictory and amateurish. No less indispensable, but much less biased is *Industrial Mobilization for War* (Vol. I; Washington, 1947), a very detailed and comprehensive history of the War Production Board and predecessor agencies.

For a view of the general industrial and economic position of the nation on the eve of war, readers may turn to Charles J. Hitch, *America's Economic Strength* (New York, 1942), a brief survey; to Fletcher Pratt, *America and Total War* (New York, 1941), which explains modern technique of warfare with emphasis on American unpreparedness; and to *Arsenal of Democracy,* by Burnham Finney (New York, 1941), a study of the industrial side of the defense program by the editor of the *American Machinist.* The relations between government and business at the outbreak of the European War are set forth in detail in *Government and Economic Life,* by Leverett S. Lyon and others (2 vols., New York, 1939–40), a Brookings Institution survey of the relations between government on one side and business, labor, and the individual on the other. Good chapters on the wartime economy of the nation may be found in Allan Nevins and Louis M. Hacker, *The United States and Its Place in World Affairs* (Boston, 1941).

Industrial mobilization is described in a variety of volumes produced during or soon after the war, many of a journalistic or tendentious or self-serving nature. Donald Nelson, the head of WPB, has defended his work in *Arsenal of Democracy: the Story of American War Production* (New York, 1946), a book which must be used with caution, but which must be used. With it should be read Bruce Catton's *The War Lords of Washington* (New York, 1948), by the director of information for WPB, a sincere and idealistic indictment of the Government for failing to use the war crisis to make our industrial machine more responsive to the needs of democracy, which casts penetrating if sometimes inconsistent light on the leading personalities involved on the home front. An expert analysis of current financial policy, written at an early date, may be found in *Fiscal Planning for Total War* (New York, 1942), by William L. Crum and others. Seymour E. Harris in *Prices and Related Controls in the United States* (New York, 1945) has furnished a lucid technical survey of a difficult topic; the writer was an officer in OPA. Beardsley Ruml deals with the relations of government and business in wartime and after in *Tomorrow's Business* (New York, 1945). A useful over-all survey of war experience, with emphasis on its lessons for peace, is presented by Luther Gulick in *Administrative Reflections from World War II* (University of Alabama, 1948). And A. H. D. Kaplan in *The Liquidation of War Production* (New

York, 1944) summarizes a searching study made by the Committee on Economic Development.

For a general treatment of the problems of modern warfare readers may turn to Hanson W. Baldwin's *The Price of Power* (New York, 1948), which studies all aspects of the subject, including the question of organization. Major-General G. M. Barnes's *Weapons of World War II* (New York, 1947) is technically expert and well illustrated. The development of the air force, with its accomplishments in the war, is treated by Harold B. Hinton in *Air Victory: the Men and the Machines* (New York, 1948), a book produced under the auspices of the National Air Council. In *The Merchant Marine and World Frontiers*, a competent study by an officer of the Maritime Commission, Robert E. Anderson traces the rise of the large wartime marine and explores the problems which it raised for the future. The production of airplanes is described by Frank J. Taylor and Lawton Wright in *Democracy's Air Arsenal* (New York, 1947); while a similar examination is given to the development of American armored force by Mildred H. Gillie in *Forging the Thunderbolt* (Harrisburg, 1947). The tremendous American achievements in wartime building are graphically summarized by Van Rensselaer Sill in *American Miracle: the Story of War Construction around the World* (New York, 1947).

On the work of the American farmer during the war, two books are especially useful. They are *Agriculture in an Unstable Economy* (New York, 1945), by Theodore W. Schultz, which deals with farm labor, prices and income, and governmental programs and controls (the author is an expert in agricultural economics); and *The Farmer in the Second World War* (Ames, Iowa, 1947), by Walter W. Willcox, which gives careful statistical treatment to production and prices, with incidental attention to government policy. A book valuable for a broad view of American industry as it emerged from the conflict is *The American Economy*, by Sumner S. Slichter (New York, 1948), analyzing the major factors in the nation's economic life. Another stimulating volume, *America's Place in the World Economy*, edited by Arnold J. Zurcher and Richmond Page, contains fourteen papers by experts on different aspects of the subject.

American social changes during the conflict are described by Selden Menefee in *Assignment: U.S.A.* (New York, 1943), and by John Dos Passos in *State of the Nation* (Boston, 1944), both lively and perceptive. One of the black spots of the war record is treated in liberal spirit by Carey McWilliams in *Prejudice: Japanese Americans, Symbol of Racial Intolerance* (Boston, 1944). Corruption comes in for examination by Harry Lever and Joseph Young in *Wartime Racketeers* (New York, 1945). The Negro problem has of course received a number of treatments. Among the more prominent books may be mentioned Robert C. Weaver's *Negro Labor* (New York, 1946), in which a Negro labor expert surveys the social and economic advance of his race; *White Man's Burden*, by Ruth Smith (New York, 1946); and on a somewhat broader plane, *The High Cost of Prejudice* (New York, 1947) by Bucklin Moon. A distinguished sociologist, R. M.

MacIver, deals with racial discriminations and tensions in *The More Perfect Union* (New York, 1948). The contribution made by refugees to America and the problems they raised and encountered are described by Maurice R. Davie and others in *Refugees in America* (New York, 1947). The author is indebted to Frederick Lewis Allen, editor of *Harper's Magazine,* for the privilege of access to a long report, characteristically virtuoso, of the impact of war upon life in America.

Biographical treatments of important figures of the time contain invaluable material on organization and administration. Among the more useful works may be mentioned Henry L. Stimson and McGeorge Bundy, *On Active Service in Peace and War* (New York, 1948), a distinguished work, which contains much between the lines and in the record; *Roosevelt and Hopkins, an Intimate History* (New York, 1948), by Robert E. Sherwood, is a fascinating narrative sown with valuable documents and provocative of endless political analysis. *Crusade in Europe* (Garden City, 1948), by Dwight D. Eisenhower, is centered mainly on high strategy and the organization of victory, but also contains a number of valuable glimpses into the home scene. No less useful is General Lucius D. Clay's *Decision in Germany.* Carter Field's *Bernard Baruch* (New York, 1944) is an admiring biographical sketch with some data on Mr. Baruch's war labors. Russell Lord in *The Wallaces of Iowa* (Boston, 1947), and Frank Kingdon in *An Uncommon Man* (New York, 1945) have something to say in praise of Henry Wallace's wartime activities. James F. Byrnes in

Speaking Frankly (New York, 1947), while dealing almost wholly with foreign affairs, offers a few sidelights on domestic matters. And Eleanor Roosevelt in *This I Remember* (New York, 1949) and Frances Perkins in *The Roosevelt I Knew* (New York, 1946) both have material of tremendous importance on the President's handling of wartime problems, on his relations with members of his Administration, and on the enigma of his political personality.

The Morgenthau Papers, published in *Collier's*, 1947, and James Farley's *The Roosevelt Years* (New York, 1948) must be included for the definitive light they shed on pattern-making moves made by the President in relation to mobilization and to the politics of preparedness. Students of mobilization in its diplomatic setting will want to study not only the Morgenthau papers, but Secretary Cordell Hull's definitive memoirs (New York, 1948). More specifically, the unusually well informed account of *How War Came*, by Forrest Davis and Ernest Lindley (New York, 1942), must be consulted, and Walter Millis's *This Is Pearl* (New York, 1947) should be consulted. A fascinatingly meticulous narrative of our retreat down the *Road to Pearl Harbor* has been supplied by Herbert Feis (Princeton, 1950) with a detachment truly remarkable for one who served as Economic Advisor to the Secretary of State at the time. For an unforgettably provocative analysis of America's foreign economic policies during the years leading up to World War II, Judge Jerome Frank's *Save America First* (New York, 1948) is well worth while. The writings of John Maynard Keynes, and especially his popular tract *How to Pay for the War* (New York, 1940), are required reading for students of the emergence of wartime fiscal policy. *How We Went to War*, by Newton Baker (New York, 1936) notes War I experiences.

The mass of government reports is virtually overwhelming. Attention must particularly be called to the investigation of the national defense program begun by the special (Truman) Senate Committee under resolution of the 77th Congress, and continued into the 80th, with numerous hearings and reports. Harry Aubrey Toulmin, Jr., in *Diary of Democracy: the Senate War Investigating Committee* (New York, 1947), has summarized the conclusions to be drawn from the work of the Truman-Mead Committee. Of the mass of official documents on the war economy, the most valuable by far are the volumes of Truman Committee Hearings and Reports and those of the Vinson House Committee on Naval Affairs; and the Reports of Director J. F. Byrnes, of the Office of War Mobilization and Reconversion, which are incomparably and indispensably lucid, comprehensive, and accurate. Both wartime mobilization and postwar adjustment are treated by the Senate Committee on Military Affairs, 78th Congress, 2d Sess., Senate Report 1036. The House Military Affairs Committee also investigated the war effort and presented much data on it; see, for example, 79th Congress, 1st Sess., House Report 728. National defense migration is discussed in the House (Tolan) Committee Reports of 1942, especially in House Reports 2396 and 2589. Stockpiling, contracts, labor relations, agriculture, price controls, and relaxation of the anti-trust laws to stimulate war effort were among the topics with which Congressional committees or subcommittees dealt at length.

For a highly professional analysis of the functional and structural problems involved in home front mobilization, as well as a scholarly history of the evolution of the modern War and Navy Departments, the *Report to the Secretary of the Navy on Unification of the War and Navy Departments and Post War Organization for National Security* (U. S. Government Printing Office, Washington, 1945), prepared under the direction of Ferdinand Eberstadt, is invaluable. It served as the blueprint for the organization of the Department of Defense and allied bodies. An equally indispensable companion volume is Bernard Baruch's *American Industry in the War* (New York, 1941), which summarizes the Elder Statesman's experiences of World War I and his recommendations for preparing for World War II, but does not contain the text of either the Industrial Mobilization Plan or the confidential modification of it prepared by Mr. Baruch and Mr. John Hancock for the War Resources Board in 1939.

As this book was going to press, Dr. Herman Miles Somers published a definitive treatise on the structure and function of the Office of War Mobilization and Reconversion (*Presidential Agency*, Cambridge, 1950). Factual and impartial, it presents a wealth of detailed information supporting Dr. Somers's conclusion that Justice Byrnes, in his relations with individual branches of the military as well as with the Joint Chiefs of Staff, maintained a clear civilian dominance over all home front issues, effectively refuting Nelson's shrill reiteration that this was impossible.

Also published as this book was going to press was the definitive treatise on *The Navy and the Industrial Mobilization in World War II* by Professor Robert H. Connery (Princeton, 1951). Professor Connery has drawn upon a rich reservoir of the primary memoranda which accumulated in the Navy's industrial mobilization apparatus during World War II. His case history is accurate and comprehensive. It must be regarded as laying a strategic cornerstone in the structure of the country's new literature on industrial mobilization. In particular, it merits close scrutiny by all students for its review of the contribution to industrial mobilization techniques made by Secretary Forrestal and his team of co-workers; and it provides invaluable guidance to students of the evolution of the Controlled Materials plan. Its discussions of such technical aspects of World War II's industrial mobilization as renegotiation and forward-pricing are major contributions.

No bibliography can be complete which does not give uniquely honorable mention to the classic treatise on "The War Production Board: Administrative Policies and Procedures" by John Lord O'Brian and Manly Fleischmann (*The George Washington Law Review*, December, 1944). Mr. O'Brian served as General Counsel to the War Production Board during World War II, and Mr. Fleischmann, his assistant, returned to Washington late in 1950 as National Production Administrator. This searching analysis not only reviews the problems posed by the industrial mobilization of the war from their legal aspect, but is an informative and wise account of the evolution of the operational attitudes and techniques which set the pattern of victory on the home front. No less important, it documents the experience of World War II which a remarkably able administrator and lawyer found himself charged with responsibility for applying to the new crisis confronting the country in 1950–51.

All professional students of the subject will feel obliged to familiarize themselves with the highly technical, but basic studies published by David Novik and his associates of War II. Their pioneering statistical studies were instrumental in making CMP the success it was. They are (1) WARTIME PRODUCTION CONTROLS by Novik, Anschen and Truppner (New York, 1950), (2) WARTIME INDUSTRIAL STATISTICS, Novik and Steiner, (Urbana, Illinois, 1950), and (3) INDUSTRIAL REPORTING EXPERIENCE OF THE WPB—Novik and Steiner, (Journal of the American Statistical Society, September and December, 1948, April and June, 1949). This formidable body of work was drawn upon to good purpose— and, happily, by the same team of technicians—when NPA applied the CMP technique to the crisis of 1950–51.

INDEX